COMMUNITY

A SOCIOLOGICAL STUDY

COMMUNITY

A SOCIOLOGICAL STUDY

BEING AN ATTEMPT TO SET OUT THE NATURE AND FUNDAMENTAL LAWS OF SOCIAL LIFE

BY

R. M. MACIVER, D.Phil.

ASSOCIATE PROFESSOR OF POLITICAL SCIENCE IN THE UNIVERSITY OF TORONTO

Jeter les bases abstraites de la sociologie—tel est le but manifeste et déjà presque sympathique aux foules, déjà escompté par leur optimisme impatient, vers lequel convergent les efforts des esprits réfléchis de l'époque.
De Roberty, *Nouveau Programme de Sociologie.*

Nous assistons aujourd-hui à l'avènement de la sociologie, qui est le commencement d'une ère nouvelle dans la philosophie même.
Fouillée, *Le Mouvement Positiviste.*

BENJAMIN BLOM, INC.
Publishers New York 1971

TO MY FATHER

First published London, 1917
Reissued 1971 by
Benjamin Blom, Inc.
New York, N.Y. 10025

Library of Congress
Catalog Card Number 70-172924

Printed in the
United States of America

PREFACE

I HAVE entitled this work *Community*, because that term expresses best the object which social science as such endeavours to study. It is in community, the common life, that the interests represented by the specific social sciences are bound together, made integral, and thus amenable to a more comprehensive science. The work which follows seeks to be an introduction to this wider science. The vast extension of social knowledge due to research into the life of primitive and barbaric communities, as well as to recent study of all the great forms of civilised association, political, economic, educational, ecclesiastical, and so forth, increases at once the difficulty and the necessity of the synthetic science of sociology. Community resembles a country recently discovered—or rediscovered—and suddenly overrun by explorers. Its mountains are being measured, its lakes fathomed, its plains surveyed, its fauna and flora investigated; but there is still scarcely any clear comprehensive chart of the whole country, based on the stores of information supplied by so many diligent explorers. Perhaps it is too early yet to expect a satisfactory map of the country, but only through successive attempts can that result be at last attained.

Detail has therefore been ruthlessly abandoned for the sake of comprehensiveness. It seemed to the author that the most essential features of community are the most often misconstrued. There is nothing about which men's minds are more confused than about the vaster social questions, such as the relation of community to its associations, of the great associations to one another, of the State to all the rest—nay, such as the very meaning of community, its essential nature and laws, its life, growth, decay, and immortality. To understand the essential social relations is to find the focus, at which the objects of investigation show, in the degree of their nearness and according to the power of our glasses, their true outlines. Our glasses may not be powerful, our vision may not be keen—but even so to determine this focus should always be within our power.

In an early essay I remarked that there was no definite science of society beyond that contained in such specific studies as economics and politics. That view I now believe to be wholly mistaken, and I hope that this present volume adds one to the many disproofs of it revealed by the recent progress of the subject. There was some excuse for the contrary opinion, for many a vain and specious formula has been set forward in the name of sociology, many a hollow generalisation has been declared an eternal social law, and too frequently the invention of terms has taken the place of the discovery of principles. But the stars fulfilled their courses unmoved by the imaginations of astrologers, and community works out social law despite the errors of us who profess to study it. Community is not only a real, it is a vital subject of study.

In these early days of social science we have begun by arguing about community with something of that simplicity of conviction which the early Greek philosophers possessed about the universe. Some have said that in community all is struggle, others that all is adaptation, some that selfishness rules, others that common interest prevails, some that environment is supreme, others that race is the master of environment, some that economic interest is the primary determinant, and others that the law of population determines economic law. Finally,

some have thought to resolve " the mystery in the soul
of State " by naming community a supermechanism or a
superorganism, while others discover it to be in reality and
no metaphor a supersoul. By no such apparent simplification shall we attain the true synthesis of community.

The author is firmly convinced that social science will
never advance except by freeing itself from subjection
to the methods and formulæ of both physical and biological science. As it has a subject-matter of its own, so
it has a method of its own. Social relations can never
be adequately stated in quantitative terms or understood
as expressions of quantitative laws. Certain writers have
declared that unless we can formulate the laws of society
with the same exactitude with which we formulate the
laws of physics, our subject is no science. It is unprofit-
able to quarrel over names. If men care to reserve the
title of science to those subjects which admit of quantitative statement, they may be permitted the reservation.
But many kinds of *knowledge*, and among them those most
worth knowing, will then remain outside the sciences.

The greater portion of the work is concerned with what
seem to the author to be the fundamental laws of social
development. A necessary result of this method is that
many questions of moment are left undiscussed. I had
originally intended to add a book dealing with those
problems where no clear law is yet, to the author at
least, discernible. To such a sphere would belong, to
take one of many instances, certain questions connected
with the sex-life of our times. But I have found that
the consideration of such questions would have extended
the work beyond reasonable limits, and have reserved it
for a possible further work.

Since this work was written the one great catastrophe
which overshadowed community in our times has fallen.
What the restoration will be no man yet knows, but so
great a social cataclysm assuredly marks the ending of
an epoch. In the light of this event I would recall nothing

of what I have written concerning the place of war in the world of civilisation. Militarism has been the enemy of modern social development, and on the other hand all social development makes militarism more evil. For it makes greater and broader the social structures which war pulls down, and it makes deeper and more universal the sense of community which war confounds. If we cannot overcome militarism, in all we do to build a greater civilisation we are preparing greater offerings to the powers of destruction. Were the great nations of Europe not interdependent, they would not at last have been brought all together—in war! The terrible irony of history now points the lesson.

A small portion of this work has already appeared in the form of articles contributed to *The Sociological Review*, *The Philosophical Review*, *The Political Quarterly*, and *The International Journal of Ethics*. I am indebted to The Carnegie Trust for the Universities of Scotland for aid given me, in the form of a Research Grant, towards the study of the literature, especially foreign periodical literature, devoted to the subjects discussed in Book III. My obligations to many authors will be apparent from the text—it may also be that I owe most to those authors to whom I refer only by way of criticism. I am under a very special obligation to Mr. James Turner, Assistant to the Professor of Moral Philosophy at Aberdeen University, who very kindly read through both typescript and proof, and has aided me greatly by his careful and critical supervision ; and to my wife, who has, besides the invaluable aid of encouragement, rendered much service in the preparation of the work for the press.

R. M. M.

KING'S COLLEGE,
ABERDEEN, *Sept.* 1914.

CONTENTS

BOOK I

INTRODUCTION

CHAPTER I

THE MEANING OF SOCIAL FACT AND SOCIAL LAW

CHAPTER II

COMMUNITY AND ASSOCIATION

CHAPTER III

THE PLACE OF SOCIOLOGY AMONG THE SCIENCES

BOOK II

AN ANALYSIS OF COMMUNITY

CHAPTER I

FALSE PERSPECTIVES OF COMMUNITY

CHAPTER II

THE ELEMENTS OF COMMUNITY

CHAPTER III

THE STRUCTURE OF COMMUNITY

CHAPTER IV

INSTITUTIONS

BOOK III

THE PRIMARY LAWS OF THE DEVELOPMENT OF COMMUNITY

CHAPTER I

THE MEANING OF COMMUNAL DEVELOPMENT

CHAPTER II

THE SUPPOSED LAW OF COMMUNAL MORTALITY

CHAPTER III

THE FUNDAMENTAL LAW OF COMMUNAL DEVELOPMENT

CHAPTER IV

PROBLEMS CONNECTED WITH THE FOREGOING LAW : (1) THE CO-ORDINATION OF COMMUNITY

CONTENTS

CHAPTER V

PROBLEMS CONNECTED WITH THE FOREGOING LAW : (2) THE UNITY OF THE INDIVIDUAL LIFE

CHAPTER VI

SECOND LAW OF COMMUNAL DEVELOPMENT : THE CORRELATION OF SOCIALISATION AND COMMUNAL ECONOMY

CHAPTER VII

THIRD LAW OF COMMUNAL DEVELOPMENT : THE CORRELATION OF SOCIALISATION AND THE CONTROL OF ENVIRONMENT

CHAPTER VIII

APPENDICES

BOOK I

INTRODUCTION

CHAPTER I

THE MEANING OF SOCIAL FACT AND SOCIAL LAW

§ 1. Social fact.

What is a social fact ? Many volumes have been
written on sociology which have not answered, or have
answered wrongly, this preliminary question. It is true
that in the study of defined and specific social problems
we need not pause to discuss the meaning and delimitation of social fact as such. But a general science of
society is vain if we have no answer, or a mistaken one,
to this question. The very first proof that a science of
society is possible must be a satisfactory working definition of social fact.

Sociology is often said to be concerned with social as
distinct from individual phenomena. " What a man does
without having learned from the example of another
person, walking, crying, eating, mating, is purely vital ;
while walking with a certain step, singing a song, preferring at table one's national dishes and partaking of
them in a well-bred way, courting a woman after the
manner of the time, are social." This passage from M.
Tarde is quoted with much approbation by Professor
Ross, who adds :

" If the social is not the vital, neither is it the individual
psychic. So we might add as supplement to Tarde :
' When one fears the dark, delights in colour, craves a
mate, or draws an inference from his own observations,

that is merely psychic. But when one dreads heresy, delights in " good form," craves the feminine type of his time, or embraces the dogmas of his people, that is *social*. " Social " then are all phenomena which we cannot explain without bringing in the action of one human being on another.' " [1]

This is all very unsatisfactory and very confusing. Nothing a man can be or do is entirely uninfluenced by " others," and all we can rightly distinguish is the immediacy or remoteness of certain influences. Society for every man is origin, atmosphere, environment, life. How can he think or be at all out of relation to society ? Alike the expression of his organic needs and the expression of his inmost individuality take social forms. Why then should it be a social phenomenon to dread heresy and presumably not a social phenomenon to embrace heresy ? Even were the heresy " anti-social," it would still not be non-social, since heresy no less than orthodoxy is a way of responding to social environment. Or again, if a man fears the dark, why should that be " merely psychic " (whatever that may be) ? Has he not inherited the instinct from ancestors who knew good cause for fearing the terror by night ? Strangest of all is the statement that sexual attraction is not a social phenomenon. If a man craves a mate, is a craving which is itself the very foundation and beginning of all society, and owes its strength in each to an endless process of social selection, the less social because it is " vital " ?

The trouble is that in the world about us there are no facts which we can single out as social facts and thereby distinguish from others which are " purely " individual, or " vital," or " psychic." Whatever a living being thinks or does has both an individual and a social aspect. An individual aspect, for it can never be adequately explained

[1] Ross, *Foundations of Sociology*, pp. 6-7.

simply as a social product ; every man's thoughts and
opinions, his loves and hates and fears, his activities of
every kind, are social relationships shot through, made
concrete and actual, by his character of individuality.   A
social aspect, for actions and thoughts are all *resultants*,
the responses of complex beings, having social origins and
socialised characters, to conditions of environment themselves somehow and in some degree socially determined.
Every man's character is personality woven of individuality and sociality ; every man's environment consists of
his fellow-men and the world of his fellow-men.   His
actions and thoughts must therefore, every one of them,
be in some kind and degree social phenomena.   But we
are not on that account compelled, as sociologists, to make
our study comprehensive of all human thinking and doing.
No one would argue that the moralist, because he finds
that the moral factor enters into all human activities,
must therefore study equally all human activities.   As he
abstracts, so must we.   As he looks for the forms and
laws of morality, so must we look for the forms and laws
of that yet more extensive element, sociality.

*Wherever living beings enter into, or maintain willed
relations with one another, there society exists.*   All such
willed relations are the primary social facts, and their
consequences are the secondary social facts.   As these
relations and their consequences reach to the world's end
and through all time, determining every possible activity
of man and all other living things, it is clear that society
is an element or function of life itself, present wherever
life is found, but present *in a greater or less degree*.   As
we shall see later, the greater the likeness to one another
of the related beings, the intenser is the social life :   a man
may find society in the company of a dog or of a savage,
but his social relations become most complete when he
finds a world of social beings most akin to himself ;   and

we shall see also that the higher the life of each individual
being the more highly is it socialised.

It is, perhaps, better here to speak of *willed* than of
purposive or *mental* relations. I believe that all willing
in man and beast is in its degree purposive, and that all
life is conscious life in its degree. But the term " purposive " tends to be limited to actions motived by clear
and definite purposes, and much of our activity is obscure
and seeming-blind. Much of it is too shallow to merit
the term " purposive " as it is usually employed, much
of it, perhaps, too deep. For this reason the term
" willed " seems preferable. It is wise for us to avoid
the interminable discussion as to the relation of " instinctive " and " rational " activity. However we distinguish them, if we distinguish them at all, both are
activities of will as above defined. If in the study of
organism we pursue the question of instinct far enough,
we reach the obscure boundaries where mechanical reaction seems to verge on living response. But in the
study of society there arises no such problem. Every
social fact consists in or arises out of a relation of wills
to one another.

Again, it is better to say " willed " than merely " conscious " (or " mental ") relations. If living beings are
merely conscious of each other—supposing such *mere* consciousness possible—they have entered into mental but
not social relations. A relation becomes social in so far
as it involves *interdependent activity* on the part of the
beings related. Now all activities of a living being may
be called activities of will, whether the living being be a
termite or a man or a god. For willing is simply the
self-determined acting of a living thing, its being itself
in action. Social willing is, therefore, the correspondent
" being itself " of each of a plurality of beings in relation
to one another in the endless and continuous situations

determined for each by the presence and activity of the others. Life is pervaded by society.

We may now summarily distinguish the main *types* of social fact.

These fall into two great classes, (*a*) social relations proper—the actual interrelations of wills—and (*b*) social institutions, which are not actual interrelations of wills, but the determinate (and therefore willed) forms in accordance with which men enter into social relations. The distinction is very important, and the confusion of the two classes has led to curious errors. A law or a code of laws, a form of government, a class or caste system— these are not actual relations of men, but the conditions and consequences of relationship. Social relations are activities, the threads of life ; social institutions form the loom on which the threads are woven into a cloth.

The chief distinctions to be found among social relations are as follows, and it is obvious that the kinds of social institution will correspond :

(1) There are infinite kinds and degrees of likeness between individuals. Strictly speaking, sociology is concerned with the likenesses of individuals only so far as they involve or arise out of relations between individuals, groups in which the likes are brought together or whence the likes result. These groups, as we shall see, fall into two great classes which we may call the communal and the associational, according as the like qualities determine a whole common life or merely a form of association within that life : a city, say, or nation on the one hand, a church, say, or trade-union on the other.

(2) There are infinite kinds and degrees of difference between individuals. These, again, are objects of sociological study only in so far as they create social relations. These relations are of two types, relations of hostility, the conflict of differences, and relations of reciprocity, the

harmony of differences. Complementary differences are the source of vastly important social unities, just as antagonistic differences are the source of fundamental social oppositions. Among social relations of interdependence we may name those of husband and wife, parents and children, teacher and pupil, governor and governed, employer and employé, buyer and seller. These are but some of the more obvious forms. Subtler forms of interdependence emerge continually with the development in every social sphere of the principles of the " division of labour," and with the general differentiation involved in the whole process of civilisation.

(3) There are definite ways in which the likenesses and differences of men combine to produce social relations. We may say that certain social relations are on the whole due to the essential likenesses of men, others to the essential differences of men, but along these lines we will never advance to an adequate knowledge of society. All social relations are in some degree resultants of the likenesses and differences of men. Social life reveals an endless process of adjustment, and men's purposes and interests combine and cross in the most intricate ways. This is seen more clearly if we turn from the actual relations to the resultant institutions. None of the complexer social structures can be credited to the simple operation of either like-mindedness or felt interdependence. Take, *e.g.*, the form of the State at any given period. This is an age-long construction resulting from the convergences and conflicts of a thousand interests and purposes in the members of a community. It is an easy thing to describe the resultant, the system, the form ; it is an infinitely difficult thing to reveal its genesis and growth out of the complex social relations of the members of the successive generations, in their varying degrees of station, character, opportunity, and power.

A word may be added in conclusion as to the meaning and value of social statistics. In the strictest sense these statistics—totals, averages, ratios, graphs, and functions —are not social facts, they are merely symbolic of social facts, and must be interpreted in order to yield them. It is the frequent difficulty and uncertainty of interpretation which leads to the common opinion that " statistics will prove anything." We may illustrate this need of interpretation by taking the simple case of averages. In the first place it is only measurable things which can be averaged, such as heights, weights, head-ratios, while the essential social facts, *i.e.* social relations and social institutions, are not directly measurable. Cephalic indices and all the other " biometric " facts are in strictness no more social facts than meteorological figures are social facts. The biometric facts are intimately related to social facts, determining and being determined by them, but meteorological facts are also intimately related to social facts. Alike they are data to be interpreted by the sociologist, but the former remain biological, the latter meteorological. The necessity for this distinction will appear in the next section. Again, the average always gives a delusive appearance of exactitude. Suppose we are told that the average height of three people is 5 feet 10 inches. This does not tell us anything about the height of any one of these people, nor yet about their relative heights. They may be 5 feet 11 inches, 5 feet 10 inches, and 5 feet 9 inches respectively, or they may be 6 feet 4 inches, 6 feet, and 5 feet 2 inches respectively, or any other series whatever which added and divided by three gives 5 feet 10 inches. Of course, the longer the series the greater the probability that the mean or average value will *reveal* a social fact about, say, the race or stock to which the individuals belong, or about the effect of certain socially-created conditions on the organisms of these exposed to them. But this fact is not expressed by the average, it is an inference or interpretation, and so with all other kinds of statistics.

It must not be concluded that statistics are, therefore, of little sociological value. On the contrary, they are most significant. They are not only of immense importance for the solution of questions of practical administration, they can, *rightly interpreted*, give us glimpses not otherwise obtainable into the most secret and spiritual mysteries of society. We have greatly to lament the fact that only for very recent times are accurate social statistics available. The knowledge of the increase or decrease over a given period of the birth-rate, marriage-rate, death-rate, suicide-rate, illegitimacy-rate, to mention only what are called " vital statistics," would throw more light on that period than volumes of historical records. The dry bones of figures become to the true sociologist a standing army of living witnesses, revealing social processes hidden for ever from his direct gaze.

§ 2. Social law.

We are now in a position to determine the meaning of social law. There are, of course, laws of society as there are laws of all animate and inanimate nature. Where there are no laws, there is no reality, no world, and where there is no knowledge of laws there is no experience, no understanding of the world. There is no chaos in the world, for the forms of law interpenetrate everywhere ; and the chaos remaining within our experience takes on order in the degree of the growth of knowledge. As we advance in knowledge we see that all things are related to one another, that the world is all threaded with identities and reciprocities, that every particular conforms in every aspect to a principle holding for other particulars as well. Such principles are laws. But there are different *kinds* of law for different kinds of reality, and we must not seek in social science—as some do—for the kind of law we can discover in mathematical or physical or chemical science. If we so seek, we shall seek in vain— we shall only rediscover the laws of mathematics, physics, or chemistry, and be as far as ever from attaining the knowledge of society.

The student of society must understand very clearly the nature and the kinds of law, for social law is most

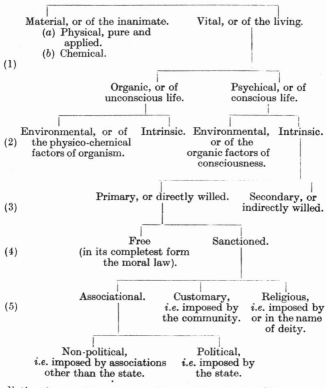

LAW.

(1) Material, or of the inanimate.
    (*a*) Physical, pure and applied.
    (*b*) Chemical.

Vital, or of the living.

(2) Organic, or of unconscious life.

Psychical, or of conscious life.

Environmental, or of the physico-chemical factors of organism.

Intrinsic.

Environmental, or of the organic factors of consciousness.

Intrinsic.

(3) Primary, or directly willed.

Secondary, or indirectly willed.

(4) Free (in its completest form the moral law).

Sanctioned.

(5) Associational.

Customary, *i.e.* imposed by the community.

Religious, *i.e.* imposed by or in the name of deity.

Non-political, *i.e.* imposed by associations other than the state.

Political, *i.e.* imposed by the state.

distinctive and most complex, unique in itself yet conditioned by every kind of law within the cosmos. In

our social life all the laws of all reality are together operative, yet its proper law is set sharply over against all other
laws. To understand the meaning of social law it is
necessary to understand the meaning of all law ; without
that understanding nothing but perplexity and confusion
will reward our study. I have, therefore, as shortly as
is consistent with comprehensiveness, drawn up the foregoing classification of laws, which should be thoroughly
mastered by every reader who seeks to be a genuine
sociologist. The table is elaborated only from the point
of view of the student of society, but it is in itself valid
for all points of view.

A short commentary will make the classification clear.

(1) Every kind of reality has its proper law, and the
great division of laws corresponds to the great division
of reality. There is one law for the unity of inanimate
nature, and one law for the unity of living nature. These,
for want of better names, I have called respectively
" material " and " vital " law. If we find that the
division of nature into animate and inanimate is one
of kind and not of degree, then there is a distinction of
kind between their respective laws. The law of the inanimate world is, so far as we know it, the law of invariable concomitance or sequence, the fixed order of material
nature. It is in itself, and is so revealed where it exists
pure, *i.e.* in the world of the inanimate, inviolable, eternal,
and exceptionless. The law of the living is on the other
side revealed in the will of the living, unstable, relative,
riddled with changefulness and imperfection. The difference is therefore profound, and especially so between
material law and that form of vital law which we have
called " sanctioned " law. The one states *It is so*, an
eternal fact, the other commands *Thou shalt* or exhorts
Thou shouldst. It would seem as if here the difference
were too great to admit the comprehension of both under

one genus. Yet it is not without reason that both types
are called by one name. The " sanctioned " law will be
found to fall under the great form of vital law, and both
forms, material and vital, are in their kind and degree
principles of uniformity, revealing the universality of many
particulars. Not only so, but the law of the animate
reaffirms within its own sphere the law of the inanimate.
The one reveals the material world, and the other reveals
the world of life.

We may contrast the distinction between material and
vital law with the distinction between the two great
forms of vital law. If all life is one wherever it is found,
if self-consciousness is but more consciousness, and consciousness but more life, if instinct is but a limited
intelligence, and the purposes of men but completer
manifestations of the impulse that moves in plant and
animal—then no sharp division can be drawn between
organic and psychical law. We may call organic the law
of living creatures in so far as they are not, or seem not
to be, guided by conscious will. It is the principle of life
where life is present in less degree or less developed form.
If this be true, then even the lowest life may have its
psychical character, though hard to trace, even as the
highest life retains an organic character. Thus while we
draw a distinction of kind between material and vital
law, we draw a distinction only of degree between organic
and psychical law. We understand life best if we assume
that the will and purpose which is the conscious master
of its highest activity is but more of that will and purpose
which works darkly even in the turning of a plant towards
the light.

(2) Starting from this principle, we are enabled to
arrange all kinds of law in a graduated series. For in
what we understand as organic life there is always operative physical and chemical law, not in their simplicity,

but under the partial and temporary dominance of life. It is only the dead organism—what was, but no longer is an organism—that is entirely explicable in physico-chemical terms, and it is so explicable because it is dead. The dead body, ceasing to be an organism, becomes a physico-chemical fact. The living organism is something more—it has, but is not, its physico-chemical conditions. Vital law neither supersedes nor remains in isolation from material law, but is in a sense built on the foundation of that law. Further, as life becomes more complex and fuller, its higher manifestations seem in a similar though not an identical manner to be built on the living structure of its lower being. Within either part of vital nature, the organic or the psychical, we find a twofold enquiry, one concerned with the way in which organic or psychical life is determined by the laws of its environment, the other concerned with the intrinsic nature of organic or psychical life. Thus within the organic sphere we can distinguish the intrinsic sciences of botany, zoology, physiology, and biology, from the science of organic chemistry, and from those scarcely-formulated sciences which study the effects on organism of climate, habitat, and other physical conditions. (It must not, of course, be supposed that the former sciences are studied in isolation from the latter— in the nature of the case they cannot be—the point is that we cannot explain organism in terms of these conditions, or, in other words, we cannot "explain it away.") Similarly, in the psychical sphere the sciences which are intrinsic for organism become now extrinsic or environmental, and in particular we distinguish the science of psycho-physics from the science of psychology proper. There are great difficulties involved in the interpretation of the fact that every kind of vital law is thus dependent on or conditioned by laws of another kind, but the general relationship seems clear.

To express this truth in another way. Laws may be arranged in inverse order of dependence and of quantitative exactness. Just as the law expressing the actual behaviour of a stone in motion (applied physics) is more complex than the law expressing the relation to one another of the sides of a triangle (abstract physics), so the law expressing the mode of growth of a plant (organic law) is more complex than that expressing the movement of a stone, and the law expressing the growth of a mind (psychical law) is more complex than the law of vegetative growth. The stone is a mere physical object, the plant is a physical object and something more (though not by way of mere addition), the man is an organic object and something more (though, again, not by way of mere addition). The social being has at once a physical nature subject like the stone to physical law, an organic nature subject like the plant to organic law, a psychical nature subject to psychical law and, therefore, to the law of psychic interrelations, *i.e.* to social law. The social being is thus in a sense the focus of all the laws of the universe, and thus, from the point of view of our knowledge, laws take on more and more, as we pass from pure physics to sociology, the aspect of *tendencies*. Not that causal relations are less binding in the latter sphere, but that they are more complex. A science like geometry, able to rule out all non-geometrical facts in its study of the bare spatial framework of the world, can give quite absolute results. But a social science can never rule out any facts. Whatever is not the intrinsic nature of social law is its extrinsic condition, whatever is not end for it is means. Even were the law of the living of the same rigid character as the law of the inanimate, it would still be far more hard to attain, for it is far more complex.

Even were the law of the living of the same rigid character—but the most significant fact for the understanding

of social law is that in no case is the law of the living one
in kind with material law. Even in that region of life
which seems as blind as the working of material nature,
we shall search in vain for the simplicity of material law.
" Iron sharpeneth iron, so a man sharpeneth the countenance of his friend "—here are two laws set side by
side, one physical, one social. For the moment they
seem parallel. Iron does not will to sharpen iron, and
the friend's countenance is sharpened whether he will or
no. Yet the measurable effect of iron on iron is worlds
apart from the unpredictable effects of the meeting of
wills. There are no " iron laws " of society.

This is more obvious in respect of imperative laws of
whatever kind. If we are able to obey laws, it is because
we are able to disobey them. " In the sweat of thy
face shalt thou eat bread "—there are many to whom
this law literally applies, yet it has not for them the
necessity of material law, or even of organic law. There
is no eternal and inviolable sequence here. " One must
live," said the prisoner guilty of stealing bread. " I do
not see the necessity," the judge replied. They spoke of
different kinds of necessity, of different kinds of law.
The imperative law states not what will be, but what
must. The material law states the " outer necessity,"
the imperative law states the obligation based thereon,
the " inner necessity."

(3) We are now able to explain the distinction between
the directly and the indirectly willed laws of conscious
life. It is a distinction generally overlooked and yet is
one of great significance. There are certain sciences many
of whose laws seem to lie midway between the inner and
the outer necessity—we might instance sciences so far
apart as philology and economics. Certain laws of these
sciences gain their seeming-iron character because they
are in one way or another not direct and immediate forms

of willing. They are rather resultants due to the partial convergences or oppositions of men's wills. Take for illustration the economic law—the specific conditions under which alone it holds good need not concern us— that as the demand increases the price rises. Men do not directly will this law as they will, for instance, a political law, yet it is the immediate consequence of their willing, and as such it is subject to the fluctuations and uncertainties of will. It is due to the interrelation of wills as certainly as, though in a different way from, political enactment. The increased demand for an object is the willing of those who lack it to possess it or the willing of those who possess some to possess more of it. But these will also to buy as cheaply as they can, and over against that will there stands the will of others to sell as dearly as they can. Now the fact that, other things being equal, men always buy as cheaply and sell as dearly as they can, may be regarded as primary or directly-willed law, but the fact we are here considering, the fact of increased price answering to increased demand, cannot be brought under the same category. It is rather a resultant, itself unwilled, of men's willing, and as such it must be regarded as more and not less dependent on will than the law which expresses the direct fiat of one or many minds.

(4) Law may be called free or sanctioned according as it expresses autonomous activity or formulates imperative enactment. Of the former type the moral law is the completest instance, as of the latter the law of the state. The former, properly understood, is determined simply by the sense of right or inner obligation, the " inner necessity " ; the latter is imposed under a sanction other than the obligation to performance resident in the sense each has of the value to be achieved by performance. For every " inner necessity " of each is variable and

thwarted by other necessities, inner and outer, of his own and of others ; each is bound up with others so that he cannot without their aid fulfil his ends. For such fulfilment legal and other systems, the institutions of society, are a prior necessity. These men must first establish, must first will, before they can attain the nearer objects of their wills. And each society so organised must will the coercion of those errant members who fail to respect, for themselves and others, the values in the name of which imperative laws exist. For those who remain unbound by these values other necessities must be found, in the last resort the inexorable outer necessity.

Men see, dimly or clearly, the necessity of imposing a central order on their inter-relations, so that the ends they severally pursue may be so far as possible harmonised and thus made more attainable, and so that the common ends springing from their common natures may be more effectually attained in organised activity. Thus they impose as organised societies, in dim or clear knowledge, a new kind of law, determinate and sanctioned, expressive of their general desire that the law of will should be as binding as the law of the outer world.

If you desire to be healthy, you must fulfil these conditions—so runs the law of health. *If* you desire to be wealthy or happy, you must fulfil these conditions—so run the laws of wealth and of happiness. *If* you desire to pursue in peace and order with all men your private and common ends, *and if* you desire to avoid the penalties annexed to disobedience, you must fulfil these conditions —so runs the law of the State. If you desire—the appeal is to the will, and behind all the *if you desires* of all socially-imposed imperatives there lies the impelling and selective and co-ordinating *you ought* of the moral imperative.

All vital law is in some way the law of the will of living beings, but the greater the life the more autonomous the

law. The blinder life of man is, indeed, one with his
conscious life, but as his will emerges more and more into
the light of purpose he becomes more and more the master
of material law. In that higher activity physical and
organic law remain as binding as before, but they are now
become ministers to conscious purpose. This purpose—
implying at once power and choice—is the liberating factor
which turns nature's necessity into man's opportunity,
and the whole evolution of man is a process of liberation
in which his very awareness of his subjection becomes the
condition of his mastery. The teleological law based on,
limited by, and yet controlling physical and organic law,
is the social law proper. It is as men purpose in relation
to one another that they build the great structures of
community. Purposive activity is a cause of causes, yet
neither mingles with nor abrogates other causes.[1] It
exists in various degrees in the various stages of life, and
where it exists all other laws are in that degree subordinate. This is the mystery of teleological law that,
though it always remains pure, though no effect can ever
be regarded as the *resultant* of teleological and other
causes, yet this supervening vital law has power within
the sphere of material law.

The law of purpose runs through all life, it is the revelation of life. To know what a being seeks is to know
what that being is. It is the ultimate explanation. As
our organic desires reveal our organic nature, so our

---

[1] To take a simple illustration, if I seek to drive a ball to a certain
point and the ball is deflected by a cross-wind, the path of the ball
must not be regarded as a resultant of my purpose and the wind.
On the physical side it is the resultant of various forces acting on
the ball, and to add the purpose to these physical forces is needless
and indeed meaningless. If you ask again not how the ball got there
but why, the answer is—because I willed it to go somewhere else. If
I had allowed for the wind and succeeded in attaining the desired spot,
the physical series of causes would still as always be complete. The
How is answered similarly as before, the *Why* is answered thus—
because I willed to send it there !

spiritual desires reveal our spiritual nature. The simple
phrases in which we sum up our purposes are themselves
no explanation of them. A man spends his days pursuing
some end of service or of knowledge. It is, we say, love
or patriotism or ambition, but are we saying anything
more than that the living being lives in and by seeking
these ends, and can we say anything more ? The fulfilment is not in the attainment but in the pursuit, not in
the short hour of success, which if it comes is usually
unvalued, but in the long hours of striving. Our most
rational purposes still so much resemble the blinder forces
of organic nature that it is perhaps wiser not to sum up
clear intentions in terms of further motives but dimly
understood. We still know better what we seek than
why. The difference of instinct and intelligence is simply
the degree in which we know the larger behind the immediate purpose, the degree in which we know ourselves
and the laws of our being. It is the nature of life that
as it increases it should increase in knowledge of itself.
The teleological law becomes clearer as life develops, and
as it becomes clearer it becomes freer, until we can conceive the highest life as one of perfect self-knowledge and
of perfect autonomy.

Such is the dominance of teleological law that in the
process of society every physical and organic factor of
human life becomes transformed into a value beyond the
mere structure and function. Consanguinity comes to
mean pride of race or family, creating social stations and
traditions. Marriage is raised beyond its organic function
to mean all the intimate values and satisfactions of the
home life. Physical contiguity comes to mean more than
a physical fact, it is interpreted into the value we attach
to our life within a town or district or country. Every
physical and organic factor becomes enhanced into a value.
In this way we are all idealists. All society depends on

the recognition of facts as values.   The activity of every
association is the pursuit of the ends it is realised as
serving.

It will now be evident that the discovery and formulation of the laws we have called free—as well as of those
secondary laws which reveal the immediate interrelations
of men's purposes—is the difficult and important task of
social science.   The laws of associations lie ready-made
before us, but they are merely materials for our study,
not the laws we seek, being themselves forms of organisation based on individually determined purposes.   They
may be quite arbitrary, revealing no true social purpose
but only the interest of the few or the folly of the many,
and when they are not arbitrary they are but the truer
reflection of the deeper-working self-determined purposes
of men.   They are empty forms unless the wills of men
give them validity, static expressions of a dynamic will
which changes, creates, and destroys them.   The ultimate
social laws are recorded in no statute-book, but must be
diligently sought in the history and experience of our
actual life.   The ultimate social laws are those which
reveal the interrelations of the purposes of living beings,
their conditions and their consequences.   To those who
understand the true relation of " individual " and " social,"
it will appear no paradox that the fundamental social laws
are thus individually determined.

(5) The significance of the subdivisions of sanctioned
law will be made clear in the succeeding chapter.

CHAPTER II

COMMUNITY AND ASSOCIATION

§ 1. The general relation of community and association.

One of the greatest of the difficulties which at the present day beset the social analyst is the confused nature of his vocabulary. Unlike the students of most other sciences he must accept the terms of everyday life. These terms are lacking in all precision, and if the sociologist is to avoid disaster he must not hesitate to refine them to his own purposes. This is the case with the essential terms of our subject-matter, the terms society, community, association, and State. The looseness with which these terms are often used even by professed authorities is remarkable, and the results most unhappy. That must be our excuse if at the outset we insist, in spite of popular usage, on limiting each of these terms to a single and definite meaning.

Society, the most general term of all, I intend to use in a universal or generic sense to include every willed relationship of man to man. If, then, we distinguish community, association, and State from society, it must be by delimiting the former as special kinds or aspects of social fact. The essential distinction here involved, one of the utmost importance, is that between community and association.

By a community I mean any area of common life, village, or town, or district, or country, or even wider area. To deserve the name community, the area must be somehow distinguished from further areas, the common life may have some characteristic of its own such that the frontiers of the area have some meaning. All the laws of the cosmos, physical, biological, and psychological, conspire to bring it about that beings who live together shall resemble one another. Wherever men live together they develop in some kind and degree distinctive common characteristics—manners, traditions, modes of speech, and so on. These are the signs and consequences of an effective common life. It will be seen that a community may be part of a wider community, and that all community is a question of degree. For instance, the English residents in a foreign capital often live in an intimate community of their own, as well as in the wider community of the capital. It is a question of the degree and intensity of the common life. The one extreme is the whole world of men, one great but vague and incoherent common life. The other extreme is the small intense community within which the life of an ordinary individual is lived, a tiny nucleus of common life with a sometimes larger, sometimes smaller, and always varying fringe. Yet even the poorest in social relationships is a member in a chain of social contacts which stretches to the world's end. In the infinite series of social relationships which thus arise, we distinguish the nuclei of intenser common life, cities and nations and tribes, and think of them as *par excellence* communities.

An association is an organisation of social beings (or a body of social beings *as organised*) for the pursuit of some common interest or interests. It is a determinate social unity built upon common purpose. Every end which men seek is more easily attained for all when all whom it concerns unite to seek it, when all co-operate in seeking it. Thus you may have an association corresponding to every possible interest of social beings. Community bubbles into associations permanent and transient, and no student of the actual social life of the present can help being struck by the enormous number of associations of every kind, political, economic, religious, educational, scientific, artistic, literary, recreative, which to-day more than ever before enrich communal life.

A community is a focus of social life, the common living of social beings, an association is an organisation of social life, definitely established for the pursuit of one or more common interests. An association is partial, a community is integral. The members of one association may be members of many other and distinct associations. Within a community there may exist not only numerous associations but also antagonistic associations. Men may associate for the least significant or for the most significant of purposes ; the association may mean very much or very little to them, it may mean merely the source of a half-yearly dividend, or it may be the guardian of their dearest or highest interests—but community is something wider and freer than even the greatest associations ; it is the greater common life out of which associations rise, into which associations bring order, but which associations never completely fulfil. If we reflect, we perceive at once that there is a vast difference between the living together of men which makes a village or city or country on the one hand, and the association of men in a church or trade-union—or even, as we shall see, in a State—on the other. Often state-areas do not even coincide with the areas of effective community, as, for instance, when a subject-people, incorporated in an alien State, continues to lead its own manner of life. A distinction of name is essential.[1]

---

[1] The only writer I know who stresses the distinction between community and association is Professor Ferdinand Tönnies. But Dr. Tönnies employs the German equivalents in rather a different significa-tion. By " community " (*Gemeinschaft*) he means *reales und organisches*

It may be well to show how infinitely associations vary in degree of permanence and significance, and the main reason of these variations, before we consider the relation to community of the most permanent and most comprehensive of all—the State.

Men may *mass* together without becoming organised. A mere aggregation is not an association. Take the case of a crowd casually collected to watch a fire. The aggregation serves no end, each individual of the crowd could watch the fire quite as well—better in fact—if the others went away ! A common interest keeps them together, but it does not bind them to one another, it need bring no individual into social contact with any other. It is a physical and not a social contiguity. No association is dissolved when the fire burns out—or when the policeman moves the crowd away ! But suppose the crowd had resolved to fight the fire and had organised themselves to that end. At once the aggregation would have been transformed into an association, its individuals would have fallen into social relations with one another, and the order which is attendant on social purpose would have permeated the whole. As soon as men see that any interest they share is furthered by organisation, they are preparing an association. So here an association would have come into being for an hour—and in an hour would have passed away.

Take next the case of men gathered to celebrate some occasion, say an historic anniversary. Here there is a purpose depending on and realised through association. The meeting-together is an essential element of the celebration. Time and place and procedure are predeter-

Leben, by "association" (*Gesellschaft*) he understands *ideelle und mechanische Bildung*. Thus he would say *Gemeinschaft der Sprache, der Sitte, des Glaubens aber Gesellschaft des Erwerbes, der Reise, der Wissenschaft.* (Tönnies, *Gemeinschaft und Gesellschaft.*) The distinction here seems one of degree rather than of kind as above.

mined, it is an organised association, not a casual aggregation. But the purpose may be only a trivial thing in
the life of each member of the assemblage. It brings
him into social contact, but a very transient and partial
contact, with the rest. There is a consciousness of
common interest realised in association, but it finds only
a momentary expression. When the pageant has passed,
or the bonfire turned to ashes, or the dinner and the
speeches are ended, the association dissolves. Because
the purpose was transient, the association it created could
not endure.

Consider next an association created for the achievement of some specific reform, political or religious, say
for the passing of a bill or the formulation of a creed.
Here a more permanent purpose animates the association,
and works a deeper organisation. Each member of the
association has a definite point of contact with every
other. It is because each member has a certain individuality that he is a member. If he were different in
a certain important way, he would not be a member.
And in the association each holds a definite place, determined in part at least by his individuality. (For it is
a general law of association that the deeper the purpose
at work, the more complex becomes the organisation.)
Yet since the purpose is specific and temporary, the
association which pursues it pursues its own dissolution.
When the bill is passed or the creed formulated, in the
fulfilment of its sustaining purpose the association itself
dissolves. When slavery was abolished, the associations
for the abolition of slavery were abolished also. Every
such association dies of its success.

Let us turn next to an association of a very different
type, the association of marriage. The purpose on which
this association rests is the deep foundation of all life,
and that purpose is fulfilled not in the mere procreation

of offspring and their tutelage until they attain the autonomy of manhood or womanhood—if it were, it might be dissolved when that purpose is completed, or when the association has failed to achieve that purpose. The profound purpose of the marriage-association includes the present as well as the future generations, and fulfils the lives of those who enter into it no less than it creates and develops the lives of those who issue from it. It is, therefore, a continuous and—unless perverted—permanent purpose of human life, and the association it creates is likewise continuous and permanent, strongly rooted in the heart of life.

Thus to a permanent purpose there always answers, in the nature of things, a permanent association. This appears still more clearly when we turn to such associations as Church and State. These rest on purposes more lasting than any individuals, and are thus maintained through periods of time infinitely larger than the life-periods of individuals. In so far as they are purposes necessary to the fulfilment of life, they create associations as immortal as life. And as the most enduring purposes are also those which grow and change the most, there is a continuous evolution of the greater associations.

Lastly, associations vary as much in extent as in permanence, and for the same reason. Wherever there is a character common to social beings, a common interest is implicit, an interest, that is, which can be furthered by organisation, by association. The extent of a common interest *should* measure the extent of its correspondent association. The most intimate interest is that which most directly unites just two human beings, as in the association of marriage; but at the other extreme are interests universal as mankind—the interest we call justice, for example—and the history of society is in part a history of the widening of associations (and therefore

of community) as men more and more recognise how
much they have in common with other men, and more
and more understand that every common value is protected and furthered by association. So out of the small
circles of primitive society have grown the great and
ever-widening associations of the modern world.

We have been speaking of the State as simply one
among other associations, but the State has obviously
a very peculiar and distinctive place. Other associations
are limited to the pursuit of one or at most a few interests,
the State seems to have some care for nearly every interest.
Other associations cannot on their own initiative enforce
their decisions on recalcitrant members, the State can
and does. Other associations have their members scattered over a city or district or country, the State includes
within its membership, or at least within its control, all
the dwellers within determined communal frontiers. It
is, therefore, highly important to determine the relation
of the State, first to community itself, and next to the
other associations within community.

§ 2. Community and State.

Because the State, like community, has territorial
frontiers and because it exercises control over all, or
nearly all, other associations, many writers speak as if
community and State were one. This seems to have
been the view of Hegel and is certainly the doctrine of
the neo-Hegelian writers on the State,[1] as well as of
many others to whom that epithet scarcely applies.
Here is a representative statement of this doctrine from
the late M. Fouillée : " Imagine," he wrote, " a great
circle within which are lesser circles combining in a
thousand ways to form the most varied figures without
overstepping the limits that enclose them ; this is an

[1] See Appendix A.

image of the great association of the State and of the particular associations that it embraces." (*La Science Sociale Contemporaine*, p. 13.)

We shall see later that this doctrine, which makes the State the limit of community and makes all other associations but elements of the State, is contradicted by the whole evolution of the modern State. For the present it will suffice to show that the doctrine, so strangely maintained in the face of history, is contrary to the present fact. Here we are not concerned with what the State ought to be and to include, but with what the State actually is and does include. So regarded, it is quite obvious that the State is neither conterminous nor synonymous with community. Every State has rigid territorial limits, but the modern world, marked off into separate States, is not partitioned into a number of isolated communities. We have already seen that community is a matter of degree, that it is a network of social interrelations here denser, here thinner, whose ever new-woven filaments join men to men across countries and continents. The State, unlike community, is exclusive and determinate. Where one State ends, another begins; where one begins, another ends.[1] No man can owe allegiance to two States, any more than he can serve two masters, but he can enter into the life of as many communities as his sympathies and opportunities will allow.

Quite obviously the metaphor of Fouillée is false. Let us draw our exclusive circles and call them England, France, Germany, and so on. By hypothesis, all associations fall within these circles, and do not intersect them. Well, in which circle shall we place the international economic associations without which none of the great

---

[1] We need not delay to show that the case of federal States is only an apparent exception.

States could to-day exist at all ? In which shall we place the numerous international unions, industrial, scientific, religious, and artistic ? " Without overstepping the limits that enclose them "—that is the foundation of the neo-Hegelian doctrine of the State, and it is a foundation which is false in fact.

But, it will be answered, every association, international or intranational, is controlled by the State. Intranational associations are controlled by the separate States, international associations by agreement between States. No members of any State can enter into any association whatever unless that State permits it. Thus every other association is subordinate to the State.

We may grant the contention. At a later stage we shall see more clearly whence and why the will of the State has this pre-eminence. At that stage we shall understand more fully the distinction between community and State. Meantime we must insist that there is a false inference if we say that because the State has control over every other association, therefore all other associations are absorbed into the State, are simply parts of the State, or are completely circumscribed by its frontiers. If we hold this view, the process of conflict through which modern States have attained their present democratic forms, and in especial the long agony of strife due to the opposing claims of churches and of States, is without meaning for us.

There is an easy and direct way by which we can discover the limits of the State. The essential feature of the State is political order, the *primary* instrument of the State is political law. There has been community where no State yet existed, and even to-day we may discover, among certain Eskimo peoples, for instance, primitive forms of communal life still uncoordinated within a State. Where there is no political law, there is no State. Political law is thus the criterion of the State, and in learning the nature and limits of political law we are learning the nature and limits of the State.

Political law is in its proper nature unconditioned, formulated, and mainly negative. These characters reveal the limits of the State.

It is unconditioned. The laws of other associations bind their members, but if you don't like the laws you can leave the association—unless the *State* forbids. If you disapprove of the laws of your club or business-association or trade-union or church, you can resign. If any such association tries of its own accord to enforce its laws on you, it comes into collision with the powers of the State. It can properly do no more than deny you its special benefits and privileges. So with communal or customary law, properly so-called. If you break the customs, traditions, fashions prevalent in your community, you may expect its disapprobation. It will boycott you, refuse to enter into social relations with you, but unless you break also the law of the State, it cannot otherwise visit upon you its displeasure. But if you break a political law, you do not merely lose privileges. The State will do more than deny its benefits, it will punish. It has behind it the united force of the community, the final sanction attached to no other kind of social law. Nor can you simply resign your membership of the State to escape its law. Even if you go beyond its frontiers its claims may follow you, and within the State, even if you shut yourself up within your walls, you are subject to the laws of the State, to all the conditions it may impose either directly or by delegation of authority.

Why does the State hold this unique position ? Why has it behind it the united force of the community ? The force of the law is not an ultimate thing, it is always and essentially dependent upon will. The State has this power of compulsion because its members *will* that power, because they subject themselves to its law and unite their force to maintain it. To what end ?

No man can wholly cut himself off from social relations while he remains in the world of men. We are forced from all sides, by every instinct and every need, into society, into relations with our fellows. Such relations must be *ordered*, or life is impossible. Mutual good demands mutual service, mutual forbearance and restraint. Thus wherever society exists there exists a system of obligations and rights. Society incessantly creates these reciprocal relations between every man and all other men. Sometimes they remain unformulated and traditional, as in a primitive community ruled by " unwritten law," but nearly always the most essential of these relationships of right and obligation are set out in clear formulæ, as political laws, and protected by a central authority endowed with communal power. Any body of men so organised that a central institution or government takes over the maintenance and development of the essential system of rights and obligations accepted among them is properly called a State. A State is thus the fundamental association for the maintenance and development of social order, and to this end its central institution is endowed with the united power of the community. It is not meant that the members of a State consciously realise why they give or permit it this final authority—if they did they would never have permitted the endless perversions of government—but only that as their political consciousness emerges, as they ask themselves why they should contribute this might to the State, the answer appears in this form. As the State develops, as its members grow in social wisdom, its power rests more and more on its service of that end.

Subjection to law is political obligation, which is only the reverse side of political right. Beyond law, beyond government, and beyond force lie the common ends, the common will of community. The end is here as always the revelation of meaning and the justification of existence. If the citizen owes obedience to government it must be in virtue of some social good which in turn determines the respect the government shall show to him. Political right and political obligation, as all right and all obligation, are derived from the same source and are meaningless if separated. Already we see that the State and its government are not ultimate social phenomena but rest on what is yet deeper, communal life and will.

The special limits of the State are revealed when we consider the further characteristics of political law.

In the second place, political law is expressed in definite formulæ. A political law defines certain categories of persons as coming within its scope, and prescribes for them as precisely as possible certain forms of conduct. It is obvious, therefore, that it can apply only to general situations and can enforce only *external* fulfilments. Thus the State is at once outside large spheres of human activity. It cannot control motives save indirectly. It can enjoin actions, or rather activities, but not the spirit of their fulfilment. But large classes of action are wholly dependent on the spirit in which they are fulfilled, and many associations exist simply to foster types of ideal or spiritual values. The State *cannot* determine these associations, and it *should not* prescribe any of those actions which derive their only value from the spirit of their performance. The State can compel people to attend church, but it cannot compel them to worship, and therefore the former compulsion is folly. The State cannot create by its *fiat* a church or

C

an artistic or literary association. It can protect and maintain and even organise such associations—to do so may be part of its function—but it cannot, if it is true to its own nature, determine and control them. Further, in its generality and externality it cannot touch (save by way of repression) that spontaneity and initiative of individual life which is the beginning of all social process and the root of all social value. The State must, therefore, be clearly distinguished from the community which creates it. Community is the common life of beings who are guided essentially from within, actively, spontaneously, and freely (under the conditions prescribed by the laws they make) relating themselves to one another, weaving for themselves the complex web of social unity. But the State works with an instrument which is necessarily formal, prescribing the general external conditions of social life, upholding the main system of those social obligations which may be externally fulfilled. Its instrument resembles, in Aristotle's phrase, no " leaden rule " which can adapt itself to the actual mouldings of the social structure, but an unbending rod which can measure only its general outlines.[1]

Because it can determine only the external forms of conduct, the law of the State must be mainly (though by no means wholly) negative. It must for the most part be content (as the neo-Hegelians themselves are forced to admit, though they do not see the significance of the admission) to " hinder hindrances " to social welfare. It can prevent or punish wrong-doing rather than endorse right-doing. It can create for men the external social conditions necessary for the well-living of their lives. It can enforce these outer obligations without the fulfilment of which the inner obligations cannot be fulfilled. For this reason the sanction of political law is punish-

[1] Cf. *Nic. Ethics*, Bk. VI., c. 10, § 7.

ment and not reward. We reward and honour only
what the theologian called " works of supererogation,"
not the minimal fulfilment of external law.

It is needless to say that in thus stating the limits of
political activity we are not belittling the immeasurable
value of that activity. The point is that the State is
not equivalent to community, that the political association does not include and can not control the whole life
of men. The State is seen to be not community but a
peculiarly authoritative association within it. The State
is determinate, a closed organisation of social life ; community is indeterminate, an ever-evolving system spread-
ing beyond and only partially controlled within the
definite framework of any State. That framework gives
to the portion of community which it encloses a certain
unity and definition, but neither cuts it off from a wider
community of which it is essentially part nor within
that portion substitutes its own external mode of action,
its necessity, for the spontaneity that is the mark of all
life, social and other. Social life can no longer in practice
and should no longer in theory be summed up in political
life. The individual should not be summed up in his
citizenship, otherwise the claim of citizenship will itself
become a tyranny and its essential moral value be lost.
" The modern wilderness of interests " is not to be
straightened out into the simple road of citizenship.
For the main road of citizenship, which we must make
straight as possible, though it intersects a thousand
paths of social interest, cannot and should not absorb
them.

These paths of social interest do not stop at the frontiers
of States. The political interest is determinate and has
limits, the social has none. Hence for the proper understanding of international relations it is most necessary
to distinguish community and State. On the assump-

tion of identity we can have no social unity among the
nations until they are absorbed within some world-state.
For each State by its very definition is a determinate
and self-contained unit. In respect of the sphere of its
sovereignty every State is demarcated absolutely from
every other. Consequently, if political relationship were
identical with social relationship, the members of one
State would remain totally alien from the members of
every other State. Communities would stand to one
another as Spinoza and Hobbes imagined them to stand,
isolated as the pre-civil individuals of their imagination,
totally irresponsible until some contract is agreed upon,
even then totally irresponsible because there is no possible higher will to make agreement binding. But, of
course, it is in international relations that the distinction
of State and community is most clearly revealed and
that the common interests of universal society most
manifestly weave new unities in spite of political separation. A man may perhaps "denationalise" himself
(though that is hardly the proper word) by leaving his
country, but he cannot "desocialise" himself without
leaving the world of men, or at least of civilised men.

Community, therefore, and not the State, is the "world
the spirit has made for itself." "The spirit" does not
isolate itself in States, as Hegel's argument assumes.[1]
On the contrary, the growth of civilisation means the
growth of ever-widening community, the "realisation"
of social interest beyond the limits of politically independent groups. Society widens and the sense of com-

[1] Hegel is rather confusing on this point. For instance, he says
(*Gr. der Phil. des Rechts*, § 330) that the State is "not a private person
but a completely independent totality," and yet immediately adds
that it is related to other States (331) and instances the nations of
Europe as "forming a family on account of the universal principles
of their legislation, their ethical usages, and their civilisation" (339).
How can "completely independent totalities" form a family? See
further Appendix A.

munity grows. In particular, the privileged classes of the different peoples, the authors of most past wars, become more and more allied by social intercourse, by common commercial and intellectual interests. M. Tarde has pointed out how classes of men whose occupation, even if in a competitive way, brings them into constant association with one another, develop a friendlier spirit towards one another than classes not subject to this socialising influence. The same holds of peoples. It is not civilisation but intercivilisation that develops mutual sympathy between States. The highly socialised Greek cities, because each held to an ideal of autonomy and self-sufficiency, the ideal of " completely independent totality," were not intersocialised, and, accordingly, displayed the intensest hostility to one another. But the aloofness of Greek states is impossible in the modern world, which is pervaded by intersocialising influences of literature and commerce. Common ideas and common trade have formed everywhere social bonds which cut across the line of States, and have made western Europe, looked on as a whole, an effective community. Thus an educated Englishman comes to have more in common with an educated Frenchman than he has, say, with an English agricultural labourer. The alien, shut out from his State, may yet have a closer social affinity to him than his fellow citizen. And yet the prevalent political philosophy blindly declares that " the State " is " the world the spirit has made for itself," and that " between State and State there can be no consciousness of common good " !

If we turn for a moment from fact to ideal—two things which the neo-Hegelians constantly confuse—we may admit the desirability of a wider political co-ordination of community than at present exists. This is to be achieved not by our going backwards and cutting off the bonds of relationship which make community wider in area than any single State, but by our going forward on the road of federation and making a union of States great enough to comprehend the existing intercommunity. The recognition of likeness of interests, purposes, and needs is increasing and not diminishing in the people of different nations. It is the State that is inadequate, not community that is overstepping its due bounds. The State must always, as we have seen, remain inadequate to comprehend and regulate *all* community. But it is more inadequate than need be, so long as the political relations of States are capricious and unco-ordinated. At present civilised States are like masters who maintain splendid order and discipline within their workshops, and thus feel free to go out and racket in the streets.

§3. State and other associations.

We have seen that a State is not a community but a peculiarly authoritative association within community ; we may now discuss briefly how States and other associations are related. Here, it must be noted, we are considering not what is but what ought to be, not the facts of this relationship, but an ideal which may in any particular State be wholly or partially unrealised. We too often assume that all actual States conform to a single type which we can identify as " the State." In fact, States present and past have adopted every possible attitude towards the other associations, sometimes heedless of them, often partial to some and repressive of others, sometimes repressive of them all, sometimes allowing certain associations (the church in particular) to share or usurp its own proper authority, and sometimes not admitting the same associations to their own proper place. All, therefore, that we can do here is to show in an introductory way how the State—by which we mean any and every State—*should*, in the light of the social ends which it can serve, stand in relation to the other associations which also after their kind pursue social ends.

If the State does not absorb into its own life of organis-ation the other forms of social life, the worlds of art, science, religion, and social intercourse, not to speak of the family life, in what relation does it stand to these ? In the first place, because, as we have seen, the State preserves and upholds through its organisation the very existence of society, that being its primary end, it has a certain superiority of control, not merely of influence, alike over the partial organisations and over the free life of community—a control which in no way contradicts the essential claim to spontaneity made by that life. Suppose the state-authority finds that the teaching of certain religious doctrines is calculated to undermine the security of society, then it may forbid the teaching of these doctrines, and if it is right in its conception of the social danger and does no counterbalancing evil by interfering, it is right also in its interference.   Suppose again that the state-authority finds that some economic association deprives its workers of the opportunity to live a reasonable healthy life, again it may interfere.   It has the same right over associations of individuals as over unassociated individuals.   It has to protect the whole against antagonistic acts of both alike, not only against deliberate acts of encroachment but also against such general and unintended social wrongs as deforestation, as the vitiation of the air-supply, the water-supply, and the sun-supply.   Only thus can it fulfil its primary function as the guardian of community.

But of course state-action has a much wider area than that just indicated.   Individualistic writers like Mill and Spencer limited the State to that kind of action, and so gave away their case. The State possesses the most complete, powerful, and centralised of all organisations. There seems no clear reason why the community should not take all advantage of the greatest organisation it has built. There seems no clear reason why this central organisation should not be utilised for the furtherance of all social ends which it is able, without detriment to any more important ends, to further. Take, *e.g.*, the economic life fulfilled by myriad economic associations. To a certain extent, as experience shows, state-organisation can develop that life without destroying its spontaneity—and so we find the State regulating forms of contract, controlling coinage, determining the conditions of limited liability, establishing banks, even assuming entire control of those industries which, so to speak, bind all other industries together and make their free development possible, the industries of intercommunication. Or again, take family life. The family is not simply an element in the State, as Plato wished it to be, but essentially something more. Yet the State does not merely recognise and protect the family. It claims a certain control, for the benefit of both family and State. It regards marriage itself as a political institution *so far as* to insist on certain regulations and conditions, and it defines to some degree the rights and duties of relatives, making them legal and not merely moral rights and duties. It might reasonably, to the advantage of both family and State, prohibit the marriage of people suffering from certain forms of disease or insanity, though here, as always, the limit of State-intervention becomes a difficult *practical* problem. Some of these problems will meet us at a later stage.

The State, we see, may control an association while yet the association remains voluntary, being, that is, no mere part of the political organisation, being freely established, freely entered into, freely directed, and in some cases freely dissolved, by its members. The right of free association is a most important factor in the development of community, and of the State. It mediates between the necessity of political government and the casualness of wholly unregulated social relations. It ensures the expression and furtherance of those specialised interests of culture and doctrine, of art and science which are so precious in our lives. It saves the State from the alternatives of stagnation and arbitrary control, It provides a ground for endless experiments in social organisation. The voluntary association leads the way, the State follows, often taking over the organisation of those voluntary associations which have been bravely but inadequately endeavouring to supply a universal or necessary public service. The provision of hospital and other medical and charitable service is a case in point. These services, so necessary to the community, were almost invariably established at the first by voluntary associations, but gradually the need for a broader basis of organisation was realised, and they are now in great part undertaken by the State. In such a case the State comes in, not to destroy, but to fulfil the work of the voluntary association, and so long as it acts in that spirit it cannot overstep its bounds.

It is to be noted that in the degree in which the State assumes its proper function as above indicated the distinctive character of associations other than political becomes clearly revealed. In the classical and mediæval worlds the distinction of community and State was never completely realised, and consequently the meaning and value of the other associations were often misunderstood. To illustrate : the Greeks tended to find their whole fulfilment in the life of the polis, which was both city and State, and in consequence the family-association remained unhonoured, unliberated, and unfulfilled, to the irretrievable loss of Greece. Again, the mediæval States, failing to give precision and limit to the political authority, failed also to give precision and limit to other associations, such as the church or the gild. Take the gild as an example. Mediæval gilds present a striking contrast to modern associations whether of capital or of labour. The gild was hierarchical, exclusive, often owning a peculiar monopoly within the community, pursuing no one clear interest but a medley of indeterminate interests. A trade union or an employers' union is a voluntary association, an association of likes, of members who are regarded as possessing equal rights within it, who have a common interest uniting them as an association, and who usually pursue in singleness of aim that common interest. Thus in place of the old complex associations of the middle ages—inadequate, arbitrary, and often compulsive, because of their confused relation to the State —there have arisen the simple voluntary associations of to-day, each with a place of its own within the community, each with a definite relation to the State and a definite autonomy, each limited to one kind of interest and composed of members who are alike in respect of that interest.[1]

It must not be inferred that in the modern world the respective places of State and voluntary association are to-day adequately and harmoniously assigned. In the western States political evolution is certainly in advance of political theory on this question, but it is still far from being complete. In some directions, especially in the industrial sphere, as we shall see later, the need exists for a completer control by the State over the liberties of associations ; in others there is needed a completer liberation of associations from political control. For

[1] Cf. Fournière, *L'Individu, l'Association, et l'État,* chap. 1.

example, medical, scientific, educational, and other properly non-political appointments are in our own country still too largely determined by political (or rather party) considerations, and are often, as everybody knows, given to less qualified candidates because they are of the right party-colour. It is folly that the selection of the head of a medical school or of a university or of a church should be determined by such considerations, and it is bad both for the association and for the State.

It must also be admitted that the associations themselves do not always recognise the limits of their proper spheres. The greater associations have in the past frequently transgressed their bounds. The church in particular has often claimed a compulsive power which is not its own but the State's alone. And the curious idea is still entertained by some that the inhabitants of a country must, presumably because they may be supposed to belong more or less to one original stock, have a single religion co-extensive with and limited by its confines— a Church of Scotland peculiar to and co-extensive with Scotland, a Church of England peculiar to and co-extensive with England, and so on. (But even the vegetation of different countries is often the same—and human beings think !) Again, a trade-union sometimes attempts to coerce non-unionists into the association, though its proper right is limited to the denial of its privileges to those who refuse to enter. Or again, to cite a more harmless instance of transgression, 'when a university confers its honorary degrees, which should stand for distinguished services to literature, art, or knowledge, upon men who have otherwise made themselves distinguished names, say as soldiers, diplomatists, or merchants, but who, in respect of the ends for which a university stands, may be mere barbarians, it too is forgetful of its sphere. Such a lack of discrimination is bad for the association, because it obscures the meaning and lowers the value of the honour when conferred on the true man of science or seeker after wisdom.[1]

We have shown in mere outline that every association, including the State, is an organised form of social life within community, that each has its distinctive place and meaning, while community is greater than any of them, greater than all of them together. We may now conclude this introduction by showing how community, and not any or all of its associations, can be and is the object of our present study.

[1] The habit of the university to decorate diplomatists, military men, city dignitaries, etc., is peculiarly foolish, since for them nearly all other honorary distinctions, titles, and orders exist, and it is ridiculous and superfluous to extend to these the one distinction which stands for service in the sphere of learning—or stands for nothing.

CHAPTER III

THE PLACE OF SOCIOLOGY AMONG THE SCIENCES

§ 1. Sociology and the special social sciences.

When a newcomer, bearing approved credentials, is introduced into an old and exclusive circle, he proceeds next to find his place within the circle. This process of adjustment the newcomer sociology has been undergoing within the circle of the sciences. Our subject is community, and the science of community is sociology. We have shown that community is a reality which no study of the particular associations will ever explain, since it is greater and more comprehensive than any, itself the common matrix of them all. We have shown thereby the credentials of sociology, and it remains to show its place and status among the sciences, in particular its relation to those sciences whose claims the claim of the newcomer may be thought to disturb or challenge.

We may divide these latter sciences into two classes. On the one hand there are sciences which are at least as generic or universal in character as sociology and yet seem to occupy much the same ground. These are the sciences of ethics and psychology, and the problem of their relation to sociology is most significant. On the other hand there are special social sciences, sciences dealing with special kinds of social fact, and, therefore, clearly less general than the science of community as a whole. We must arbitrate here between the claims of the generic science and the claims of the specific sciences. This latter problem is the easier of the two, and may be resolved before we seek an answer to the deeper problem.

Just as particular associations have at times sought to sweep within their bounds the whole life of community, so have particular social sciences sought to comprehend the whole study of community. In particular men have made this claim of comprehensiveness on behalf of the sciences of politics and economics, claiming with misguided enthusiasm that all social phenomena are fundamentally political or economic. But there have always been obstinate facts which resist inclusion under either of these genera, and have rendered vain all such partial syntheses. The social sciences have their sphere within sociology, just as associations have their sphere within community. The specific social sciences are *sciences of associational forms of life*, and, therefore, can never ascend the throne reserved for sociology, a throne tenantless until she enter into her kingdom.

The purposes men pursue, and in the pursuit of which they build associations, are most numerous and complex, but they can be reduced under a limited number of categories. To definite kinds of purpose correspond definite forms of association, and these in turn give order and precision to the correspondent social activities. Hence there arise within social life great distinguishable series of facts which are studied by distinct sciences. The special social sciences—politics, economics, jurisprudence, the study of the associational aspects of religion, education, art, literature, and every other activity of men—exist as such owing to the relative isolability of certain kinds of social fact, the relative interdependence of social phenomena belonging to the same series and their relative independence of social phenomena belonging to other series.

It may suffice if we consider in this light the best formulated of all the special sciences, *viz.* economics. *Mutatis mutandis*, the result of our consideration will hold for each of the other social sciences.

The facts which fall within the economic series have a certain relative independence and interdependence. For example, we can investigate the relation of the cost of production of an article to the amount produced and to the demand, the relation of increase of capital to increase of profit, the relation of the output of precious metal to its purchasing power, and so with many far more complex relations. Not that such economic relations are really isolated, but we can suppose other social factors to remain constant while the change in one economic factor produces change in other economic factors. *In so far*, the science of economics exists as an independent study, but we must always remember that such independence is very relative and very partial. The failure to recognise this fact has been responsible for much bad economics. It has, indeed, always been obvious that the economic series was related to other definite series of social facts, the political series, the legal series, the series concerned with the growth of population, and so on ; and the investigation of these interrelationships was regarded as constituting certain frontier-provinces of economics, or perhaps common territories which it shared with politics or ethics or jurisprudence. But this is far from being an adequate statement of the case, and the interrelation of definite series of social phenomena, economic and political, economic and religious, religious and political, and so forth, forms only a minor part of the incessant interactivity of social forces. Thus economic phenomena are constantly determined by all kinds of social need and activity, and in turn they are constantly re-determining—creating, shaping, transforming—social need and activity of every kind. Hence there arises an incessant complication of interactive factors, of which we can often distinguish only the social resultant, the outcome of interactive forces whose several operations we cannot discern.

What then of the sphere of economics ? Is economics properly limited to the study of the interrelation of phenomena within the economic series, so far as such relatively interdependent relations can be discovered (1)? But this limitation would make of economics a very fragmentary science. It would be condemned to dwell in a middle region of abstraction, cut off from the knowledge of its communal source and significance. Shall we then add, as the economic text-books do in practice (though often rather half-heartedly), (2) the investigation of the prior social determinants of economic phenomena, so far as definite determinations can be established—the study of varying climatic, cultural, religious, political, and other conditions as economic determinants ? If so, must we not add (3) the investigation of the prior economic determinants of other social phenomena—for instance, the study of industrialism as affecting morals, class-spirit, the status of women, religion, or international relations ? The profound unity of communal life renders it impossible wholly to separate (2) and (3), and, therefore, I assume that economics, if it passes beyond (1), is bound to study both of these ; but its interest would of course be one-sided. As a specific science it is seeking throughout to learn more about the nature of economic phenomena, not directly about the other social series with which the economic is so intimately bound. Otherwise it would lose itself in the vaster study of community.

Let us then assume that we have here found the sphere of economics. We have found it to be constituted of a complete study of one and a partial study of two other series of social relations, the three being relatively and in different degrees isolable within the world of social phenomena, and thus capable to a certain extent of independent study. But we must see that by their very nature these series form part of a greater system within which they arise and without which they would be meaningless. Take the simplest and most seeming-independent set of economic relations you please, and consider how it implies the whole world of social relations. Take the simple law of demand : " the greater the amount to be sold, the smaller must be the price at which it is offered in order to find purchasers." [1] But the ratio, as every economist points out, varies very greatly according to the kind of article ; according as it ranks as a luxury, a conventional necessity, or an absolute necessity ; according to the power of custom and fashion, the standard of civilisation and intelligence within a community. So that in our investigation of the economic question we are led into the widest realm of social, moral, and even religious relations. We are led in particular to the consideration of certain fundamental social laws which are common determinants of many specific types of social phenomena, to the consideration of the nature of custom, of social imitation and suggestion, of group-feeling and group-thinking, of temperamental and cultural unities and differences, of social conflict and co-operation. But it would needlessly enlarge the study of economics if it undertook a complete investigation of all these phenomena, and it would mean a needless overlapping of studies, since the other social sciences have equal grounds for investigating the same phenomena. These belong therefore to the general sphere of sociology as distinct from the definite spheres of the specific social sciences.

[1] So formulated by Marshall : *Principles of Economics* (6th ed.), p. 99.

D

In the wider sense sociology includes the special social sciences. In the narrower sense, as a distinctive study it investigates all those social relations which are too broad or deep or complex to fall within the scope of any one of the specific social sciences. For the diverse associational activities which give rise to the several social sciences are but aspects of the great communal unity, depend on one another in most intricate ways, and unite to produce resultants which can be called by no other name than communal. The common determinants of all specific activities, their greater interrelations and their communal resultants, constitute a subject-matter the study of which is the heroic and endless task of sociology. It is concerned with the nature and development of community. Here there lies still a vast territory to be explored. For we have in the special social sciences been investigating, so to speak, the flora and fauna of the country, but the soil itself, whence they alike spring and whereon they are alike sustained, we have largely ignored. Or, to change the metaphor, we have been examining the diverse coloured threads interwoven into the web of community, and have scarcely noticed the pattern which they weave. But no study of the threads, of the specific series of social facts studied by the social sciences, will yield a true knowledge of that pattern, of community itself.

Community is the object of our study. The special sciences consider the special associational activities in themselves, sociology considers them as aspects within a common life. We cannot live in mere economic or political or ecclesiastical associations, we do live in a community of which economic, political, and religious life are very necessary and real aspects. The need for this synthetic study is indubitable and is becoming realised. Mr. Gomme, the author of *The Village Com-*

munity, lays it down as a " fundamental proposition "
which he regards as "the true basis of anthropological
research," that " enquiry into the culture and condition
of primitive man . . . can only be conducted by considering each item of culture which is the subject of
enquiry in association with all other items of culture in
the same social group." (*Sociological Review*, Vol. II.,
p. 321.) If this principle holds of primitive communities,
it surely holds with equal force of the greatly differentiated
communities of civilisation. The differentiation makes
the task not less necessary but more difficult.

Some twenty-three centuries ago Plato wrote a great
dialogue on the city-community and its right ordering.
We agree to call it *The Republic*, but it is in fact, as it is
strictly in name, a work on the community of the city[1]
(πολιτεία). It is not simply what we understand as a
treatise on political science, it is too concrete and comprehensive for what we usually understand as a treatise
on ethics, discussing as it does the principles of economics,
politics, family life, religion, education, philosophy, art,
and literature. Plato saw all these as factors of one common life, bound together within the unity of that life.
The Republic was the first and greatest of sociological
treatises.

But the unity which Plato's comprehensive mind had
found soon disappeared. It was partly that the social
world itself was differentiating, even when he wrote, into
something too complex to be contained under the form
of the city, partly that his successors had not the power
of their master to discover a new synthesis of community.
The greatest of Plato's disciples wrote a series of separate
treatises on the different aspects of social life. In particular he wrote one treatise on ethics and another on

[1] As usual, the translators of Plato nearly always render πόλις as
"State" instead of "city," thereby losing the orientation of the original.

politics, *without being clear about the relation of the one to the other*.[1] The co-ordination was lost, and men have continued down to our own days to treat as separate studies economics, politics, religion, education, and so forth, while little or no attempt has been made, until quite recently, to show their interrelation and their basis in communal life.

Yet *The Republic* was the greatest achievement of Hellenic thought, and the greatest achievement of our thought to-day might well be a like synthetic inter-pretation of our greater and more complex world. The growth of sociology since the time of Comte is a witness that men are beginning to realise again that there is a unity of social life, and are seeking to restore the lost synthesis of community.

§ 2. Sociology and ethics.

Is there a *science* of ethics ? If we turn to the authori-tative works on ethics we find that they are devoted primarily to the question, What is the supreme good or the supreme good for man ? All the other problems which they raise, the ground of ethical obligation, the meaning and relation of the virtues, the relation of the good of the self to the good of others, are subsidiary and imply the previous solution of that central problem. But we discover soon enough that there *is* no body of accepted doctrine in respect of that problem, and that in the nature of the case there can be none. For if I say that happiness is the supreme end of life and another gainsays me, what way can be found of deciding between our claims ? If I meant that men as a rule do seek happi-ness before everything else, my statement might admit of verification or refutation, but if I mean that what

[1] Contrast Aristotle, *Nic. Ethics*, V. 2. 11, *Politics*, III. 4. 4, and IV. 7. 2, with *Nic. Ethics*, X., chaps. 7 and 8.

men *ought* to seek is happiness, how can that statement be controverted except by an equally dogmatic statement that they *ought not* to seek it ?   Now the distinctive character of ethics is that it is concerned with the question of *ought*, the question of right and wrong, good and bad. It is concerned, that is, with a question lying beyond the bounds of scientific procedure, beyond verification, beyond induction, beyond actuality.   Therefore, we can have a history of ethics but no science of it.   Instead of a science we must be content with a philosophy—or rather a series of philosophies, varying according to the insight and character of each philosopher, a series whose ethical contradictions and antagonisms can never be dissolved by any scientific procedure.   All ethical claims are claims of worthfulness, and we can neither confirm nor refute them save by our own estimate of their worth. In so far as they may mistake the true relation of means to ends, in so far as they may maintain that a system or mode of action contributes to some end to which in fact it does not contribute, we may convict them of scientific error, but in so far as they maintain that an end is good *in itself*, how shall we refute them if we disbelieve—save by denial ?

Systematic ethics is, therefore, a philosophy, while sociology is a science.   This general distinction gives the clue to those specific problems of relationship which have needlessly agitated many minds.   Philosophy and science can live quite well together, even though their representatives quarrel.   The physicist must willy-nilly be a metaphysician also, and he is never so much one as when he derides metaphysics.   Similarly, the sociologist is an ethical philosopher also and he can never divest himself of his philosophy.   His ethics is conditioned by and to some degree dependent on his social experience ; it is none the less not to be identified with his sociology.

I have said that ethics is a philosophy and not a science. But besides the metaphysical ethics of the schools there is the applied and practical ethics of the moralist—the social reformer. The latter is interested primarily in the actual means by which ethical ideals have been and can be realised, and especially in such re-organisation of social relations as will create a social environment favourable to these ideals. Here we have an objective side of ethics, an investigation into the relation of social means and ends. Such an investigation is so far sociological, concerned with the nature and conditions of social fact, and any science—for here we can speak of science—which systematises such investigations is certainly a branch of sociology. One might instance the science of education, penology, hygiene, and the rudimentary science of eugenics.

These are, *so far as they study the relation of social means to ethical ends*, specific social sciences.

So far—but they are something more than that. We shall have to insist at a later stage that no individual is completely explained in terms of his social attributes, and that, therefore, the ethical can never be identified with the social. This fact renders the relationship more complex. For ethics need not consider right and wrong conduct simply in relation to its social effects, even although we take it for true that all right conduct promotes and all wrong conduct depresses social welfare. To be true to one's own self may *involve* doing justly by all other men, but the conceptions are not identical. The greatest ethical systems (like the greatest religions) lay stress on the individual character as end in itself and not merely as means. They find the sanction of conduct rooted in the nature of the being whose conduct it is, the effects on others being regarded as secondary, the consequence of an inner rightness. Thus, strictly speaking, practical ethics may pursue the problem of good and evil beyond the fields open to sociology, and in so far may prove more than a branch of it.

The sociological interest lies in the question how far existing social conditions, the actual relations of men to men, further or retard the realisation of ethical ideals and how far social conditions can be altered for their completer realisation. If we set up different standards of value the antagonism is ethical, not sociological. For whatever the standard be, whether we accept, say, the ordinary doctrine of men that equity and altruism are good ends to pursue, or the doctrine of Nietzsche, that mastery and self-assertion are more to be desired, we can with equal impartiality investigate how far the existing conditions of society are favourable or unfavourable, and how they can be made more favourable, to either end. Were I a Nietzsche I would as sociologist enquire how the might of the strongest can be most conserved in, or in spite of, society. Were I a Schopenhauer I would enquire how society might best defeat itself. Were I a Tolstoi I would enquire how social conditions might most be made to conform to a certain ideal of the simple " natural " life. Were I a Bismarck I would seek the conditions under which peoples can become hardened into world-powers. At a certain point our sociologies will take different directions according to our ethical ideals. Not that where our ideals conflict our sociologies will also conflict, but rather that we are answering different sociological questions. It is our social interests that conflict. The conflict of ethical ideas is, therefore, no ultimate problem for sociology. In so far as these conflict the sociologists will ask different questions and *therefore* find different answers.

Why, it may be asked, should sociology be involved in the uncertainties of this ethical conflict ? Why cannot it confine itself simply to the social facts, the causes and

the consequences, without naming them good or evil?
The fuller answer to this question will appear later.
Meantime we may remark that the question would not
be asked at all were it not for an analogy drawn from the
" material " sciences. These, we suppose, are concerned
purely with facts and laws, not at all with values. I
believe that our " material " sciences are more entangled
with values than we usually imagine, that we cannot
study even stars or rocks or atoms without being somehow determined, in our modes of systematisation, in
the prominence given to one or another part of the subject,
in the form of question we ask and attempt to answer, by
direct and human interests. The facts are not, but they
have, values. In the study of all human phenomena,
on the other hand, the facts, or some of them, not only
have, but are, values. There is no *ought* in chemistry,
no chemically good or evil results and combinations :
there are no geologically good or evil types of rocks. In
all such sciences there is no teleology and no pathology.
But wherever the principle of life is found, the striving
towards a fulfilment envisaged or still unknown, there,
in plant, organism, mind, inevitably facts become more
than facts, something more compulsive and more arresting.
Wherever life exists, attainment and failure, growth and
decay, good and evil exist. Those who would make
sociology a " natural " science, unconcerned with values,
would leave out of account the special characteristics of
the world of which it treats, in a vain attempt to ape
those sciences where such characteristics are unknown.
We are overmuch inclined to see in physical science the
type and model of all science, and to imagine that mea-
surement alone is knowledge. Purposes are incom-
mensurate ; the movements of thought among a people
cannot be estimated by counting heads ; the power of
personality is not to be measured like the power of an

engine ;   institutions are ideal constructions without
quantitative length or breadth.   The things most know-
able are the things least measurable, purposes, passions,
desires, and the complex social world built out of their
conflicts and co-ordinations.   You can have no adequate
interest in society unless you are interested in it as
fulfilling human values.   Its essential forms have been
shaped by men's purposes, and its development is wholly
dependent on the development of these purposes.   These
purposes have all an ethical character.   The very existence
of society means ethical purpose in its members.   The
sociologist who has no ethical interest, no interest in
social conditions as relative to values, is a dilettante.
He is like a grammarian who studies the letters and
syllables of words but never thinks of the words themselves as meanings.   It is a possible method, and there
is some knowledge to be derived that way—but it is not
the knowledge of community.

So long as the sociologist never confuses what he wants
to be with what is, never lets his inevitable subjective
valuation distort objective fact, his sociology and his
ethics will live together in peace.   Putting it in the most
summary form, we may say that sociology is concerned
with facts as values, ethics with values as facts.

Finally, it may be well to insist here, in view of later
discussions, that it is a false view of ethics which limits
its interest to a few social relations specially singled out
as "moral."   Every question of values is an ethical
question, and every purpose of men is relative to a value.
Ethical activity is thus peculiarly comprehensive.   It is
not a species of activity co-ordinate with economic or
political or even religious activity.   It builds no specific
association in the way that religious activity builds the
church or economic activity builds the industrial system.
It is not a specific type of activity at all, for it may be

revealed in all the specific types. Ethical activity is wider in its range than any other, it is literally universal, revealed in every activity of life. In its pure form it is the most intimate and individualised and free of all activities, and it makes unending demands on every social organisation. Yet even if every association, even if community to its outermost bounds, conformed perfectly to these demands, the ethical spirit would still be partially unexpressed in its social constructions. It is more than the critic, it is the creator and maintainer, the destroyer and renewer of all values. From the conscience of the individual, where alone it resides, it proclaims a law for the universe itself.

§ 3. Sociology and psychology.

On no question is current sociological doctrine in so confused a state as on that of the relation of sociology to psychology. When the question is raised we are generally put off with such statements as these, that psychology is " concerned with " the individual mind and sociology with the interaction of minds, or—even vaguer—that psychology " deals with " the individual and sociology " deals with " the group, or—perhaps worst of all—that psychology is " the science of the association of ideas " while sociology is " the science of the association of minds." Statements like these merely confuse the issue.

Nor can we lay all the blame at the door of the sociologists. Some psychologists define their subject-matter in a way which adds to the confusion. Thus psychology has been recently defined as " the positive science of the conduct of living creatures." [1] This definition is intended to meet a not very serious difficulty connected with the usual definition of psychology as " the science of mind "

[1] W. M'Dougall, *Physiological Psychology*, p. 1 ; *Psychology* (Home University Library), p. 19.

or " the science of consciousness," and is itself open to more serious objections. The qualification " positive " is meant to distinguish psychology from " normative " studies such as logic and ethics, but since men often act this way or that because they believe they *ought* to act so, since they sometimes draw conclusions because they find them *valid*, the present writer at least fails to see how a positive science of conduct can be built which fails to investigate principles so essentially determinative of conduct. However, we may leave the psychologist to settle that issue with the students of logic and ethics. There is a broader objection which concerns us more directly. If conduct be the *distinctive* subject-matter of psychology, then psychology is an encyclopædic science of which sociology (including all the special social sciences) is a part. The author of this definition illustrates the conception of conduct or behaviour by the case of the guinea-pig returning to its hole, the dog seeking its home even from a great distance, the exile returning to his country after many years. But other sciences than psychology take cognisance of these phenomena. Are zoology, anthropology, and sociology simply branches of psychology ? Or are they not *positive* sciences ?

The source of confusion here involved may be revealed as follows. Every thing a living creature does or suffers, every event in history or experience, is a psychical phenomenon, and cannot be understood except in terms of the purposes and needs and passions of psychical beings. Herein alone is " vital " law clearly distinguished from " material " law. " Any external circumstance whatever which we designate as social would be a puppet-show, as void of intelligibility and meaning as the interplay of the clouds or the intergrowth of the branches of trees, did we not, quite as a matter of course, recognise psychical

motives, feelings, thoughts, needs, not merely as bearers
(Träger) of these externalities, but as their reality and as
alone of intrinsic interest to us." [1] All conduct, properly
so called, is therefore psychical, *but psychology is not
therefore the science of all conduct.*

For conduct has a double character. It is the activity
of a mind in relation to a world other than itself. Subject
is always in relation to object, the mind is always in
relation to its world. The relation is indissoluble, mind
apart from object is as utterly beyond our comprehension
as object apart from mind. Here is where the difference
between psychology and all other sciences—and the
essential difficulty of psychology—is revealed. The other
sciences study this world of objects—not merely material
objects, for our ideas and imaginations, our mental
constructions of every kind, our institutions and social
forms, are also objects of mind. The study of its objects,
material and immaterial, is the proper or natural direction
of mind. It is the treatment of objects as objects. But
psychology essays a more perilous task. It seeks to
know mind, the knower; it seeks to complete the
objective world of science by making the essential
subject itself an object, and an object to itself. The
task has only to be stated for us to realise its extreme
hazardousness. In so far as we can know mind at all,
it must be through some kind of analysis of its realisations
in subject-object relations. Psychology, in other words,
can study the mind only in its relation to objects; but
psychology is interested never in the object as such,
always in the object as itself manifesting the character
of the subject which perceives, thinks, knows, feels, or

[1] This passage is from Professor Simmel's remarkable *Soziologie*
(p. 21), one of the few works which appreciate the bearing of our present
question. But I do not think that Professor Simmel's conclusion,
which makes sociology a study of abstract social relations, is adequate
or necessary.

wills it.   Where the object of mind is material (or physical)
there is little danger of our confusing the sciences which
study the objects of mind with the science which studies
mind itself.   But where the object of mind is in some
special sense the work of mind, a grave danger arises,
and here it is especially important to distinguish the
science of the mental object from the science of the sub-
ject-mind, to distinguish, say, ethics, logic, sociology,
and philosophy from psychology.   The only object which
the psychologist could study *for its own sake* would be
mind as object, were it possible, as some psychologists
seem to believe, for mind to be object either to itself
or to some other subject ;   and that object is totally
different in character from what we call the " content " of
mind, from the concept which is in its very nature object,
not subject.   The study of these concepts—for their own
sake, in the systems which they form—is not psychology.

When, therefore, we study laws or customs or any social
institutions, in order to attain a knowledge of these things,
we are not psychologists but sociologists.   Forms of
association or community are in their nature objective
things, just as truly as forms of speech or types of art
are objective, just as truly as colours or sights or sounds
are objective.   They are what mind thinks, not what
mind is.   They reveal mind, being the stuff of its manufacture, but they are not mind, and their laws are not
the laws of mind.   Even the so-called laws of thought
are not the laws of the behaviour of mind.   They are
laws of the behaviour of objects.   " A thing cannot both
be and not be "—that statement is about things, not
about minds.   Were it a statement of the behaviour
of mind, we might suppose that, if minds were different,
a thing might both be and not be ;   but the same sup-
position is equally true or equally false in respect of every
statement about things.

The confusion arises from the fact that some sciences may be regarded as throwing a more direct light than others on the nature of mind. Sociology in especial gives aid to psychology, just as psychology gives special aid to sociology. Human needs and purposes create social structures. What is it on which our attention is focussed ? If the nature of social structures, as created by and as fulfilling men's needs and purposes, then we are sociologists. If the nature of mind as revealed in the structures which they have built, then we are psychologists. It is a difference of attitude in regard to a common material. The study of these social relations is a sociological study, but it provides the psychologist with data whence he may derive psychological fact. Man's activity as a social being, like man's activity in every sphere, throws light on the character of mind. Men cannot dig or build or analyse or philosophise without revealing their essential minds—still less can they enter into relation with their fellows without so doing. Men are not always digging or building or philosophising, but all men are always revealing themselves as members formed within and active within a society.

Psychology when it studies mind as revealed in social relations is often called " social psychology," an expression which has given rise to much misunderstanding. For, of course, social relations are the social relations of individuals. There are no individuals who are not social individuals, and there is no social mind that is not individual mind. Hence " social " psychology is rather an aspect than a branch of psychology, since there is no individual psychology from which it can be demarcated. Again, it is often said that " social " psychology and sociology are either wholly[1] or in great part[2] identical. But we must bear in

[1] See, *e.g.*, Karl Pearson, *The Grammar of Science*, p. 527.

[2] See, *e.g.*, Ward, *Pure Sociology*, p. 59.

mind the distinction of attitude already referred to. The psychological interest is distinguishable from the sociological interest. This is easily seen in practice. If we compare, for example, Mr. McDougall's *Social Psychology* with the *Social Psychology* of Professor Ross, we see that the former is interested in social phenomena mainly from the psychological point of view, the latter mainly from the sociological point of view. The one is interested directly in the social relations of men, the other is on the whole more interested in the light they throw on essential mind. Both are interested in the conduct of living creatures—psychology has no monopoly in that—but the attitude is different, and that makes a world of difference to the result.

BOOK II.
AN ANALYSIS OF COMMUNITY.

CHAPTER I

FALSE PERSPECTIVES OF COMMUNITY

§ 1. Introductory.

The failure to understand the true distinction and the creation of false distinctions between " individual " and " social " is a main source of sociological error.

There are no individuals who are not social individuals, and society is nothing more than individuals associated and organised. Society has no life but the life of its members, no ends that are not their ends, and no fulfilment beyond theirs. There is no conflict between society and *the* individual, between the welfare of society and the welfare of *the* individual. The quality of a society is the quality of its members. There is no social morality that is not individual morality, and no social mind that is not individual mind.

A recognition of these simple truths is a first step in the understanding of society. Yet they are often denied and more often ignored. And the reason, strange though it may seem, is the hold which bad metaphysics has upon us, even—or especially—on those who abjure metaphysics altogether. Many of those who regard a society as other and more than the members who compose it, might be surprised to learn that their doctrine rests on one or other or both of the two oldest metaphysical delusions known to the history of thought, the delusion that relations are in some way independent or outside of the things related in them, and the delusion that the type exists somehow by itself, " transcendental " to its members !

A society consists of beings *like* to one another in various ways, in some ways like-minded, in some ways like-bodied also. Thus one can conceive a type of which each is an instance or embodiment. All " share " a common nature. Now the one metaphysical delusion is to regard this common nature, this abstract type, as somehow substantial and real in itself. We first substantiate it, and then empty into it the whole worth and value of the mere individuals who " embody " or " exemplify " it. We make flesh and blood and soul that which the sculptor *symbolises* in stone and the artist caricatures on paper. The sculptor embodies in stone his *conception* of Britannia, the artist draws on paper his *conception* of John Bull, but many of us, quite unreflectingly, regard our conceptions not as abstract or symbolic or representative, but as real. It is not possible here to explain the metaphysical character of this fallacy, it must suffice to point out its existence and the misunderstanding which it creates. It is an error that pervades both popular and systematic thinking on society, and it is as common as it is rarely noted. One acute social observer has recently commented upon it. Speaking of certain people whom he supposes guilty of this fallacy he says : " They were, in the scholastic sense—which so oddly contradicts the modern use of the word—' Realists.' They believed classes were *real* and independent of their individuals. This is the common habit of all so-called educated people who have no metaphysical aptitude and no metaphysical training. It leads them to a progressive misunderstanding of the world."[1] (H. G. Wells, *The New Machiavelli*.) This fallacy is so

---

[1] I fear the author is too optimistic as to the effect of metaphysical training, since many of our metaphysicians have fallen into the same error.

wide-spread and takes so many forms that we shall have frequently to refer to it.

Again, a society consists of beings *related* to one another in various ways, some superficial, some deep and vital. Into social relations men are born, in them they live and develop. None lives or dies to himself, and all are bound up in one unity by reason of their social relationships. It is when men reflect on this essential fact that they fall, so often, into the second metaphysical delusion. They come to think of these social relations as literally *ties* between man and man, somehow outside the beings they bind together, as railway-couplings are outside the carriage they connect. It is extraordinarily difficult, owing to the poverty of language, to talk of relations without making this false implication. The result is, as we shall see presently, that men come to think of society as " greater than the sum of its parts," as in some way independent of its " parts." This false conception of society disappears in a true estimate of the meaning of relations. Consider for instance the " bond " of kinship, say as between father and son. Here fatherhood as a relationship is an element in the personality of the being we call " father," just as sonship is an element in the personality of the being we call " son." Or take the relationship of friendship. We speak of the *ties* of friendship, but the ties are the reciprocal sentiments felt by each towards the other of the beings so related. The ties exist *in* the personality of each, and there alone. Or take a political relationship, that of governor and governed. There can be no governor where there is no governed, and *vice-versa*, but governorship is an activity *of* the one, and subjection to government a corresponding passivity and activity *of* the other. Social relations, in a word, are simply those elements and functions of personality in each which are dependent on the elements and functions of personality in others. Society is therefore not relations, but beings in their relationships. It follows that there is no social function which is outside of the functions of personalities. Society is in us, in each of us, in some degree in all, in the highest degree in the greatest of us.

Having seen the bases on which they rest, we may now examine the special errors into which men have been misled in the general interpretation of society.

§ 2. Community as organism.

We may take the oldest first. It was very natural that when men first came to reflect on the life of a community, they should have been struck by certain features of it wherein it resembled the life of an individual animal or organism, the persistence of the whole though members pass away, the division of function between the members serving the welfare of the whole, the dependence of every member on the " corporate " unity of the whole. From the observance of these and other resemblances—as they were observed for instance by Aristotle and St. Paul— it was only a step to the " explanation " of society in terms of organism, and the establishment of a complete and intricate analogy. This " explanation " took whimsical form in such mediæval writers as Nicolas of Cues, who found that in the political life the offices of state are the limbs, the laws are the nerves, the imperial decrees the brains, the fatherland the skeleton, and the transient human beings the flesh![1] Thence the conception of community as a kind of organism passed into the modern world, finding countless expressions from the days of Hobbes and his " Great Leviathan " until Spencer and Schäffle arose in the fulness of time, and squandered upon it their power and ingenuity.

[1] Cf. Gierke, *Political Theories of the Middle Age*, n. 79.

Yet it requires only a little analysis to detect the falsity of an analogy which has wrought harm, not only in the study of general sociology, but in ethics, politics, psychology, and economics as well. There are, indeed, as we have already admitted, several very significant resemblances between community and organism. But it is a false and pernicious deduction which regards community as any *kind* of organism. To prove this statement it is unnecessary here to enter into the details of the analogy. One or two general observations will suffice.

(1) There is one essential difference between a community and an organism which destroys all real analogy. An organism is or has—according as we interpret it—a single centre, a unity of life, a purpose or a consciousness which is no purpose or consciousness of the several parts but only of the whole. A community consists of myriad centres of life and consciousness, of true autonomous individuals who are merged in no such corporate unity, whose purposes are lost in no such corporate purpose. This difference was admitted by Spencer himself—there was "no corporate consciousness" within society—but had he realised the far-reaching significance of that admission he must have transformed his whole philosophy. For this central difference determines a thousand other differences, and reveals the analogy as merely superficial even where it seems most apt. A community does not act in unity like an organism, or maintain itself like an organism, or grow like an organism, or reproduce like an organism, or die like an organism. The central difference renders the whole analogy vain.

(2) We know better the meaning of society than the meaning of organism ! When we say "organism" do we include the consciousness which, at least in the case of animal organisms, gives it form and meaning, or can we somehow "abstract" the organic from the con-

scious life ? What are we to say of the relation of an
organism to its environment ? Is it merely mechanical
reaction or is it indeed an intelligent *response*—" quasi-
intelligent " like all " quasis " begs the question ? Is it
physico-chemically determined, or is it " free " ? If the
determination be purely mechanical, the failure of the
analogy is obvious ; and if it be other than mechanical,
must it not be purposive ? If then it be purposive, we
have already reached the stage of mind, and are speaking,
properly, not of bodily but of mental and spiritual powers.
Let us then take organism in this wide sense as having an
end or purpose—not merely a function—to which all its
parts, cells and organs, contribute. Still the central
difference makes analogy vain. For if the analogy is to
hold, the parts must have ends or purposes as well as the
whole—the cells must have purposes (if you regard the
cells as the elements in organism corresponding to
individuals in community), or the organs must have purposes (if it is these that correspond), and the purposes of
the elements must give meaning to the whole, since in
community it is the purposes of the individuals which
alone give the purpose of the whole. But it is exceedingly
difficult to speak of cells or organs as having purposes.
Kant indeed defined an organism as " a whole of which
the parts are reciprocally ends and means." Means,
certainly, but how ends ? Shall we say the heart is an
end for itself, or the liver, or the brain ? Is not such a
conception itself sociomorphic, derived from human
society and nowhence else, true of human society and of
nothing else ? It is in human society that we understand
the meaning of " reciprocal ends and means," in the interactions of men who through interaction fulfil their individual and common purposes. So we are here first of all
interpreting organism in terms of society, and then reflecting the analogy back again. Which is as perverse as to say

of a man that he is a very good likeness of his portrait!
Only that in this case the likeness does not hold !

When the biologists have told us whether an organism
is an engine or a chemical compound or a spirit or an
"entelechy" or all together, we shall better understand
the analogy it bears to a communal group—but before
that we may have gone a long way in the direct understanding of community !

(3) Sometimes men find the analogy to lie between
state and organism, sometimes between community and
organism, but generally they confuse the two. Now
community is a matter of degree, with no set bounds,
whereas organism is a closed system. Is the city of
Edinburgh a social organism ? But it is part of the
community of Scotland. Is Scotland an organism ?
But it is part of the community of the United Kingdom.
Is the United Kingdom an organism ? But a wider
community envelops and is enveloping it. Organisms
within organisms, and not as parasites !

We cannot run away from these difficulties by merely
prefixing an adjective, and speaking of " social " or
" spiritual " or " contractual " organism. The prefix
only adds to the confusion. This is very evident in the
case of the prefix last mentioned. It is a *contradictio in
adjecto*, an implied denial of those very characters which
make an organism what it is. By calling society a
" contractual organism " Fouillée sought to reconcile
the current opposition between organism-theories and
contract-theories of society.[1] But the opposition is
factitious and should be resolved not reconciled. There
ought to be no opposition between contract-theories and
organism-theories. Contract, as we have already seen,
is relative to association, and not to community. It is a
most important conception for the understanding of the

[1] *La Science Sociale Contemporaine.*

unity of associations : it does not in the least, any more than the organism-theory, explain the unity of communities. A community is not a constructed organisation, it is a life.

We shall see presently that the unity of society, unlike that of organism, depends primarily not on the difference but on the likeness of its members. It is a unity of autonomous self-determining members seeking in a common life the same kind of fulfilment. Difference is necessary for its development, but is secondary—the basis is likeness.

§3. Community as a mind or soul.

Community is not an organic, it is a spiritual unity. It rests on the common and interdependent purposes of social beings. But community is not therefore to be thought of as a greater mind or soul. There are two forms of spiritual unity, one the indissoluble unity of the single mind, the other the unity—or rather the harmony—of minds in social relations. The two forms of unity are totally disparate, yet nothing is more common, or more fatal to a true perspective of community, than the confusion of them. Because a community is a union of minds, it is not therefore itself a mind. Such a statement seems so obvious, and yet the contrary statement is explicitly made by distinguished sociologists such as M. Durkheim, and distinguished psychologists such as Mr. William M'Dougall. The latter for instance writes as follows :

" When the student of behaviour has learnt from the various departments of psychology . . . all that they can teach him of the structure, genesis, and modes of operation, of the individual mind, a large field still awaits his exploration. If we put aside as unproven such speculations as that touched on at the end of the foregoing chapter [the view of James that the human mind can enter into an actual union or communion with the divine mind], and refuse to admit any modes of communication or influence between minds other than through the normal channels of sense-perception and bodily movement, we must nevertheless recognise the existence in a certain sense of over-individual or collective minds. We may fairly define a mind as an organised system of mental or purposive forces ; and in the sense so defined, every highly organised human society may properly be said to possess a collective mind. For the collective actions which constitute the history of any such society are conditioned by an organisation which can only be described in terms of mind, and which yet is not comprised within the mind of any individual ; the society is rather constituted by the system of relations obtaining between the individual minds which are its units of composition. Under any given circumstances the actions of the society are, or may be, very different from the mere sum of the actions with which its several members would react to the situation in the absence of the system of relations which renders them a society ; or, in other words, the thinking and acting of each man, in so far as he thinks and acts as a member of a society, is very different from his thinking and acting as an isolated individual.[1]

This passage contains two arguments in favour of the hypothesis of super-individual " collective " minds, neither of which can stand examination.

(1) The " definition " of a mind as " an organised system of mental or purposive forces " is totally inadequate. When we speak of the mind of an individual we mean something more than this. The mind of each of us has a unity other than that of such a system. When two of us enter into any arrangement whatever, there arises in some sort a system of " mental or purposive forces," or,

---

[1] *Psychology* (Home University Library), pp. 228-9.

more strictly, a certain relation of the purposive forces *of each mind* to those of the other. But why are we to call the inter-relation of " mental forces " a mind ? Does the system so created think and will and feel and act ? Does it perform a single one of those operations which we recognise as the work of that essentially active thing, a mind ? If a number of minds construct by their inter-activity an organisation " which can only be described in terms of mind," must we ascribe to the construction the very nature of the forces which constructed it ? That is surely impossible. Must we then, alternatively, postu-late a mind which thinks the whole construction ? In that case " collective mind " would think the whole structure of the collectivity of which it is presumably the subject ; the " collective mind " of England, for instance, would think the whole complex structure of the English community. Unfortunately that greater mind does not communicate its thinking to individual minds, else they might learn directly from the subject what they com-prehend only painfully and imperfectly from the study of that structure which is its hypothetical object ! Again, social organisations occur of every kind and every degree of universality. If England has a collective mind, why not Birmingham and why not each of its wards ? If a nation has a collective mind, so also have a church and a trade union. And we shall have collective minds that are parts of greater collective minds, and collective minds that intersect other collective minds. But all these " minds " lack the integrity and isolation and unity of action which are essential to the very conception of mind.

(2) The second argument is an obvious fallacy. If each man thinks and acts differently as a member of a crowd or association and as an individual standing out of any such immediate relation to his fellows, it is still

each who thinks and acts ; the new determinations are
determinations still of individual minds as they are
influenced by aggregation. When sheep play follow-my-
leader, we do not attribute the movement of the flock to
a flock-mind. When men aggregate, especially as casual
unorganised aggregations, each mind responds in a
peculiar way to this special crowd-environment, as it
responds in a peculiar way to every kind of environment.
The environment changes with the response of each who
forms a constituent of it, and the change in turn occasions
a new response of each, and so on. Thus a peculiarly
rapid process of mental change takes place in the members
of a crowd. Each becomes to a degree susceptible and
imitative. The mood of each is assimilated to that of
each other. To the onlooker it seems as though waves
of emotional agitation swept through the crowd. Each
is less than himself, not surely because he has become
part of a greater mind, but because the effect of aggregation is to evoke in each a certain emotional response at
the cost of rationality. There is no structure of organisation within which the individual can find shelter for his
individuality against the overpowering cumulative influence of mass-suggestion and mass-imitation. But this
is merely an extreme instance of the obvious fact that
every mind is influenced by every kind of environment.
To posit a super-individual mind because individual
minds are altered by their relations to one another (as
indeed they are altered by their relations to physical
conditions) is surely gratuitous.

(I have taken this extreme case because it is to such
types of activity that men generally point when asked to
exemplify the conception of " collective mind." Strictly
speaking, it is no such thing. But it is interesting to note
that this case which most *suggests* a non-individualised
social mind forms one of the lowest and not of the highest

social manifestations. It is the contagious psychical influence that moves a herd of buffaloes or a human crowd, the mood that responds to the waving of flags, the beating of drums, the shouting of the loud-voiced orator, the appeal of the impassioned extremist. It is the contagious psychical influence that carries a man out of himself, but rarely to a higher level, nearly always to a lower. It is an influence that nearly all students of society regard as evil, to be counteracted by education in self-control, the retainment of individuality.[1] The crowd is passionate, stupid, merciless, and immoral. When its passion is just the crowd acts like a fool, when unjust like a raging beast. It understands only the simple and clamant and spectacular. It can destroy, but it cannot create. It chooses a Barabbas before the Christ.)

It is important to clear out of the way this misleading doctrine of super-individual minds corresponding to social or communal organisations and activities, and therefore it may be well to go a little deeper in our analysis. Strictly speaking we can hardly even say that, at least under normal conditions, minds or mental processes *interact*; they are rather interdependent, determined indirectly by the activities of other minds. Such determination is of two kinds; the more immediate, where by symbolic communication—language, gesture, art—the thoughts and purposes of one mind are represented to others, and so affect the thoughts and purposes of others; the less

[1] Cf. Ross, *Social Psychology*, chap. v. Simmel (*Soziologie*) quotes Schiller's epigram, " dass leidlich kluge und verständige Leute in corpore zu einem Dummkopf wurden," and states that the experience of English trade-unions shows that mass-meetings arrive at the most wrong-headed decisions, in consequence of which the system of delegates has been in large measure substituted. The conduct of men as an unorganised mass and their conduct as an organised society differ in a remarkable way. This is well illustrated, as a trade-union leader has informed me, by the case of the dock-labourers of London. Before they became organised they were at the mercy of mob-orators, but these amateur students of group-psychology lost their ascendency when the dockers' union was properly constituted.

immediate where each, by the physical operations through which its purposes are pursued, alters thereby the conditions under which others must act for the fulfilment of their purposes, and so indirectly alters their purposes and thoughts as well. The interests of all are thus interdependent ; they harmonise so that they can best be attained for each through the co-operation of all, or they conflict, so that the attainment of his interests by one means the negation of the interests of others. In all community there is a vast complex of co-operative and competitive forces out of which spring, as resultants, its common properties, its customs and institutions. But to the resultant unity there need correspond no unity of mind. Often when we fail to perceive the complexity of the process from which social institutions or movements result, especially when they are hidden from us in the scantily-recorded life of the past, we readily resort to a simplified explanation, as if they were the direct expression of a single purpose. Our knowledge of the complexity of the social process in the present should make us wary of these conclusions.

But, it will be said, there are purposes common to many minds, and these express themselves as co-operant activity in the formation of common institutions. Certainly, and as will appear later, these common purposes are the first foundations of all society. Here it is necessary only to point out that the common or type element in many minds does not constitute a common or type mind in the sense of a super-individual entity. There is no more a great "collective" mind beyond the individual minds in society than there is a great " collective " tree beyond all the individual trees in nature. A collection of trees is a wood, and that we can study as a unity; so an aggregation of men is a society, a much more determinate unity : but a collection of trees is not a collective tree, and neither is a collection of persons or minds a collective person or mind. We can speak of qualities of tree in abstraction from any particular trees, and we can speak of qualities of mind as such, or of some particular kind of mind, or of mind in relation to some type of situation.[1] But in so doing we are simply considering the character-istic or like elements of individual minds, as we might consider the characteristic or like elements discoverable in individual trees and kinds of trees. To conceive, because of these identities, a " collective " mind as existing *beside* those of individuals or a collective tree beside the variant examples is to run against the wall of the Idea theory ; it is to give a *prima-facie* obvious but demonstrably false answer to the haunting and unanswer-able question : Can the identities we find in individual things,—type, stock, race, whatever the identity be,— exist only in conception or idea, while only the individual things themselves exist " in nature " ? False, because the answer is got by supposing the abstract to be concrete also, the attribute to be substance also ; false because it is an attempt to image the invisible moulds of things in terms of the things moulded, to give to forms the qualities of substance in the mistaken belief that so they are rendered more comprehensible. Fortunately, the sociolo-gist has no call to answer the real metaphysical question involved, since it does not arise in his sphere alone, and until men speak of the unity or activity of super-individual tree or animal or stone, we may well refrain from speaking of the unity or activity of super-individual mind.

It will now be clear that when we speak of the will or the mind or sentiments of a community, we mean no mystical

[1] It is in this sense we speak of the " mind " of a race, the " soul " of a people, and so on. We do not mean by it anything super-individual or transcendental. But we should not speak in this connection of a " *collective* mind," any more than we speak of a " collective soldier " when we mean an army or a " collective tree " when we mean a wood.

will or mind or sentiments. We are speaking of the like willing or the like thinking or the like feeling of social beings. If I love and honour my country, it is the love and honour of a mind, of a uni-centred spiritual being. But if a country loves and honours one of its members, that multi-centred love and honour is a very different thing. He loves it as a unity, but it cannot as a unity love him in turn. Many hearts may beat as one, but the heart-beats are still many. In a sense, perhaps in more senses than one, that is true of community which Spinoza said was true of God—if we love it we cannot hope for a love reciprocal to our own. The unity which we love does not as such think or feel. It has no unitary mind or will or heart.

Appropriately enough, the only thorough-going attempt to conceive a community in terms of a communal mind was made in the *Republic* of Plato.[1] But Plato did not think of a super-individual mind as existing beside or beyond individual minds ; he rather regarded the minds of the members of a community as together *constituting* a greater mind like in every respect to the smaller. The community is " the individual soul written large." We can understand the microcosm of the individual if we understand the macrocosm of community, and *vice versa*. If there are three parts of the individual soul, there are three classes of the community. As the parts of the soul are related to one another, so should the classes of the community be related to one another ; as there is a reasoning part of the soul which ought to control the rest, so there is a reasoning class of the community which ought to control the other classes, and as there is an appetitive and again a " passionate " element in the soul, so there is an appetitive and again a passionate class in the community.

[1] See *Rep.*, pp. 368, 369, 435, 441.

F

If taken at all literally, this is both bad psychology and bad sociology. It is bad psychology, because you cannot " divide " mind into self-subsistent faculties. We think with our whole mind, feel with our whole mind, will with our whole mind. Reasoning, feeling, willing, perceiving, believing, desiring—these are all complex activities in which the whole mind, not mere " parts " of it, is active. To speak summarily, each involves the predominance of an aspect, not the pure functioning of a part. And it is bad sociology, because you cannot make the classes of a community correspond either to aspects or to parts of mind. The analogy breaks down. You cannot have one class which merely or even mainly thinks, another which merely feels. (As it is, Plato's classes—the philosophers, the guardians, and the workers—do not really correspond to his divisions of mind into reasoning, passionate, and appetitive parts.) The great defect of any such conception is that it obscures the true unity of community. For classes so distinguished are related only by way of difference, each fulfilling its nature in contributing specifically distinct functions, like the separate parts of a machine each shaped differently to the service of an end not its own,— nor yet that of the whole machine.

The nearest approach to the fulfilment of such a conception would be some " aristocratic " state where classes become castes, a state where unity rests, as it indeed rests for Plato, merely on a " justice " which sees that each part fulfils its own distinct function, " does its own business." For justice is a principle of partition, the assigning to each that which is his own and no one else's. Difference of function—in a narrower sense—is indeed essential within a community, but beyond the difference involved in external function there must exist, as we shall see, an inward likeness. Society is not simply or primarily the harmony of differences, but the union of likes. The likeness is ultimate, and therefore justice is not the deepest ground of social unity nor the completest social morality. It is only the superficial social relationships—and these only when fulfilled in a superficial manner—which rest on mere difference, as the relation of master to servant, employer to employee, buyer to seller. There the exchange of a *quid pro quo* may be all that is involved in the relationship. But in a true community the ruler makes laws for himself no less than for the governed to obey, the imposer of taxes imposes them on himself as well ; so the true priest confesses as well as hears confession, and the true doctor prescribes for his patient only what in like circumstances he prescribes for himself. The relations of difference remain, but they imply an identity of nature in the members so related, a relation of likeness on which the relation of difference is founded. Likeness of nature involves likeness of ends and likeness of goods. Therefore you cannot split up a community into classes corresponding to distinct and exclusive elements, whether of mind or of anything else.

All community is a web of likenesses and differences, of what is common and what is diverse in the members of it. It is thus a system complex and wonderful beyond the complete understanding of any of its members. But we must not invent a communal mind to think that greater system. The bonds of society are in the members of society, and not outside them. It is the memories, traditions, and beliefs of each which make up social memories, traditions, and beliefs. Society like the kingdom of God is within us. Within us, within each of us, and yet greater than the thoughts and understandings of any of us. For the social thoughts and feelings and willings of each, the socialised mind of each, with the complex scheme of his relation to the social world, is no mere reproduction of the social thoughts and feelings and willings of the rest. Unity and difference here too weave their eternal web, the greater social scheme which none of us who are part of it can ever see in its entirety, but whose infinite subtlety and harmony we may more and more comprehend and admire. As a community grows in civilisation and culture, its traditions are no longer clear and definite ways of thinking, its usages are no longer uniform, its spirit is no longer to be summed up in a few phrases. But the spirit and tradition of a people become no less real in becoming more complex. Each member no longer embodies the whole tradition, but it is because each embodies some part of a greater tradition to which the freely-working individuality of each contributes. In this sense the spirit of a people, though existing only in the individual members, more and more surpasses the measure of any individual mind.

Again, the social tradition is expressed through institutions and records more permanent than the short-lived members of community. These institutions and records are as it were stored social values (just as, in particular, books may be called stored social knowledge), *in themselves nothing*, no part of the social mind, but the instruments of the communication of traditions from member to member, as also from the dead past to the living present. In this way too, with the increase of these stored values, of which members realise parts but none the whole, the spirit of a people more and more surpasses the measure of any individual mind. It is these social forces within and without, working in the minds of individuals whose own social inheritance is an essential part of their individuality, stored in the institutions which they maintain from the past or establish in the present, that mould the communal spirit of the successive generations. In this sense too a community may be called greater than its members who exist at any one time, since the community itself marches out of the past into the present, and its members at any time are part of a great succession, themselves first moulded by communal forces before they become, so moulded, the active determinants of its future moulding.

And as with knowledge, so with its concomitant and its product—power, power as stored in all the contrivances whereby man has harnessed nature to his service. Those means of knowledge and of power are the *capital* of community, capital which is taken over by each successive generation and increased in the measure of the wisdom of each—a true inheritance. This capital is the apparatus, the property of community, external to it as an individual's property is external to himself. It is none the less of incalculable significance. Without it our history would be an endless succession of futile beginnings. This has been well emphasised by an American sociologist : " Our prehistoric ancestors of the stone age, and of still earlier times, dragged out their miserable lives with little or no capital of any kind. And what should we of western civilisation do, if, at birth, we were thrust into the midst of the primitive struggle for existence ? What would distinguish us from our prehistoric ancestors ? Nothing of moment. Prehistoric men could not invent the telegraph, discover the differential calculus, build a sky-scraper, nor construct a steam-engine : and we, if removed at birth from all contact with civilisation, with its accumulated capital of all kinds, could not surpass the achievements of our primitive ancestors. We too, growing up from birth wholly outside the influences of civilisation, should live the life of primeval men." [1]   Our native " inheritance," that self-hood which we are or will attain, would be a frustrated and unavailing potentiality in the absence of those *means* to knowledge

[1] Wallis, *Examination of Society*, p. 273.

and to power which are in all literalness our social inheritance.

All these facts we may gladly admit. They are of the very greatest import, but that import is wholly mistaken if we invent as the bearer of those great and secular traditions some mind that is other than and beyond the individual minds in whose interdependent activities they have in the past been born and in the present are being maintained.

§ 4. Community as "greater than the sum of its parts."

The facts we have just been instancing are often regarded, even by those who reject the doctrine that community is either an organism or a soul "writ large," as at least proving that community is somehow more than its members, "greater than the sum or resultant of its parts." As this looser interpretation is also misleading, and falsifies our perspective of some practical problems of community, it may be well to devote to it a little consideration.

When we speak of a community as greater than the sum of its parts, we are still thinking in terms of some analogy, since the expressions "sum" and "parts" are not directly appropriate to society. Of what other things can we properly say that they are more than "the sum of their parts"? If we turn to those who apply the expression to society, we find that they make use of such similes as this: Bronze has a hardness which belongs to neither tin nor copper nor lead, its constituents; in like manner the character of a society differs from the characters of its components, the individual men and women. Or again they say: A body consists of parts, of organs, but the whole body is something more than the sum of its organs. Here we have the two types of instance which suggest the statement that a society is "greater than the sum of its parts."

Let us look at the first type. The analogy is that of
the chemical transformation of elements when they enter
into composition. But the " parts " here are not the
parts of the compound, they are the elements, yet uncompounded, which unite to form it. We are asked to distinguish such a chemical unity from a mere mechanical
one, which presumably is not " more than the sum of its
parts." Thus M. Durkheim, in his advocacy of the
society-greater-than-the-sum-of-its-parts doctrine says :
" I do not at all deny that the individual natures are the
components of the social fact. The question is whether,
in uniting to give birth to the social fact, they are not
transformed by the very fact of their combination. Is
the synthesis purely mechanical or chemical ? There
lies the whole question."

Shall we ever learn to study society directly in itself, and
not in the distorting mirror of analogy ?   The " whole question " as asked by M. Durkheim is mere confusion.   In the
case of chemical composition we are first given the elements
uncompounded. They enter into combination, passing
through a process of modification, and a new unity results.
Here not only is there no analogy whatever to social
process, but it is not even true that we have found a whole
which, in the required sense, is " greater than the sum of
its parts." For all that M. Durkheim and those who use
similar expressions mean is that the character and properties of the whole resulting from the chemical process
are different from the character and properties of any of
the several constituents *as they existed before entering into
the combination*. But the constituents so understood are
in no sense *parts* of the resulting unity, the copper and
tin and lead are not parts of the bronze. It is a still
greater confusion to say that community is greater than
" the resultant of its parts." Further it is easier to show
that there is no analogy between the chemical process, or

any other process which gives resultants properly so called, and the social process. We can find one only if we fall back on some obsolete "social contract" doctrine of society which discovers men existing in some void out of society and brings them in. If individuals never exist out of society, where shall we find the non-social lead and copper and tin which make the social bronze? In truth men are constantly being changed in the social process, but the social process was there from the first, and it is continuous and endless.

The second type is based on the organic analogy, that fruitful mother of social misconceptions. Here one may be brief, in view of what has been already said concerning that analogy. Organs are essentially relative to the unity and function of the organism, and to speak of the "sum of its organs" is mere nonsense. An organism cannot be greater or less or in any relation whatever to the pure figment, the "sum of its parts." Any argument resting on such an analogy is worthless.

There is no "sum of individuals," no "sum of the parts" of a community. The social relationships of every individual are not outside him, they are part of his personality. How can you sum things if part of their being consists in their relationships to one another? To talk of a "sum of individuals" is to think first of individuals as abstract, relationless, desocialisable beings. Understand individuals as concrete beings whose relations to one another constitute factors of their personality, and you realise that these *are* society, these and these alone— and the metaphysical confusion which leads you to look for something beyond this, something beyond these unsummable social individuals, passes away.

There is a true distinction out of which these false distinctions may have arisen. For every association, every organised group, may and does have rights and obligations which are not the rights and obligations of any or all of its members taken distributively but only of the association acting as an organised unity. We may therefore, *in reference to any particular association*, distinguish associational (more loosely " social ") and individual rights. What then are the former ? They are the rights of the members of the association, or of those whom they elect for that purpose, to act in a certain capacity, in a certain predetermined way, in order to attain certain common ends of all of them. To attain these ends, a principle of organisation, limiting and directing the activity of the members, is imposed by the wills which create the association. And so of duties. This is simply an instance of the general case, that all rights and duties are relative to particular situations. As a unity the association may become a " juristic person," a " corporation," and from the legal standpoint the character of unity so conceived is very important. But we must beware how we substantiate the " juristic person " as integral mind or living body, when, as the old legal saying made plain, *it* can suffer for *its* wrongdoings the pains and penalties of neither. The " juristic person " is a real *unity*, and therefore more than a *persona ficta*, but the reality it possesses is of a totally different order of being from that of the persons who establish it. What endless debate the writers on jurisprudence would have been saved could they only have found for an associational unity some other term than that of legal *person!*

Let us not conceive community either as mechanism or as organism or as soul : for the unity of which we are thinking is not mechanic or organic or even psychic, it is properly named only with its own name, it is communal.

§ 5. The practical results.

I have dwelt so long on these false analogies because in more or less subtle ways, under forms of expression too rarely examined, they prejudice our study of social questions. They are the sources of that most misleading antithesis which we draw between *the* individual and society, as though society were somehow other than *its* individuals. Writers of a certain cast of mind are fond of speaking as if the interests of society and of " the individual " (not of some individuals) were antagonistic. Sometimes they maintain that " the individual " ought to be subordinated to society, sometimes that " the individual " ought to be delivered from society. One well-known writer finds in the transition from a supposed age in which " the individual " was the pre-eminent factor to a supposed age in which society is the pre-eminent factor the whole explanation of social evolution.[1] Again, these analogies seem to be responsible for those curious distinctions between the " actual " and the " real " will of the community which enable some writers to preach autocracy in the name of democracy.[2] In a word, they stand in the way of a true appreciation of that intricate weaving of individuality and sociality which forms the not-to-be-unravelled web of life. Analyse these misleading analogies, and in the revelation of their falsity there is revealed also the falsity of this essential opposition of individual and society. Properly understood, the interests of " the individual " *are* the interests of society. We are here talking not of two distinct things but of two aspects of one thing. Oppositions there are within society innumerable and endless, but these are all partial, to be construed in a very different manner. They will be discussed in their proper place—here we need only show

[1] Mr. Benjamin Kidd.
[2] See Appendix A.

in conclusion how the doctrine of *essential* opposition distorts our practical philosophies.

It leads to one of two extremes, equally false though not equally dangerous. One is the common doctrine emphasised by Comte and by Fichte that right conduct is that in which the individual utterly forgets himself and remembers only his community. "There is but a single virtue," said Fichte, " to forget oneself as individual. There is but a single vice, to look to oneself." Noble as this ideal sounds, it is open to a serious criticism. We must insist, in the face of misinterpretation, that the service of one's fellows or one's country or one's race is not the complete end of life, nor fitness for such service, " fitness for citizenship," the complete end of education. To make such fitness or service *the* ethical ideal is to reason in a circle, and is to darken the very meaning of that vital fitness for service. It is to reason in a circle, for if the fulfilment of each lies in the service of all, each becomes a means to the ends of others who yet are themselves but means. All serve an end which is no one's end, and therefore not the end of the whole. Each man may find his welfare through social service, but his end is not therefore social service. It is not what he is *for*. Nothing extrinsic can be a man's fulfilment—or a people's. If we serve the welfare of " the race," yet the race consists of successive generations and the successive generations are also individuals. If a social ideal be not fulfilled in the lives of individuals present or to come, where is it fulfilled ? And again, it is to darken the meaning of service, for to serve others as individuals or as an association or community is to strive for the well-being of one's fellows : that well-being consists in definite conditions and activities of life, and these ends for others, if they are true, are ends for each. Speaking generally, it is only because they are ends for me, because they are good things I have already

attained or am on the way to attaining, that I can seek
to help others to attain them also. In seeking others'
good we can find our own, but we can seek for others only
what we have already in some measure attained for ourselves. The level of the individual gives the worth of
his social interests. The service of the unworthy is
unworthy service, and the love of the unworthy is unworthy love.

As individuality develops the more within society, the
more do we need a right understanding of individuality.
The social person is the only pure unit we *know*, others
are only relative. Sum up his social relationships, he is
more than these. Understand his environment, he may
not be there, he goes in and he goes out. Explain him by
heredity, you are explaining him by himself. All values
are finally personal, values of personality, and in the
service of personality alone are laws and institutions
justified.

As the one extreme doctrine sinks the person in his
social relationships, so the other and more dangerous
extreme elevates him beyond social relationships altogether. This is the " amoralism " of Thrasymachus and
of Nietzsche, which regards the laws and institutions of
society as the cunning of the weak to bind the strong,
advantageous to the weak but prejudicial to the strong.
The doctrine is contradictory and suicidal, and is perhaps
best accounted for as a reaction against the other extreme
view just considered. The complete refutation of it was
given long ago by Plato, who showed that the social
virtues are not merely " another's good " but one's own.
(*Republic*, Bks. I.–IV.) In other words social relationships are not external things, not nets in which personality
is enmeshed, but functions of the personality of each, the
fulfilment of which is the fulfilment of personality. Once
let us understand that social relations do not lie somehow

between men but only *within* them, and we can never be guilty of so fatal a confusion as that of Nietzsche and his Greek forerunner.

We must not indeed suppose that the interest of every individual will always coincide with the interest of his society. There may be genuine conflicts of interests in which an individual has to choose between his own greater good and the good of his society. We cannot go so far as to say with Fouillée: "Tout ce que je vous dois, je me le dois ; ce que je fais pour vous, je le fais pour moi, ce que je fais contre vous, je le fais contre moi . . . Mon suprême désintéressement est mon suprême intérêt, le parfait amour d'autrui est le parfait amour de moi-même." (*Les Elements Sociologiques de la Morale*, p. 282.) These are noble words, and bear witness to the profound inwardness of social relations. Yet there remain social disharmonies, social sacrifices, and social tragedies.

This much at least we can say without fear of exception or contradiction. As all individuality comes to fruition in society, so all individuality must in some way give itself up to society. To find itself it must lose itself. A profound sense of final failure accompanies all individuality which detaches itself from social service. One of the most essentially gloomy novels of the age—more essentially pessimistic than many which merely preach pessimism—is Mr. Arnold Bennett's *The Old Wives' Tale*. A sense of frustration, of the mere inevitable process of individual life through wanton experience on to the ludicrous conclusion of old age and death, of the meaninglessness of a world which breaks down what it builds, pervades its pages. It is because none of its characters give themselves up to a cause larger than themselves, social or ultra-social. In this the novelist reads more truly— whether he sees the alternative or not—the destiny of detached individuality than do the swarm of quasi-

optimistic writers who also seem to find nothing in life
but egoistic motives. This truth is notably stated by
Mr. Bernard Shaw in the following passage : " Put your
Shakespearean hero or coward, Henry V. and Pistol
or Parolles, beside Mr. Valiant and Mr. Fearing, and you
have a sudden revelation of the abyss that lies between
the fashionable author who could see nothing in the world
but personal aims and the tragedy of their disappointment
or the comedy of their incongruity, and the field-preacher
who achieved virtue and courage by identifying himself
with the purpose of the world as he understood it. . . .
Bunyan's coward stirs your blood more than Shakespeare's
hero, who actually leaves you cold and secretly hostile. . . .
This is the true joy of life, the being used for a purpose
recognised by yourself as a mighty one." (*Man and
Superman.*)

Only in society is personality at home. Only in a
highly developed society can the social initiates, the
children of society, develop their potentiality ; only in
serving society can the developed member attain the
further fulfilment of life ; and it is only the finely developed
personality, with the self-determination, initiative and
sense of responsibility which characterise such development, that can create and maintain fine and deep social
relations. Society is nowhere but in its members, and
it is most in the greatest of them.

CHAPTER II

THE ELEMENTS OF COMMUNITY

§1. The objects and subjects of community.

Having in the preceding chapter rejected certain false accounts of the nature and meaning of community, we have next to reveal its true character. We have to turn from analogical reasoning, which nearly always misleads, to the direct analysis of those communal factors which build or determine the complex structure of communal life.

All social relations, we have seen, are psychical relations, relations of minds. Whatever their physical and organic bases, it is psychical laws alone that directly bind man to man in society. This is the starting-point of all knowledge of community. Community is no greater mind, but it is created by that activity of men's minds in which they relate themselves incessantly to one another.

Now the great distinction of psychical from all other relations is that the former are not mechanically or externally determined—but are motived. It is because we seek, clearly or dimly, from prescience or instinct, some end, some fulfilment of ourselves or others, that we relate ourselves to one another in society. Here we discern already the two polar factors, distinguishable in analysis, indivisible in actuality, of all human activity ; on the objective side the *interest*, that for the sake of which we will the relations of community, on the subjective side, the *will*, the active mind for which the interest exists.

It is as men will in relation to one another that they create community, but it is by reason of, for the sake of, interests.

(It should be noted here that when we call interests the objects (or objectives) of our wills, we do not identify interests with the material or other objects by means of which they are attained. Thus when we seek food, the interest in food is not to be *identified with* bread and meat, but is instead the satisfaction of hunger. In fact no material object can constitute an interest, but only the satisfaction of its possession or use, whatever satisfaction it brings or is capable of bringing.)

These two factors of all activity, whether it be called social or not, are, we must repeat, essentially correlative. Where interest exists, there will exists, and *vice versa*. Every relation of men's interests is a relation of men's wills. There is no will without an interest and no interest apart from a will. It is very important to bear this truth in mind when we seek to analyse community. By so doing we shall avoid the duplication and possible confusion involved in a separate and abstract discussion of social mind or will on the one hand and social " forces " or interests on the other. Throughout this chapter I propose to speak mainly in terms of interests, but of interests always regarded as objects of our wills, of our minds as active. It is advisable to lay stress on the aspect of interest, for the more objective we can be, the more complete will be our analysis.

But first it is necessary to explain as clearly as possible what we understand by interests, and to show that this term is the most satisfactory which our vocabulary contains to describe those objects of our wills which are the determinants of all our relations to one another.

By interest we shall always mean some object which determines activity. Hence it is more than mere desire, it is more than the mere consciousness of a present lack of satisfaction, more than the mere knowledge of the way to a state of completer satisfaction. The prisoner who knows that escape is hopeless feels no less the unhappiness of durance, but that feeling stimulates no longer any interest. Even when to the consciousness of a possible satisfaction there is added the knowledge of an available way to its attainment, there may still arise no active interest. The contemplated satisfaction may not be pursued, it may be ignored either in favour of other satisfactions or as itself unworthy. I may be conscious of poverty, but if I can be rid of it only at the cost of actual preferred ends of mine the desire for wealth may never involve activity, may never create an interest.

Nor can we say that interest is always preceded by a sense of lack and constituted by a desire to relieve it. This common view is bad psychology, and leads to a false and mechanical conception of the nature of conduct. Our concrete experience contradicts the abstract notion that life is a succession of endeavours to fill successive emptinesses. Let a man reflect on his own conduct during a day or an hour, and he must feel the inadequacy of such an account. Often the ultimate motive of action *is* the interest, behind which we can find no prior sense of lack. We are so made that we pursue this end or that, when the possibility of its attainment is brought to our consciousness ; we pursue it before the thought ever emerges of the deficiency its non-attainment would involve, or before the deficiency itself ever creates a conscious sense of lack ; we pursue it because we want it, not merely or necessarily because we dislike the sense of its absence. To fulfil an interest is not the same as to destroy it. The interest in food is eliminated when a man has starved to death, it has not been fulfilled. Interests are fulfilled only in the maintenance of a desired

G

state of consciousness, of a way of life. Interests are indeed the spurs of life, but they do not drive it to its own annihilation. It is not in terms of emptiness and fulness alone that we shall understand the great motive forces of community.

I propose to follow Ratzenhofer in consistently calling these motive forces *interests*. This term seems for our purpose more serviceable than any other. The term *social force* is itself too indistinctive, and too readily suggests mechanical or impersonal power. The term *desire* is too subjective, it is also too comprehensive since what we require is a term for such objects of desire as determine activity ; these latter have also a certain permanence and stability and correlation which the term *desire*, unlike the term *interest*, does not suggest. The terms *purpose* and *end* refer too exclusively to rational objects of the will, to determinants of conduct whose meaning stands revealed in the light of self-consciousness.

For we must note that our interests vary infinitely in the degree of their clearness or rationality. We may realise their meaning in the whole scheme of existence or we may be blind to everything beyond the immediate fulfilment of our desire. Much of our life, much of our social activity, seems almost as lacking in prescience as is the work of bees, almost as much the driving of some necessity we do not realise or understand. In much of our activity, particularly that which we label "instinctive," we find a resultant which we neither foresaw nor desired to produce. In so far we act much like the Creator in *Genesis*, who, having done his work, sees that it is good. But a great and ever-increasing and dominating part of social life reaches into the sphere of deliberate purpose. These purposes may be shaped by the same needs that guided our blinder activity, but they are sought and attained in directer ways, by the conscious adaptation of means to ends. With the growth of these clearer interests community is revealed as existing for their realisation, and its institutions become more and more directly adapted to serve them. It is a question of degree, since all social relations are psychical. Society rests not on the common organic principle of all that lives but on the peculiar type of connection and interaction which mind always creates, but which grows ever completer as man comes to realise his place in nature and his capacity of fulfilment through social relations.

The interests of men, so understood, are the source of all social activity, and the changes in their interests are the source of all social evolution. Interests increase and differentiate ; some are eternal, others change and pass, and as they grow stronger or weaker they transform the associations they have created. Always it is interest that is prior. Community comes into being because interests are realisable only in common life. Community is not all psychical relationships of human beings, for war is also relationship. But the interests realisable in community outweigh the dissociating interests, the interests realisable only by conflict. Thus the permanence of community is assured. We shall see later that the socialising interests increase continually *where life itself increases,* while the desocialising interests diminish continually. Thus the expansion of community is assured.

§ 2. Forms of relation between wills or interests.

We may now proceed to an analysis of those general relations between men's interests on which depend the permanence and expansion, the strength and degree of community. As before we shall speak mainly in terms of interests, merely repeating that, wherever a relation exists between the objects of the wills of different men, there too a relation must exist between these wills themselves.

There are in the first place two great classes of interests (as also of the forms of thinking and willing which correspond to these) which must at all hazards be kept distinct in our thought. The confusion of them has vastly retarded sociological reasoning, and it is part of the nemesis attaching to uncritical discussion that however we now distinguish them our terms can only with difficulty be kept free from wrong associations. When each of a number of beings pursues an interest like or identical *in type* to that which every other pursues, say a livelihood, or reputation, or wealth, or any other interest which is for each discrete and personal, we may call the interests they severally pursue *like* interests. Such interests do not necessarily involve any community, any social relationship, between the beings who will them, however like the interests are. The interests of all the beasts of the field when they seek their food create no unity, and were there food enough for all would create no conflict. The interests of all are identical in type, but there is no common interest. When, on the other hand, a number of people all pursue one single comprehensive interest of them all, say the welfare or reputation of town or country or family, or again the success of some business in which they are all concerned, we may call that interest a *common* interest. The pursuit of the common welfare of many remains a common interest, no matter what ulterior interest may inspire that pursuit. The consideration of motives may lead us into a further sphere of like interests, as when men seek the welfare of their community for the sake of some direct or reflected glory it brings themselves, but the interest itself remains common. Often the attainment of like interests is sought through the establishment of a common interest, as when men form a trading company.   Here the common interest, that in the welfare of the company as such, as a single indivisible organisation, is secondary, the like interests being prior.   In other cases the common interest is primary.   The common interest is always a directly social interest, the like interests are always egoistic.   And the two form the inextricably entwined motives of the greater part of our activity.   But it is for that very reason we must keep them distinct in our analysis.   Otherwise we shall find in social phenomena a simplicity they do not possess.

By secondary common interest I mean that interest in associational or communal welfare which is itself dependent on a further exclusive interest, as when men seek the good of others because of the advantage or glory it brings themselves.   Primary common interest is that which is dependent on no such further interest.   Primary and secondary common interests are the mingled sources of all our social activity.   The love of an association or community is very often like the love of many parents for their children, whom they love as a kind of extension of their own individuality, as a kind of property.   Even when the primary interest is predominant, the secondary interest supports it.   The two are not so much kinds of common interest as its factors.   In all our relations with others it is difficult to evade the promptings of the intrusive self-interest.   The psychologist finds in his sympathy with the sorrows of others an element of reflected sympathy with himself conceived as in a like situation, in his efforts to relieve the sufferings of others a desire to attain also a certain self-satisfaction and to banish a cause of self-pain ; he finds his sympathy with the happiness of others crossed by pangs of envy if the same happiness has passed him by, and his efforts to bring happiness to others stimulated by the reflected happiness the endeavour brings to himself.   The mind of man is infinitely too complex to admit of " single-mindedness " : it has been shaped by infinite experiences that reach out of all imaginable time. It is only a lunatic, a man whose past has suffered violent dissociation from his present, whose motives are ever simple. To have *absolutely* simple motives *is* to be a lunatic, for not even genius can ever attain to such simplicity.

We can now make some further distinctions. Like interests fall within the wider class of *discrete* interests, *i.e.*, interests as pursued by each for his own personal or individual fulfilment. It is better to call these interests " discrete " than " individual," since of course all interests are individual in one sense, *i.e.*, that they are all interests of individuals. When several persons pursue discrete interests which yet are like or identical in type, we have *like* interests ; when they pursue discrete interests which differ in type, we have *unlike* interests. Unlike interests are interests which, so far as those who pursue them are concerned, lie in unrelated spheres of activity and so do not involve or create any direct social relations. For example, the interests of philately and astronomy need never bring the philatelist and the astronomer into social relations. But such isolation of interests is always relative. Again, intermediate between like and unlike interests are the very significant class of *complementary* interests, partly like, partly unlike. When the interests of two or more persons, while not wholly alike, are yet interdependent, involving reciprocal service, we may call them complementary. The most obvious examples are sexual interests, but others of very great importance are revealed in the division of labour within community and in the whole fabric of reciprocal rights and obligations. It is obvious that complementary interests do most easily and immediately create common interest.

A further distinction, within like interests, has already

been implied. Men may pursue their like interests in
social isolation ; their interests may run *parallel*, involving,
for the individuals in question, no contact whatever.   Or
again their pursuit of like interests may bring them into
relationships either of conflict or of harmony.   When
two or more persons pursue an object of such a character
that the attainment of it by one involves in so far the
failure of the others to attain it, we have *conflicting*
interests.   In the simultaneous pursuit of such an exclusive object, there results, as Kant said, the kind of " harmony " involved in the pledge of Francis I. to the Emperor
Charles V., " What my brother wants " (*i.e.* Milan),
" that I want too."   But on the other hand many objects
which men seek, each for himself, are yet either expansive
through co-operation, or at any rate such as to be more
easily attainable by each through the co-operation of all,
and under these conditions the like interests are *concordant*.   Co-operation increases, conflict diminishes, the
objects to which the like interests of men are directed.
This fact that like interests may lead either to harmony
or to conflict, that these attitudes are in some measure
alternatives, has vast significance for the evolution of
community.

Finally, in view of the importance, especially from the
standpoint of political science, of a clear terminology as
a basis for the discussion of social willing, we may insist
once more that the relations of wills are best understood
and explained if we start from the objective side, the side
of interests.   If we substitute the term " will " for the
term " interest," the definitions given above will then be
adequate for the subjective aspect.   Thus when each of
a number of beings pursues an interest like or identical in
type to that which every other pursues, we may call their
several wills *like wills*.   Again, when a number of people
all pursue one single comprehensive interest of them all,

we may call their willing in so far a *common will*. And so for the remaining distinctions we have made.

It is essential to remember that "interest," as used throughout this work, means strictly that which is the object of will. For "interest" may be used in a wider sense, as equivalent to advantage or welfare, whether that advantage is or is not willed by those whose advantage it may be. But unless that advantage is the object of *some* will, it is not an interest as above defined. The failure to distinguish these two meanings has brought confusion into political theory. If "interest" be used as meaning simply "advantage" or "welfare," then something may be an individual's or a community's interest which he or it not only does not pursue, but even repudiates. It is a perfectly legitimate use of the term "interest," but it is not legitimate to pass from the one meaning to the other and speak of such an "interest" as representing the "real will" of individual or community. We shall avoid this confusion by using the term in one sense only, viz., as that which actually motives will. Again, if we use "interest" as equivalent to "welfare," we can no longer pass from the "general" or "common interest" to the "general" or "common will" as if these were equivalent or co-extensive. A single individual may seek the general welfare in a way unregarded by his community, but we shall then call his interest (the object of his will) not a common interest, but an interest in common welfare. It becomes a common interest, as we use the term, when it is pursued by him and others in concert, not discretely but through their joint activity.[1]

---

[1] The failure to make these distinctions leads Dr. Bosanquet into confusion in his account of the " real " and the " actual will " in *The Philosophical Theory of the State*. A similar confusion was involved in Rousseau's account of the " will of all " and the " general will." The " will of all " is " merely a sum of particular wills ; " whereas the " general will " " regards only the common interest," and " what generalises the will is not so much the number of voices as the common

We may now map out the whole field of interests, from the standpoint of social relationship, as follows :

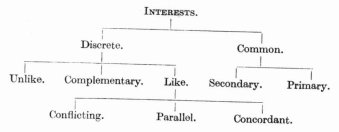

§ 3. The kinds of common interests.

We have next to enumerate and classify the various types of interests which create and sustain community and its associations. The task has often been attempted in recent years, and various helpful classifications have been made.[1] If we do not adopt any of those it is because none of them is made from the point of view set out in the introduction of this work. A completer classification than any yet offered is necessary for our purpose. Interests are the springs of community, and a comprehensive classification of them is a necessary preliminary to the study of it.

Our concern here is with interests as common and not as discrete, for it is common interests which are the sources of community. All like interests are potential

interest which unites them." Here then he meant by the " general will " the will corresponding to the interest in general welfare, which, of course, on any particular issue may not be the will of the whole community, since many members of it may be considering only particular interests, and these may be opposed to the general welfare. But, again, he says, " the will is either general or it is not ; it is either that of the body of the people, or that of a portion only." Here obviously the will is called general because it is that of the whole community. The transition from one meaning to the other has led to much sophistical writing, by no means in the *Contrat Social* alone. For a completer analysis of these fallacies see Appendix A.

[1] Perhaps the best of these classifications is that of Lester Ward, *Pure Sociology* (2nd ed.), p. 261.

common interests ; in so far as that potentiality is realised community exists.

Like interests pass by endless transitions from the most universal, shared by all men, down to the most particular and intimate. All men are alike in respect of certain fundamental interests. We all have like organic needs, needs of food and drink, air and light, clothing and shelter. As these are needs of all living beings, they create like interests for all living beings. But every like interest, as we shall see more clearly at a later stage, is best secured for all when all whom its pursuit brings into contact pursue it in common, under regulated social conditions. The universality of like organic needs is thus in the long run a mighty socialising force.

Some psychical interests seem equally as universal as are organic needs. For example, justice and liberty (properly defined) are interests of all men, demanding and creating social unity—though not yet in the measure of universality. But on the whole the more specific psychical interests are not so universal as the specific organic interests. If we adopt Aristotle's distinction of " life " from " good life," we may say that universal like interests are those on which "life " depends, while the particular like interests of men reveal their varying conceptions of " good life." Men seek power, distinction, adornment, knowledge, and endless forms of spiritual satisfaction, but not with the unanimity of their pursuit of organic necessities.

The like interests of likes become in part the common interests of likes. In so far as men realise that likeness of nature or of interest means potential common interest, in so far as they realise the value of community, they create associations for its furtherance. In the classifica-tion which follows interests are viewed in relation to the associations which they create. These associations answer to (a) the whole complex of communal interests, or (*b*) some less extensive group of interests, or (*c*) single specific interests.

(*a*) A community is a social unity whose members recognise as common a sufficiency of interests to allow of the interactivities of common life. We have already seen that community is a matter of degree, and that it is most readily determined by territorial boundaries. For local contiguity not only permits the conversion of pre-existent like interests into common interests, but itself ensures the operation of biological and psychical laws which constantly weave new common interests.

The completest type of community is the nation, and when a nation is allowed free expression it creates an autonomous State. Within the State there are established, corresponding to the narrower communities within the nation, the local governments of district and town. The State and its sub-divisions are associations, organised *forms* of society. Communities must create associations in order to uphold communal interests, associations which pursue these interests in specific ways. And the State is the greatest of associations because it upholds, in its specific political way, the greatest recognised complex of common interests, those of a determinate community.

(*b*) When a group is held together by a complex of interests, but itself is constituted as a portion and not the whole of any community, it is usually called a class. A class may have some one predominant interest round which the others cluster and which gives its name to the class. Thus we speak of governing classes, in terms of a predominant political interest, of leisured classes, working classes, professional classes, agricultural classes, and so on, in terms of their respective economic interests. Or again we distinguish classes as upper, middle, and lower, in terms of social status. To constitute a class, a group must have a complex of common interests, and these common interests must distinguish them from other groups of the community possessing other, and it may be antagonistic, common interests. The extreme of this opposition is revealed when classes constitute castes.

A class in turn pursues its complex of interests through associations. Being only an element in a community, its members cannot constitute a state, but they create associations, of which the type is the political party, which seek to control the policy of the State. We may include here also those associations which foster and are held together by group-sympathies or " class-spirit," that general sociality which exists between the members of any group.

(c) Men are not content to pursue common interests merely in so far as these form complexes of greater or less completeness. They come more and more to establish associations for every common interest in its specificity. Only by the help of such associations can the endless degrees and varieties of likeness (and thus of community) in interests be adequately recognised and furthered. Wherever men discover that they have any common interest, the ground is prepared for the corresponding association. It is in the line of evolution that these associations should grow continually in extent, in number, and in singleness of aim. Already they present a vast and bewildering array.

It is exceedingly difficult to classify, completely and without cross-division, these specific interests and the associations which they create. One obstacle to classification is the lack of definite names for the various groupings of social phenomena. A more serious obstacle is that interests lie behind interests in the most perplexing ways. We have, for instance, an interest in wealth, but it is in general for the sake of further interests which wealth may serve. Or we have an interest in knowledge, but it may be for the sake of the wealth which that knowledge may bring, and thus ultimately for the sake of the further satisfactions which wealth may acquire—or it may be for the sake of knowledge itself. Or again, we may have a political interest which is determined by an economic interest, and so on.

Reflection on this difficulty leads to the first division of specific interests, that into ultimate and derivative. For, although any specific interest whatever *may* be derivative, *i.e.* may exist as an interest because it is a means to some ultimate interest, yet some are essentially derivative and others are in their proper nature ultimate.

Of derivative interests the two great classes are the political and the economic. The political interest is directed towards the character of that great organisation of society which upholds liberty in order, the condition of the fulfilment of all other interests, and whose policy and direction is of vital significance for these other interests. It is for the sake of these that the political interest, in all its degrees and forms, exists. The economic interest is in like manner derivative. This interest is so universal simply because it too is a means of all ultimate interests. It is in no way limited to the field of industrial and commercial activity, but it is bound up, in one way or another, with the pursuit of *every* interest. If men paint or preach or philosophise they usually expect to derive from that work, besides the satisfaction it may bring, the means of satisfying their other interests, just as certainly as if they cultivated the land or manufactured goods or bought and sold. Man has many ultimate interests, and he can satisfy them only if he adds these derivative interests to the rest.

Of ultimate interests the two main classes are those based on organic needs and those based on psychical needs. We may, for the sake of conciseness, call these respectively organic and psychical interests, but we must in so doing remember that all interests are psychical, the interests of minds. But some interests are created by organic needs and some by non-organic needs. There is no line of demarcation between the two, they pass by subtle transitions into one another. They are inter-dependent and are indeed meaningless apart. Again, interests of the one type may be made the means to interests of the other; we have derivative organic interests, dependent on ultimate psychical interests, and we have the reverse order of dependence. But both types may be pursued, and usually are pursued, though not in equal degrees, as underivative.

Organic interests are best divided, for our purpose, into sexual and non-sexual. The former have a social signifi-cance and a character of complementariness which dis-tinguish them sharply from all other organic interests. The term " sexual " is here used in a wide sense, to include all those interests which we ascribe to sexual love, family affection, and the spirit of kinship. Non-sexual interests comprise our interests in food and drink, in exercise and recreation, in clothing and shelter, in whatever fulfils all the other organic needs.

From these we pass to psychical interests. These are both difficult to distinguish, at the border-line, from organic interests, and are themselves so interwoven and complex as to render classification difficult. The following line of distinction seems the simplest and may be adequate for our purpose. We adopt the psychological distinction between knowing, feeling, and willing as *aspects* of mental activity, and distinguish interests according to the predominant aspect in each case. (1) There are interests in which the intellectual aspect predominates, the scientific, philosophic, and educational interests in the discovery, systematisation, and communication of knowledge. To discover, to systematise, and to communicate, these are interdependent activities and form a unity of interests. They create the multitude of scientific associations, whose labours have both widened the horizons of our knowledge and are in especial the source of those technical utilities which are constantly transforming our whole social world. We must add to these the specifically educational associations, which, however diverse and comprehensive their aims, can pursue them in one way only, by imparting knowledge.   (2) There are interests in which the emotional aspect dominates, the artistic and religious interests. The former creates a multitude of associations, artistic (in the narrower sense), musical, dramatic, literary ; and the latter creates that most significant association, the church.   (3) We may add to these the interests in which the aspect of will predominates, the interests in power, prestige, and self-assertion.   These do not directly create specific associations, owing to their lack of content or definition, but they are always actively at work shaping associations, determining both their internal structure and their modes of operation. They are especially important as determinants of the derivative interests, for government and wealth are in a peculiar way at once the forms and the sources of power.

All specific common interests of men fall within the scheme we have outlined above. Every one of these interests, it must be noted, may be pursued either as primary or as secondary, either for the sake of the common good involved or for the sake of the private advantage it may bring to the pursuer ; and usually the two motives are inextricably blended. It is therefore a mistake of analysis to add the " egotic " as a kind of interest comparable with, say, the organic interests.   Egoism and altruism are not kinds of interests at all, but rather ways in which we relate ourselves to our interests.   Even the interests in power and prestige may not be " egotic." The power sought after may be that of family, class, or nation, and even when we seek power for ourselves it may be for the sake of any of these. Again, it is a mistake to place the " ethical interest " alongside, say, the scientific or artistic. If we speak of an ethical interest at all, we must count it as general and not as specific : for ethical activity works in and through all interests, their universal and final determinant.

As we have said, it is only in later stages of social evolution that specific interests are demarcated and create specific associations. In primitive community they exist only as complexes of interests. This does not mean, of course, that in civilisation these complexes are broken up; on the contrary, they become greater and completer. Differentiation never means the dissolution of unity but only the revelation of its character.

We may, in conclusion, present our results in tabular form as follows, showing both the kinds of common interests and the associations which correspond :

INTERESTS	CORRESPONDING ASSOCIATIONS
A. General	
The interests of sociality, dependent on general (group or communal) likenesses.	Associations of social intercourse and camaraderie, clubs, etc.
B. Specific	
I. Ultimate	
(a) Interests based on organic needs	
1. Non-sexual	Hygienical, medical, and surgical associations. Agricultural, industrial, and commercial associations.
2. Sexual	Marriage and kinship associations, the family.

INTERESTS   CORRESPONDING ASSOCIATIONS

(*b*) Interests based on psychical needs

Culture interests		
	1. Scientific, philosophical, and educational	Scientific and philosophical associations; schools and colleges.
	2. Artistic and religious	Associations of art, music, literature; the theatre; the church.

      3. Interests in power and prestige

(All interests under *B*. I. may be combined in any number and degree to form complexes of interests, *i.e.* group and communal interests. Both singly and thus combined they create derivative specific interests.)

II. Derivative, of which the chief types are :

(*a*) Economic   Nearly all associations under *B*.

(*b*) Political

    (1) The state and its subdivisions. (Corresponding to communal interests.)

    (2) Political parties. (Corresponding to group interests.)

    (3) Associations for the political furtherance of specific interests.

    (4) All associations, legal, judicial, etc., directly dependent on but not simply parts of (1).

§ 4. The oppositions and harmonies of common interests.

Every social phenomenon emerges out of the meeting of interest-determined wills, out of their collisions and above all out of their harmonies. In the understanding of these collisions and harmonies lies the understanding of community.

We must, therefore, investigate the nature and degree of opposition and harmony which exist, in mere fact or of necessity, between the interests classified in the preceding section. It will appear as the result of our investigation that while oppositions of interests are necessary and ubiquitous they are yet subsidiary to a still more universal unity of interests. The deepest antagonisms between interests are not so deep as the foundations of community. Every opposition on analysis turns out to be partial, not absolute. What is true of the whole universe, that differences prove to be but differences within unity, is true of our social world.

We have to apply to the interests classified in § 3 the distinctions set out in § 2. We have seen that likeness of interests may lead either to opposition or to harmony. Here is the great source of social oppositions, and here is perhaps also, if we go deep enough, the final source of social harmony. Mere unlikeness of interests never creates either conflict or harmony, only indifference. Unlike interests of different persons or groups must depend on a more ultimate likeness before it brings them into contact. Conflict and harmony spring out of the common nature of those who enter into such relations. Difference of interests leads to oppositions only because it leads to coincidence of like interests. Even the most primitive savage, who hates all aliens from his tribe, hates them, so far as he reasons at all, not because of their difference alone—what is absolutely unrelated to him would be absolutely indifferent to him—but because that difference implies the antagonistic pursuit of interests they alike possess.

In order, therefore, to understand the oppositions and harmonies of different interests we must go beyond that difference to a unity or likeness of nature which in their several ways these interests serve. For every individual

there is always present the necessity of choice between
conflicting interests of his own ; for every community
there is always a conflict of interests among its members,
its associations and groups. Intra-individual conflict
and harmony of interests is relative to the unity of
the individual being, social conflict and harmony to
the likeness to one another of the members of community. The latter is our direct concern, but it must be
preceded by a consideration of the former. Under what
conditions, we must ask, do the specific interests conflict
and harmonise within the individual life ? A brief consideration of this question will throw light on the question
of social harmony and conflict.

1. *Intra-individual conflict and harmony of interests.*
Let us consider in this regard the specific interests as
classified above. *Essential* organic interests, it will at
once appear, are in their nature harmonious and not
conflicting. The unity of the organism binds them
together. The welfare of the whole organism is found in
the welfare of all the parts. " Whether one member
suffers, all the members suffer with it ; or one member be
honoured, all the members rejoice with it." For the
individual there is, therefore, no conflict of interests in
the pursuit of organic welfare. And there is notably a
complete harmony between the two divisions of organic
interests.

Not only so, but the adequate fulfilment of both is a
necessary basis of the higher psychical life. That higher
psychical life is rooted in organic needs. Suppose
man's sexual interests to disappear, how much of art and
poetry and religion—aye, and of the sheer intelligence
that probes into the causes of things—would disappear
as well ! Suppose all his organic interests to disappear,
while mental activity somehow continued, that mental
activity would become the idlest dreaming within the

void ! If body is one and mind is one, mind and body are also one. So we can add that *essential* organic interests are in their nature harmonious with psychical interests. Despite secondary exceptions a healthy organic life is a condition of a vigorous psychical life. On the other hand, body and mind are so related that an intense psychical activity, if it be spontaneous and not imposed by outer necessities, sustains and prolongs organic functioning.

We have already implied that *essential* psychical interests are harmonious with one another. It is a confusion of thought which inspires the belief that the suppression of our emotional nature is an aid to intellectual strength. *If* our emotions are enlisted on the side of our intellectual pursuit, they are in the degree of their strength a stimulus to it. Without emotional driving we have no intellectual *interest* at all. To employ the language of Aristotle, it is never the appropriate emotion, but only alien emotions, that interfere with our intellectual interests.[1] It is, therefore, never emotion as such that is an enemy to science and philosophy. On the contrary, the highest intellectual eminence is associated with emotional intensity, and the greatest artists, poets, and founders of religion have been greatest because their intelligence was most adequate to the strong demands of their emotions. Finally, it is obvious that the interests in power and prestige are themselves spurs to all other psychical interests.

What then of the conflict of interests which eternally besets the individual life ? Let us examine one of the commonest forms of such conflict. A man has often to choose, we say, between his economic interest and his culture-interests. This is not, however, the right anti-

---

[1] Aristotle speaks in terms of " pleasure," not " emotion." ἐμποδίζει δὲ οὔτε φρονήσει οὔθ' ἕξει οὐδεμιᾷ ἡ ἀφ' ἑκάστης ἡδονή, ἀλλ' αἱ ἀλλότριαι, ἐπεὶ αἱ ἀπὸ τοῦ θεωρεῖν καὶ μανθάνειν μᾶλλον ποιήσουσι θεωρεῖν καὶ μανθάνειν. *Nic. Ethics*, VII. 12. 5.

thesis. For, as we have seen, the economic interest is derivative, the culture-interests are ultimate. The economic interest is a condition of all other interests, cultural and non-cultural. It is in no necessary opposition to either kind, being a condition of both. If it were in opposition to any ultimate interest, it would be in opposition to all, but such opposition would be an opposition between the means and the ends of life. There *is* an opposition involved, an opposition of a very real nature, but it is none the less accidental. Where there is a common means which serves many ends, the limitation of that means involves a limiting choice between ends. Here is the heart of this most significant opposition. It is an illustration of the universal principle that the limitation of means, not only economic means, but the means we call time, opportunity, physical and mental energy, imposes upon us eternal choices between ends. If we pursue one interest intensely, the more must we limit the intensity of other pursuits. If we specialise in one direction, we are thereby prevented from specialising in another. Thus partial oppositions are created on every hand. Partial oppositions, for they arise from the limitation of the common means to all our ends. Partial, because all ends of the individual spring from the unity of his nature. For what is it that must determine the choice between alternative ends ? Surely their relative values for the being to whom they are values, for the being who is himself at every stage a unity, and who is ever seeking to realise himself as a unity.

2. *Social conflict and harmony.* The pursuit of any interest by individual or group may be either an aid or a hindrance to its pursuit by other individuals or groups. This is the social significance of likeness of interests. That likeness is itself the great cause of social oppositions and the source of social harmonies.

The very fact of individuality creates an eternal possibility of opposition between the interests of every self and those of every other. The correlative fact that all individuality is socially determined and socially conditioned eternally breaks down the absoluteness of such opposition. It is instead revealed as partial and relative. All oppositions of interests are secondary to the common interest of an association or at least of a community. This we may summarily show by considering oppositions as they occur (a) within and between associations, (b) between groups within community, and (c) between communities.

(a) Within every association, however narrow or however wide the unity of interest on which it rests, oppositions inevitably arise. If men are united as to any end, they are not thereby united as to the means of its pursuit. If they are united upon the means, they are not thereby agreed as to their relative positions within the organisation so determined, and their relative shares in any positive or divisible product of the common activity. Always, within any social unity, we find the common interest but partial and imperfect. Likeness of interests is never, and from its nature can never be, transformed into perfect community of interest. But the oppositions fall within the association, they are not so great or so powerful in dividing as the common interests are great and powerful to unite. Otherwise the association would not endure.

For instance, in an economic association, such as factory or store, there must always remain a difference of interests —or, to speak more strictly, a likeness of interests not reduced to community of interest—for the different members of it. This difference is inherent in its nature. It may show itself deepest in the division of employer and employee, or perhaps of manager and workman; these are the greater cleavages, while lesser divisions scarify

the whole fabric of the association. Yet community of
interest is still stronger than difference, and the fabric
holds because that community is never cut through by
these divisions. True, on the basis of this difference,
the employees may form or enter another kind of association as well, one devoted entirely to the interest of
employees, and the employers may form or enter another
association devoted to the interest of employers. Now
between these latter associations there may seem to be
no community of interest. Certainly there would be
none if these stood alone and apart from all other
associations, but, as we have just seen, they come into
being only because other associations exist in which
employers and employees have common interests. The
antagonistic associations are not isolated or isolable,
they too are secondary to a common interest beyond the
antagonistic interests on which they rest. If we consider
the deepest antagonisms within the economic system,
the conflicting like interests of competitors, the conflicting
like interests of labour and capital, of cultivation and
manufacture, of manufacture and distribution, of supply
and demand, we see that they are all not only partial but
secondary, that *they would not exist at all were there no
prior community of interest.*

If this holds in a sphere of association where interests
are essentially derivative, where the primary common
interest is relatively least and the secondary common
interest is relatively greatest, it holds *a fortiori* within all
other associational spheres.[1]

---

[1] At the same time it is significant that the bitterest antagonisms
between associations have belonged to the associational sphere perhaps
furthest removed from the economic. They have arisen between
churches. But here the antagonism has been largely due to extra
social interests, *i.e.* to interests founded on dogmatic interpretations
of religion. This antagonism dies down as opposing dogmas cease
to hold captive the minds of men, and the spirit of religion becomes
finer, if also rarer.

(*b*) The opposition of groups within a community is more continuous and embittered the greater the complex of interests which at once unites the members within the group and separates the group itself from others. For since the members of groups must be alike in most of their interests, the extent and number of exclusive group interests indicates the degree in which the like interests of the respective groups remain unreconciled. Thus the extreme form of intra-communal opposition is that between caste and caste. Here the division is so sharp that only by the aid of adventitious interests, interests determined by tradition and religion, is community maintained. It is maintained too only at the cost of the intrinsic interests of the community. For progress is possible only through the transformation of like interests into common interests, and the exclusiveness of caste bars the way. The divisions of caste *almost* destroy the community and would altogether break it up were it not that extrinsic common interests, traditional and religious, prove substitutes for those intrinsic common interests which the caste-system rejects. There exists a community of interest, of a kind, to which even caste-divisions remain subordinate. Thus the community endures.

It is needless now to show that *class* differences are also subordinate to community of interest. But the distinction of caste and class suggests an interesting corollary. Classes *as distinct from castes* rest on true personal differences, differences of occupation, ability, character, and manners. The more they rest on significant personal differences the further are they removed from the evils of a caste system, from the disunion and stagnation it entails. Where intrinsic differences help to determine classes there is a constant transition and possibility of transition—intrinsic qualities not being simply heritable

—from one class to another, which lessens the antagonisms bred of difference. And further, in so far as intrinsic
differences determine classes, in so far it is unlike interests,
not exclusive like interests, which distinguish class from
class. The former, we saw, do not create division, the
latter are its primary causes. Intrinsic differences are
of course in significant beside intrinsic likenesses, so that
the more rational the basis of class-distinction, the
narrower becomes the range of exclusive class-interests,
and the broader the basis of community.[1]

Oppositions may arise between other intra-communal
groups than castes and classes. We may illustrate by the
very significant opposition arising out of the increased entry
of women into industrial life. A partial sex-opposition
here arises, for example, *in so far as* the willingness of
women to accept lower wages reacts detrimentally on the
employment and wages of men. But an examination of this
opposition shows at once how far it is from involving any
essential antagonism of interests between the sexes. For
women are able to accept lower wages largely because
the economic support of the family, itself more central
to women's life than to men's, falls mainly upon men. If

[1] It is not, of course, implied that our classes are absolutely or even
very largely distinct from castes. The ideal of classes founded purely
on intrinsic differences is not and never has been realised. But whereas
in eastern civilisations the chief determinant of class and status was
birth, in the western civilisation of to-day wealth is a class-determinant
of equal or perhaps greater importance, and wealth is a less rigid determinant than birth : it is concreter, and thus its claims are more easily
challenged ; itself a matter of degree it is less apt to create distinctions
of kind ; alienable, acquirable, and transferable, it draws no such
permanent lines of cleavage as does birth ; and lastly, being itself
in some uncertain degree a return for service, it is never purely a *caste-*
distinction.

We may note that a group must possess a quasi-communal character
in order to constitute a caste or class, *i.e.* the members of it must
share in some degree of common life, must to a certain extent live
together. Now in the modern world of intercommunication this
living-together, in towns at least, is chiefly determined by the type
of house inhabited, in other words, by the amount of rent the occupiers
can afford to pay. Thus writers on social classes find it easiest to
distinguish them in terms of rent, *i.e.* in terms of wealth.

then the lower rate of women's wages acts to depress the wages of men or throw them out of employment, it is the whole community that suffers : it would mean that men are less able to support or establish families, a result disastrous to the welfare of women, and disastrous most of all to the welfare of the race which lives and has its being in the common interest of men and women. As for the wider antagonism of interest between men and women which some misguided people have proclaimed, that is in reality the merest figment. The common interest of men and women is laid in the foundations of life and reaches to its pinnacles. What hurts either hurts both. If man is primitive and unenlightened, he treats woman as a chattel ; and

> " If she be small, slight-natured, miserable,
> How shall man grow ? "

The common interest of all intracommunal groups is, we may conclude, superior to the dividing interests. The interests on which community rests are greater than the interests on which the groups within it rest. The objective witness to the superiority of common interest within and between associations and groups is the very fact of the State. This greatest of associations stands for the co-ordination of all the interests of a community, thereby setting itself, in view of the incessant partial conflicts within community, a vast and endless problem, but also, in view of the greater common interest which these conflicts can not destroy, a problem progressively soluble.

(c) The fact of the State has always made it comparatively easy for men to recognise the superiority of common interest within a State-determined community. The actual limits of states have at the same time made it difficult for men to recognise the further extension of

community. But we have already seen that community
by its very nature is more extensive than any State, and
we shall see later that the disparity in extension has
grown with the growth of civilisation. For the peoples
separated by the frontiers of states have like interests,
and no power on earth can destroy or limit the law that
like interests are most attained when they have created
a common interest as well.

We need only say here, by way of anticipation, that
the only common interest which can be bounded by the
limits of a State is the interest of nationality, and that
the interest of nationality can only at one moment be
the decisive interest of a state-determined community,
viz., when some other nation, under the guidance of the
primitive nation-idea, threatens it with that armed
violence of conquest which is the prostration of all
interests.

This study of interests enables us to understand more
clearly why no metaphor derived from any other form
of unity can describe for us the unity of society. We
may perhaps think of the specific common interests as
the strong bonds uniting men to men, while the indefinite
instinctive interests of sociality and tradition resemble
the myriad fine threads of social unity. But interests
are not external bonds, not couplings which might be
uncoupled or removed while the beings remain unchanged ;
they are the interests *of* each, not merely *between* each
and every other ; they exist only as the objects of men's
wills, and they unite men in a spiritual harmony never
to be understood in any terms of physical conjunction
or organic oneness. They bind heart to heart, but they
live only in the hearts they bind ; they are common,
complementary, antagonistic, merged and opposed in a

thousand modes, yet they exist only in the activities of individual minds. It is no wonder men look round for metaphors to express so unique a unity, and it is no wonder they stumble in seeking to represent what can be understood only by itself.

CHAPTER III

THE STRUCTURE OF COMMUNITY

§ 1. Associations as organs of community.

In the last analysis community is nothing but wills in relation, if we understand by will no abstract faculty or power but mind as active. The indissoluble unity of all conscious life, that of subject and object, mind and its world, knower and known, appeared for us therefore in the form of will and interest ; and looking mainly at the objective side we were able to perceive the great forms of social unity that, though pierced by endless forces of division, cohere victoriously in communal life. How they so cohere, how the various common interests (or wills) which create associations are co-ordinated into community, this we must next consider.

First we must note that communal life is not confined within those associational moulds which answer to specific types of common interest. The life of community encompasses those forms and as it were clothes with living flesh and blood that associational skeleton. When, therefore, we have shown how associations are co-ordinated, we shall not have revealed the whole unity of community. We shall have shown merely the structure of its framework. To understand the whole reality of community we must keep in mind also the endless un-formulated relations into which men enter, relations of infinite variety and of every degree of complexity, by

whose means every man is brought into nearer or remoter
contact with every other, joined in a solidarity and interdependence which none can ever fully estimate. This
important truth has been well expressed by Simmel in
the following passage :

" Men regard one another, and men are jealous one of
another ; they write one another letters or dine together ;
they meet in sympathy or antipathy quite apart from all
tangible interests ; their gratitude for altruistic service
weaves a chain of consequences never to be sundered ;
they ask the way of one another and they dress and adorn
themselves for one another ;—these are instances chosen
quite at random from the thousand relations momentary
or lasting, conscious or unconscious, transitory or fraught
with consequences, which, playing from person to person,
knit us incessantly together. Every moment such
threads are spun, are dropped and again caught up,
replaced by others, woven up with others. These are
the reciprocities between the atoms of society, reciprocities that only the piercing vision of psychology can
investigate, which determine all the tenacity and elasticity,
all the variegation and unity of this so intelligible and
yet so mysterious life of society." (*Soziologie*, p. 19.)

Associations are the definite forms under which the
more permanent and specific types of social activity, of
relation between will and will, are co-ordinated. They
are as it were the various lines and figures standing out
on the web of community. They form an integral pattern,
as we shall see, but the integrity of the pattern is as
nothing to the integrity of the web. Community is the
whole incalculable system of relations between wills, an
association is the *pre-willed* form under which a definite
species of relation between wills is ordered. A university,
for instance, is a definite organisation ordering the research
and communication of knowledge. Men study and teach

apart from any association, but they have willed specific
organisations directing the main relations of student to
student, of teacher to taught.   And so of the greatest
associations, the industrial associations, the church, the
State.

Thus we see that every association is both an organisation within community and an *organ of community*.   The
incalculable complex of the interactivities of common
life are yet reducible under a certain number of categories,
as we saw in the last chapter, and men will corresponding
associations, giving a certain fixity and order to the
further acts of willing which fall within any given category.
Such types of willing are themselves throughout dependent
on types which fall under other categories.   Community
is not broken up into its associations.   Its unity reaches
deeper than the co-ordination of its associations.   Community is prior to its associations.   It is communal
will which creates associations.   Take the case of the
State, that completest organ of community.   Community
existed before any State.   It was the slow-developing
will of men in community to create the State which
gradually brought the State into being.   Community
was there from the first, but the State has been constructed.[1]   The State is an association men as social
beings have willed to create and now will to maintain.
There is thus a will in community more fundamental
than even the will of the State.   It is the will to maintain
the State.   If all men adopted the principles of anarchism
that will would exist no longer—there would be no State.
The State (like every other association) is a manifestation
of common will, and the will manifested in the creating
and maintaining of states and churches, industrial and

[1] As Spencer and others have pointed out, there still exist primitive
communities, groups of Eskimos, Digger Indians, etc., which show
no trace of political organisation.   Cf. Spencer, *Principles of Sociology*,
Part V., chap. 2.

commercial associations, circles of sociality, and so on, is the completest and profoundest reality which the world of community contains. It is in every sphere of its operation the nearest living approach to the ideal " general will " of the philosophers.

Every association is thus an organ, greater or smaller, of community; greater or smaller according to the strength, number, and unity of the wills which maintain it. The different associations within community are not created by separable groups, for men combine in most diverse ways with one another to maintain diverse associations. Every man is a member of more than one association and in each he forms part of a different unity. Associations are thus unities within, but they are not *units of*, community. Common interests overlap and interlace, and common willing is but the subjective aspect of common interest. How, despite these overlappings and interlacings, common interests as organised in associations are co-ordinated in one system, forms the final problem of this chapter. Before we resolve it, however, it will be well to consider more closely than we have yet done the meaning of this fact that the establishment and maintenance of every association is a manifestation of common will.

§ 2. Covenant and community.

Every association, every organisation of men, came into being through a covenant of men to establish it, and exists in a covenant of men to maintain it. Without this agreement of wills there could be no organisation, no constructed system of order and procedure. The old doctrine spoke of a *social* contract or covenant, and would have escaped the fallacies of which it is accused if it had only distinguished community from State and recognised that while all associations, the State included, rest on covenant, community itself is prior to and the necessary precondition of all covenant. A social will to establish society (or community) is a contradiction. A social will to establish and maintain the State is a great reality. It is visible in the obedience men pay to political laws determined by a majority alone ; it is visible in the continuous transformation of the State, in accordance with changes in the social will. Community is co-eval with life, associations are merely its products.

The distinction between eternal community and constructed association is vital to our purpose, and to explain community we must show exactly in what sense associations have been constructed, in what sense they are based on a covenant once prior in time, always prior in logic, to themselves. The statement that all associations rest on covenant is liable to misinterpretations. These we must remove.

In the strict sense, a contract is a definite form of agreement between two or more parties, determining their several rights and obligations in respect of some common interest, these rights and obligations being in a *legal* contract enforced or vindicated by the authority of the State. In this definite form the State at least cannot arise from or rest upon contract, and no one has ever maintained so contradictory a doctrine. The truth of the social-contract theory is that the State rests on a covenant of its members, not necessarily formulated at any time but implied in their actions as members of the State, a covenant to maintain the existing State and its laws or even (in new colonies, for instance) to establish a State and system of laws. So far the social will to establish or maintain the State is co-ordinate with the social will to establish, say, a church. But once the State has been established it exercises sometimes a limiting, sometimes a repressive, power over all other manifestations of social will. In this way the covenant on which the State rests becomes differentiated from the covenant on which any other association rests. In this way, too, the social will to maintain the State may become deeper and more comprehensive than the social will to maintain any other association. All associations are alike organs of community, but the State becomes the co-ordinating organ of them all.

In the light of this fact we can examine more closely the meaning of the basis of covenant on which every association must be constructed. We shall consider various types of association in this regard, beginning with the simplest contractual type and ending with the State.

1. As an instance of the simplest type of association we may take the limited-liability company. The phrase is significant, for the whole activity of the association is closely determined by contractual limits, the rights and obligations of its members are set out in the contract.

2. It is instructive to compare with such a type that of the club or association for social intercourse, existing not for the attainment of the economic means of life like the limited-liability company, but for some form and degree of common life. This association too is based on a covenant, it has a certain constitution, with rules and regulations to which all its members must conform. In becoming a member I most certainly covenant with all other members to observe these rules and regulations, and the observance of them is for me as for every member the condition of the social intercourse and other privileges which the club provides. But the covenant does not define the activity of the club in the same way as the contract defines the activity of the limited-liability company. You cannot define social intercourse in a charter, you cannot define or contractually limit the relations of common life.

3. Take again the case of a church. It too has a contractual constitution, in the form of articles and confessions which its members covenant to observe. But the constitution can define only in the most general way the end for which the church exists. In a word, the church is based on a covenant, but it is more than a covenant. The latter may be modified, reformulated, according to changes of thought and life within the former. Without the contractual basis the life of religion would indeed remain chaotic, yet the articles of contract are in a sense subordinate to that life, they cannot properly express it, and they almost necessarily give more attention to minor matters than to greater, to the form than to the spirit.

4. Let us next turn to a type which is most significant as leading up to the consideration of the State—the family. Marriage *involves* a contract—but how inadequate any contract must necessarily be to express the life so determined ! The contract can but rule out certain forms of action which would disintegrate the association or destroy its meaning, and insist on a few primary positive obligations which, vital as they are, are beyond measure too meagre to comprehend and express the society and life they determine. Suppose married life widens into family life, of that widened association it is true to say that the place of contract is still further restricted. The parents covenant to maintain the child, but not with the child. It is no longer a covenant of all with all. But the reason is significant. It is because the child is not yet an autonomous being with a formed character, with an autonomous will by which to enter into covenants. He is in a peculiar sense dependent upon his society. (It is because of this dependence within the family, as opposed to the autonomy possessed by the members of any other association, that we can regard the family as *a communal unit*. Biologically it is of course *the* unit of organised

group life.) When the child has become adult and autonomous, then if he remains on within the family association, it is because he now agrees to remain, and the family association again takes on a broader basis of covenant, in other words it now rests more completely on an agreement of wills. But it is very necessary to notice that this further agreement involved in the new autonomy of the adolescent members is, as a rule, unlike the marriage-contract, no formal compact but an unformulated relation of will to will; and that also, unlike the marriage-contract, it comes into being at no one moment of time but as the revelation of growth. In these two aspects the family affords a significant parallel to the State.

Some further points of importance have already emerged and may be insisted upon before we consider the crucial instance of the State. First, we have seen that contract or covenant may be the basis of an association and yet be quite inadequate to express the character of the social activity thereby determined. The terms of contract can never comprehend the meaning of a kind of life. We must not think of contract merely in terms of limited liability. Again, it does not follow that because an association is based on, or determined by, covenant, it is therefore conventional or arbitrary. Will is the subjective aspect of interest, and the more fundamental the interest the more fundamental the will. A covenant may thus be rooted in the deepest needs and desires of our nature. We must not identify what is willed with what is voluntary or optional in the sense that one may choose it or not at pleasure. On the contrary, what we will is what we are, the expression and realisation of our being. Because we have a certain nature, we will inevitably certain things, we form inevitably certain associations. Take the marriage-association, for example. This most certainly involves a covenant—but we cannot dissolve the covenant at will as we enter it at will, the reason being that it is recognised to be no arbitrary agreement. It is indeed something agreed upon, something contracted into, but it is agreed upon in virtue of needs and elements of human life which are in no sense arbitrary or transient but necessary and vital. Or take the case of the church. Here one is free to leave as one is free to enter the association. But the church (or any " voluntary " association) is not therefore arbitrary. It corresponds to a need of human nature, and so long as that need remains the will remains. Many things we will because we *must* will them, because it is our nature to will them. Such is the will to live itself. Such is the will to maintain the greater associations. New autonomous wills for ever emerge within community, but because many interests are universal the great associations which pursue them endure.

5. We may lastly apply the doctrine of contract or covenant, so clarified, to the State, showing that it too, though itself the precondition of contract in the narrower sense, rests upon an agreement of wills.

If we reject this doctrine there are but two clear alternatives open, one that political unity exists only or mainly as an unwilled accidental coherence of men, the other that it rests on force. The second of these alternatives may be at once ruled out of court. In the face of nearly all our traditional jurisprudence it remains true that there can be within a community no force which is so strong as its most common will. Force is by its very nature the servant of will. This is as true of any eastern despotism as it is of any western democracy. As Green said : " If a despotic government comes into anything like habitual conflict with the unwritten law which represents the general will, its dissolution is beginning."

(*Principles of Political Obligation*, § 90.) If a State is a
despotism it is because its members want or acquiesce in
(which also is a form of willing) a despotism. If the
many obey the one, they must have willed to obey.
There must be agreement before there can be compulsive
force, since there is no political force in the world except
that of men who unite or delegate their individual powers.
And in the long run the strongest determining force in the
world is that of the most common will within it. The
other alternative might seem at first more plausible.
No doubt the State has emerged out of a condition of
social coherence in which men scarcely realised any of the
significance of common life, in which they were ruled by
traditions and necessities they did not understand, much
as ants and bees do not understand, we may suppose, the
communities they build. But we must remember that
the State, the political organisation, has come into being ;
it is only community that has been from the first. As the
State develops its nature is revealed. " For what each
thing is when fully developed, that we call its nature."
(Aristotle, *Politics*, I. 2. 8.) We do not see clearly the
nature of the State in that primitive world where it is
almost indistinguishable from community. The State
is an organisation, a construction ; we can trace the process of its building and rebuilding, and where we find the
building completest there we should most seek for its
meaning and " form." Now, as civilisation and culture
advance, as men gain in intelligent appreciation of the
social world they make and inhabit, growing more
autonomous, less dependent on tradition and custom,—
the State becomes more and more determined by the
concerted willing of the members of community, reveals
more and more a real though unformulated covenant of
these. Of course many reputed members of every State
never, or only at rare intervals, realise this social will to

maintain it. In so far they never become social adult beings. But the State still rests on a covenant, not of all but of some. It is a social organisation, and social organisation is the creation of common will. It is those citizens who will the maintenance of the State who both make and *are* the State, the rest are merely its subjects. The broade⋅ the basis of contract becomes, the stronger and more unified becomes the State—but without some basis of contract there is no State.

We have thus shown again from another standpoint that every association is created and maintained by a social will which is prior to, more fundamental than, the will *of* the association : in a word, that every association is an organ of community.

§ 3. The universal principles of associational structure.

While all associations are organs of community, one of them, the State, stands out as co-ordinating them all. It is more than one among other organisations, it is also the organisation of organisations. We have already discussed the principle, often abused and often mis-understood, which determines the proper limits of its co-ordinating activity. Its instrument, political law, is mighty but not all-powerful, and there are spheres into which it cannot enter or can enter only to destroy. But every association has its outer as well as its inner side, every interest, however inward and spiritual, stands somehow related to external means and thus within the world of external organisation, a world that must be co-ordinated and can be co-ordinated only by the State.

It is not my purpose here to discuss the various ways in which different States seek and have sought to realise this principle of co-ordination. That enquiry belongs to the specific region of political science. I propose instead to show the universal principles of the structure of associations, with special reference to the structure of the State. By this method we shall at once complete the analysis of association and reveal the essential character of State-co-ordination.

We have seen that the social will to maintain an association is more fundamental than the will of the association itself. For example the will to maintain the State is prior to the will of the State itself. This is no mere metaphysical distinction, but a vital sociological fact. The will of the State is revealed in the laws of the State. Nearly every such law is born out of political conflict, it is scarcely ever what all the members of the State want and directly will, it is usually determined by a majority of voices or votes and is often bitterly opposed and resented by a minority. Yet it becomes the determined will of the State. (If the will behind law is not the will of the State, then there is no will of the State.) It is obeyed by those who opposed as well as by those who supported it. Why is this ? It is not merely, we shall see, because the majority has also the greater force. It is finally because there is a will more ultimate than the will of the State, the will to maintain it.

It is never the whole but at most a majority that decides the general policy of any association. This is inevitable, it is a principle rooted in the nature of men. If all men are agreed on the primary ends of an association, if there is a fundamental common interest for which it stands, there is not on that account agreement on the means by which these ends shall be fulfilled, or on the endless subsidiary interests which every association creates. The question of policy, of *how* the association is to attain its ends, has always divided and will always divide its members. So long as men differ in knowledge, in experience, in character, in temperament, in circumstances, they must differ in opinion. This is as true of the State as of every other association, and in this respect our language about the " general will " as sovereign tends to mislead us. For the State is directed not by a single unitary will like that of an individual, as the organism-theory would imply, but by a partial will somehow predominant, in the prestige, power, or number of those to whom it is common, over a partial opposing will. In a democracy it is or may be the will of a majority, and this majority-will is there the true ultimate sovereign which sets up and pulls down governments and which dictates the lines of their policy.

There are, we must now see, in every developed association three distinct kinds or stages of common will. There is first the social will to maintain the association, prior to and more universal than what we must call the will of the association, the will which decides its course or policy. It is the former that is alone truly general. In the case of voluntary associations it is indeed a universal will, a will common to all the members, in the case of the State alone it may be less than universal (since entry into the State alone is not free but in some degree compulsory), but it must still be general. Next, *within* the association there is active that policy-directing will which, always partial and always changing, is yet at every moment the supreme determinant of direction. Lastly, every association possesses not only a policy-directing will, but also a specific administrative will. Common action cannot proceed simultaneously from a great number of autonomous wills, however common their interest. Every association must have a centre or focus in which its activity takes determinate form. Such an organ is a necessary means for the carrying out of the policy of the association. In the case of the State this organ is the government, and we may call the government the *legislative sovereign*, as distinct from the majority-will which in this instance we may call the *ultimate sovereign*.[1]

It is the latter we must investigate in our endeavour to understand associational structure, and we have in the first place to fathom the measure of the instability of that will which is the *de facto* ultimate sovereign within every developed state. We looked for a general will and we have found a partial one. We look for a stable will —and we find one that fluctuates incessantly. It is no hard-and-fast majority that sits as sovereign on the political throne, it varies infinitely, so that surely every citizen is at some time in regard to some question a member of the determining majority. Yet this very instability is a factor of its success. Why do oppositions, representing a temporary minority-will, harangue and appeal ? Simply because they hope that, in the subtle process of action and re-action, persuasion and repersuasion, which constantly affects all human willing, this minority-will may be converted into a majority-will. A rigid cleavage, unmitigated by this hope, would create a deeper antagonism.

It matters not whether the sovereign we have found has none of the *a priori* attributes of kingship, no permanence, no fixity of resolution, no majesty. It may be a sovereign unworthy of the political philosopher, it is none-the-less *the* sovereign. Majority-rule is sometimes spoken of as a modern " superstition." On the contrary it has been in some sort a social necessity from the beginning, from the time when the loudest shout first carried the day. For what alternative is there ? If the autonomous members of an association are not

[1] The term "sovereignty" is at present indiscriminately used in both these senses—thus we speak of the "sovereignty of parliament" and of the "sovereignty of the people"—and this has led to much contradiction in political philosophy. In especial, it has created the contradiction between the view of Bentham, Austin, and their successors, and that of Rousseau and his successors.

unanimous—and that they can never be on any question of policy—the alternatives are to act at once by a majority-decision or to wait for unanimity till the Greek Kalends ! In fact all historical attempts to establish the principle of unanimity, as in the Roman tribunate, in the Polish Reichstag, in the assembly of German mark-proprietors, in the Cortes of Aragon, have meant the domination of the minority, that privilege of veto by which a single dissentient can frustrate the will of all the rest. Such systems were doomed to failure. They sought to establish an impossible universal will in the direction of policy and they succeeded only in making the less universal will, the will of the minority, prevail. Decision by majority is in matters of policy a practical necessity.

We may grant that it is beset by dangers. A majority of voices makes nothing right or wise. A true form of constitution can save us from the tyranny of minorities, how shall any constitution save us from the tyranny of a majority ? Only an enlightened and educated public opinion can avail us here. In the world of to-day, committed necessarily—and rightly—to majority-rule, our only hope lies in social education, in the inculcation of social responsibility, in the insistence on the value of all personality, on the primary worth of spontaneity and the secondary worth of compulsion, on the expediency of waiving those claims the insistence on which, though legally and politically permissible, would create deep or abiding oppositions and diminish the strength of community. All men feel, for instance, that the decision of vital political issues by a bare majority is invidious, and that any measure involving coercion, however justified, should have a substantial preponderance of voting power in its favour.

We may point out some further facts which reduce the invidiousness of a sovereignty so far removed from the

philosophic ideal. In the first place laws, though determined by the will of at most a majority, are in profession
and principle enacted for the welfare of the whole community. The end therefore is or *should* be universal.
It is or should be what the majority will as for the good
of the whole. When they act on any other principle and
legislate in view of a mere sectional, class, or party good
which is inconsistent with the good of the whole, their
action is false to the nature of law and false to the spirit
of obedience to law which rules in community. Law
makes a universal claim, even though it never or rarely
proceeds from a universal will. Again, though nearly
every law issues out of conflict, the system of these laws
comes in the process of revision and consolidation and
readjustment of opinion to represent not merely the will
of a partial and changing sovereign, but that deeper
social will on which the State is based. Thus the system
of the laws of a country reveals the continuous set of the
social will as it is shaped by the continuous experience
of age after age. It reveals the character of those who
form the State, the nationality, in the wider sense of
that term, of those included within the State. The
changes in that system from age to age, the transformation,
for example, of English criminal law during the nineteenth century, witness to changes in the national character. It shows that in spite of the divisions of class and
party a people has still a character, a nationality. On
the system of laws created by that unstable fluctuating
sovereign-will there is directed the constant selective
criticism of this greater if more elusive will. Parts of
the system grow obsolete, parts are repealed, but what
endures becomes the central framework of all associational life, a living and growing framework capable of
co-ordinating all the vast associational activity of community. Here at last, when we turn our attention from

that moving changing will which at every moment of time determines the direction of the State, and look to the enduring product of its activity, realising how the permanent social will has herein come to reinforce the unstable political sovereign, we have discovered the secret of the structure of community.

§ 4. Some fallacies exposed.

Our analysis of will and interest may now be applied to expose some common fallacies as to the unity, integrity, and inerrancy of common will. We have seen something of the marvellous complexity of the interests which are bound up in community, we have seen that community presents no smooth surface but one scarred by oppositions of every kind and degree, that it is directed by no integral will but by whatever will is at every moment victorious over an opposing will. These facts are too often overlooked and a false simplicity given to the social life, a false integrity to history. We may point out three forms of this false simplification.

(1) Interest lies behind interest in endless degrees of complication. Men may unite in willing some activity, some policy, and yet be determined by different interests and so far by different wills. We have seen how rarely the policy pursued by an association represents the determinate concerted willing of all its members. Yet such a rarity is common compared with the cases—if such even exist—where many men, united on one policy, have therein the selfsame interest, and seek the same particular consequence of its fulfilment. An illustration of to-day may bring this truth home. Suppose the policy of the United Kingdom in respect of free trade were changed through the election of a tariff-reform government. This change would mean that a majority of electors voted for the tariff-reform party, but behind that common act

what variety of motive would lie concealed! The majority-voters would not all have voted the same way because they all wanted tariff-reform, just as the minority-voters would not all have voted the opposite way because they all disliked tariff-reform. Concede for simplicity's sake that the question of free trade versus tariff-reform were the only issue—an absurd concession, except in the case of a referendum on a non-party question. Still variant will and variant interest would have entered, contradicting the *prima facie* integrity of the decision. Some would have voted from general attachment to party, some from aversion to the opposite party, many from personal considerations of various kinds. The remnant really desirous of the policy would have desired it from various motives and combinations of motives, that particular industries would benefit from the change, that the country as a whole would, that the change was bound up with other interests, say imperialism or militarism. And so with every measure of every government. In every State, in every association, this common will of which we speak so glibly is the rarest thing to find. There is a common will or no free association could exist. But that will is not expressed in every act of the association in such a way that we can say offhand—The association acted thus because of this or that interest. The philosophic historian is peculiarly liable to that error. He tells us so readily what the Greek or Roman or Teuton thought and willed at every juncture of Greek or Roman or Teutonic history. But history so written proves no better than what Napoleon (who made some) declared that history was, "a fable agreed upon," and the historian so writing is attributing to some fictitious unity of mind results and decisions that are born out of the partially common, partially conflicting interests of many minds. The historian so writing regards those conflicting interests as though at most they were merely motives swaying one undivided will until one strongest motive determines the unity of decision. Not in this way shall we attain to a knowledge of that sure reality of common nature which is fundamental beyond all antagonisms. If one only realised the complexity of any social system, where authority d:rect and indirect subordinates will to will ; where interests combine and clash in a multitude of ways ; where every degree of ignorance and enlightenment underlies decision ; where custom and convention, the mental habits of uniformity, are incessantly at warfare with the liberating enterprise and ambitions of individuality—we would avoid for ever the easy simplification that finds one motive behind every social decision, one will behind every social fact.

(2) Still more hazardous is the process of finding, behind the historical *succession* of events constituted by the actions and fortunes of a people, a unity of mind that, like the mind of each of us, is determined in its successive acts by its previous experiences, so that behind them we can trace a continuous policy and set purpose. Historians often exaggerate the unity of purpose which underlies the movements of an age, postulating at every stage a single-minded entity called Rome or Greece or Egypt or England, and scarcely realising the difficult problem of unity in difference set by the succession of men and generations. Again, I am far from denying the unity in the life of peoples—but I do dispute its simplicity, and wholly oppose the idea that this unity is like the unity of an individual mind ; for the latter is a single centre of experience, modified by all its past doing and suffering, the former is a common principle living in and transmitted through the multitudinous variant minds of successive generations.

(3) Lastly, a special danger besets us when we seek to

discover behind the records of a people not simply the
" mind " of that people but the " mind " of the race to
which it belongs. The danger here is that we attribute
to one factor what is the resultant of several. When we
attribute—to take one of many instances—to the Hellenic
spirit a love of autonomy, art, culture, outdoor living,
adventure, and so forth, we are certainly speaking of
qualities which to a greater or less degree (art and culture
at any rate were sought even in Athens by the few alone)
characterised some or all of the Greek communities.
But by what title do we credit these qualities to an original
racial temperament alone when we know that physical
barriers preserved isolation, that a poor soil, indented
coasts, an island-strewn sea, and rich neighbouring
continents promoted adventure, that a Mediterranean
climate, in an age when sanitary science was unknown,
made outdoor living far preferable to indoor ?   Doubtless these physical and economic factors helped to form
communal habit and outlook, so that the people spontaneously tended to activities which their conditions
necessitated. But that spontaneity itself is derivative.
There are instances of peoples which, changing their
habitat, have changed also their habits, and there are
many instances of peoples—the Hellenic itself might be
cited in this regard—whose portions, occupying territories
of different characters, have developed in correspondingly
different directions.   This will be brought out more fully
when we come to discuss certain questions of heredity
and environment.   Meantime it is sufficient to point out
that in nothing are we more liable to go astray than in
the search for the race-spirit, if by that we mean a focus
of original characters revealed as independent of environment.   To find it involves a perilous initial process of
abstraction, the almost or altogether impossible process
of unravelling the web of life and character woven by the

constant infinite reactions of circumstances and the minds of men.

One further fallacy is deserving of mention here, because of its importance in the history of the doctrine of common will. It is the doctrine of its inerrancy, sometimes held without qualification, sometimes limited to moral inerrancy. " The people," said Rousseau, " are never corrupted, though often deceived, and it is only then that they seem to will what is evil." (*Contrat Social*, II. 3.) It is an idea which in one form or another is or has been widely prevalent, having been held not only by certain political philosophers but also by the unphilosophical. To illustrate, a saying existed among the Greeks to the effect that there is a certain divinity in the voice of the multitude,[1] and in the middle ages there arose the proverb (though possibly in a somewhat different signification) that *vox populi* was *vox dei*, while there is a Moslem proverb which says outright that " error is impossible in the united deliberations of the community." There is indeed a core of truth in the idea. If it merely means that the need or the good of the community is better interpreted by the many than by the few, since a dominant minority is often perverted by selfish interests, that claim is well established by history. Or if it means that " in the multitude of counsellors there is wisdom," that also may be true in general, since reasoning and argument may count for something, prejudice may counteract prejudice, and the exposition of the partial views of each may lead to a wider comprehension of the issue by all. But taken more literally the doctrine is so obvious an error that it is strange any intelligent being should have given it credit. It is a belief resting on the illusion of the

---

[1] Cf. Hesiod, *Works and Days*,

φήμη δ' οὔτις πάμπαν ἀπόλλυται, ἥν τινα λαοί
πολλοί φημίζουσι· θεὸς νύ τίς ἐστι καὶ αὐτή,

referred to with approbation by Aristotle, *Nic. Ethics*, VII. 13. 5.

super-individual mind, strengthened by the dogmatic principle which makes for every people its own present customs and traditions sacred and best. As entertained by Rousseau and his Hegelian followers it seems to lead to the preposterous conclusion that all the individuals who compose a people may be going to hell while the people itself progresses heavenwards ! Doubtless it is less probable that many shall fall into some form of error than that one of them shall—but there is no subtle social alchemy which can transmute the errant wills of individuals into the infallible will of a community.

The same doctrine is sometimes stated in a vaguer and more elusive form. There is a proposition sometimes made by moral philosophers that the moral and the social are one. The expression is misleading. If it simply means that morality is that which, if translated into conduct by the members of a society, would ensure an ideal social order, the doctrine is true enough, it is merely a partial statement of the meaning of morality. But then the statement is misleading, for the expression, " the moral," when used without qualification, always refers to a conception of an ideal or " ought " (though the conception may be mistaken), whereas " the social " is generally and properly used as signifying the actual, the existent order of a society, which not even its component members may regard as the order which ought to exist. In other words, the moral and the moral " ought " are one, the social and the social " ought " are not necessarily one. Hence those who use the expression in the sense just mentioned would avoid needless ambiguity if in place of saying that the moral and the social are one, they said rather that " the moral " and the " ideal social " are one,—so expressed, the contention is not without justification, though as we shall see later it does less than full justice to morality. But if on the other hand the expression that the social and the moral are one means that morality consists in conformity to the existing social order, then (unless we are illegitimately using the expression " the moral " in its etymological sense, as signifying the customary, that which accords with usage) the doctrine is false for the reasons already given. Doubtless every social order embodies some elements of universal morality. Otherwise it would be no order at all, nor could the society at all exist. As Plato pointed out, without some justice, without some morality, not even a band of pirates or of thieves could keep together as a society. And yet the very perfection of the social order among thieves or pirates, the unity and coherence of their society, is the measure not of the moral good within the society but of the moral evil which they can compass. We see here already, what will appear more clearly in the next chapter, that social institutions however perfect in form are but the means to social values, the means to good and evil, to the welfare or disaster of men. The order and coherence of a society of thieves, is the means to moral evil ; the same order and coherence in a society of honest men would be the means to good. The end is all.

Not among any one people nor yet in any one age can we seek for the norm of wisdom or morality. Yet a broader and surer standard of judgment somehow comes to birth. The excess of one age is revealed to the next and in the process of action and reaction we may perhaps grasp the more comprehensive truth, the more central judgment, the profounder morality. The reaction of successive ages from extreme to extreme—profligacy to puritanism, puritanism to profligacy, dogmatism to scepticism, scepticism to dogmatism, materialism to idealism, idealism to materialism,—is a witness to no essential instability of human nature but to its essential sanity. The pendulum must swing from extreme to extreme before it can find rest at the centre. It is because it can rest only in the centre that it swings not from extreme to centre, but first from extreme to extreme. Each of us has known the satiety and revulsion which comes from dwelling long with false or partial ideals, the assertion of the more permanent against the more transient will. The same process goes on endlessly in the development of a people through its ever-fresh generations. It is really an amazing thing, and very reassuring, that for all the caprices and prejudices of individual men, and for all the blindness and narrowness of the judgments with which every age judges of its own works, there yet arises in the course of time a saner, broader, almost universal judgment in regard to these. Every age may follow some wandering fire, but a later age at length pierces the illusion. Every age may contemn or stone its prophets, but in the eyes of later generations wisdom is justified of her children. Every age may raise to ridiculous eminence some undeserving contemporaries, but the slowly yielded wisdom of succeeding ages surely dethrones them. So in the succession of generations men attain that retrospective judgment which we call in implicit trust, as though it were too sane and comprehensive to be the judgment of men, "the judgment of time" itself.

CHAPTER IV

INSTITUTIONS

§ 1. The meaning of institutions.

In the last chapter we analysed the structure of community and found it to consist of a " framework " of associations co-ordinated under the association of the State. But surely, it will be said, it is *institutions* that are the structure of community ! Surely it is these alone that give it character, that are its enduring forms, like continents of land amid the oceans of ever-dissolving, ever-recreated life ! Here we raise a question on which the text-books of social science are curiously silent, the question of the relation of institution and association. Yet the answer is by no means obvious. We speak, for instance, of the family and the church as " institutions," and they are certainly also associations ; we speak again of property as an " institution," and it is certainly not an association. Are associations then simply one form of institution ? But we would not call a small newly-established trading company an institution, though it is certainly an association. Once more we must raise the preliminary, possibly tiresome, but in a subject such as ours most necessary, question of names. What is an institution ?

We would all agree that every institution involves a certain social recognition or establishment and that nearly every institution possesses a certain permanence.

Permanence without establishment is not enough. It is, for instance, inappropriate to speak of poverty (or " the poor ") as an institution, for though the poor are with us always their poverty is not deliberately established by society. Poverty is an institution in a monastic order or among yogis, and it sounds cold-blooded to talk of poverty as an institution of the wider community simply because it implies a similar establishment. Again, the very fact of recognition and establishment implies a certain permanence. What then is it that is thus permanent, thus established ? It is not, we must see, any mere object standing in outer nature. The land on which we live, most permanent and first recognised of all external things, is not an institution. On the other hand the mode of its cultivation, of its possession, and of its inheritance, say the run-rig system, communism, entail, mortmain, primogeniture, are clearly institutions. These are, or were, permanent forms of relation between men in respect of the land, forms recognised by communities or associations. It appears then that institutions are forms of order established within social life by some common will. The qualifying phrase, " established by some common will," enables us to distinguish these from customs, which are also permanent ways in which men relate themselves to one another. It may be only a question of degree, but institution implies a more definite recognition, a more determinate will. Customs are but the habits of a community. As one man falls imperceptibly into a habit so do many men, the members of a group, form imperceptibly common habits, that is, customs. These customs may come to be recognised and instituted, they may come to be honoured, or perhaps to be condemned as a burden and restriction—or they may be as little felt by those who share them, as little known to them, as is the weight of the atmosphere. Our whole lives are threaded by unfelt, unrecognised customs, of which we can make ourselves aware only by an effort of reflection. These latter can scarcely be called institutions. They are but the raw material of institutions, and common will is for ever taking customs as they emerge into common consciousness, and *instituting* them.

The qualifying phrase, " established by some common will," also enables us to determine the relation of association and institution. An association is a body of social beings as organised for the pursuit of some common interest or interests. It stands in contrast to community, the common life of social beings. Community is any area of common life ; an association is a definite organisation pursuing some specific interest or pursuing general interests in some specific way. The distinction of association from institution should now be obvious. For institutions are forms, established forms of relation between social beings in respect either simply of one another (as in the institution of rank) or of some external object (as in the institution of property). An association is more than a form, it is the creator as well as the created, it is a source of institutions. An association has a subjective as well as an objective aspect, it too is created by common will, but it consists in wills as organised in respect of some common interest. An institution has an objective aspect alone, it is a means alone. The association may modify its institutions, may dissolve some and create others, as the State for instance is constantly doing. So the association outlives its institutions. Therefore if we are to be strict in our thinking, we should speak of the family as an association and of marriage as an institution, of the State as an association and of representative government as an institution, of the church as an association and of baptism as an institution. The association is a living thing, the institution is but a form, a means.

A difficulty in the observance of this distinction arises from the fact that some terms stand both for the association and for the institution through which it works, *i.e.* either the principal institution or the complete set of institutions belonging to the association. This is the case with the term " church," and still more clearly with such terms as " hospital " and " university." Take for instance the term " hospital." It stands for a definite system, through which medical and nursing skill is applied to suffering or disease. It may stand also for an association of doctors and nurses who supply that need. This association, we must note, is not equivalent to the institution, for the institution is a form or system constituted by the relation of the members of the association to those who require its aid. It is this relation that is instituted, it is this form of activity, this means of supplying need, which *is* the institution.

From this it also appears that institutions are not, as is sometimes imagined, external things. Sometimes we point to a building and say, " This is that or the other institution "—" This is the University, this is the Infirmary." We mean, however, that these are the buildings belonging to the institution, or the institute as we may perhaps call it by way of distinction. It is a mistake to find the essence of any institution in externality, just as it is a mistake to make conduct equivalent to its external manifestations. Institutions are organised forms of social activity, and have therefore an external aspect, an aspect in time and space.

Finally, we may note that institutions may be created either by definite associations or by community itself. We cannot attribute to the will of any specific associations the greater institutions of our common life. The State builds forms of government, but can we say that the State has equally built the institution of property, or the vast mechanism of co-operation and division of labour which is established in and beyond all associations ?   And what shall we say of that most significant institution of prostitution before which its laws are vain ?   The State protects, recognises, or at least permits many institutions which community and not the State alone has built.

§ 2. Institutions as instruments of organisation and of control.

If then institutions are the creation of common will they must have been created as its instruments, for the service of common interests.   Whatever is instituted is purposed, and therefore has its meaning only in the end it serves.   If we ask then how institutions can serve interests, the answer is, by organising and by controlling them.   *These ways of service are clearly distinct*, though in fact inseparable and interdependent, and it is highly important that we recognise the distinction.

The organising function of institutions need not detain us here.   Every extension of organisation, instituted by the further or fuller association of human wills, is an extension of the power of every will therein concerned. It places at the disposal of each new common factors of power.   It prevents waste of life by focussing and unifying activities.   It increases the sphere within which each may exchange services, select activities, seize opportunities.   When men create institutions they pursue not only their respective interests, they make themselves in so far, whether they design it or not, means to the ends of one another ; and the ideal of association is realised in so far as all men become means to the ends of one another while they remain ends to one another and to themselves.

Again, institutions are instituted customs, generally so in their origin, always so if they endure.   An institution need not always have been preceded by a corresponding uninstituted custom—we can hardly say, for instance, that political institutions such as a bi-cameral parliament or a system of proportional representation arise out of precedent custom—but if any institution endures it necessarily takes on also the quality of a custom. It thus performs that kind of service which habit or custom performs, making smooth and easy the paths of social activity, minimising the expenditure of physical and psychical energy and thus liberating it in new directions. Not only so, but because of its permanence as objective form it fulfils a service which mere habit cannot fulfil, it saves social beings from the necessity of building afresh with each generation of them the structure of their social world.

The controlling function of institutions demands our closer consideration, for it raises questions which have sharply divided the social thinkers of every age, and which have sometimes even sundered states and peoples. Yet these very conflicts, it may not be too rash to assert, have thrown such a light on the questions at issue as to guide to the only possible solution all who study them with an open mind.

Every institution has a controlling as well as an organising function. For institutions, being established forms, constitute an inner social environment. This environment, like any other, reacts upon those who are exposed to its influence, and so the relation of institution to social life becomes very complex. They do not merely reflect and express social life, they modify it profoundly ; they do not merely fulfil men's purposes, they are means by which these purposes are determined. Who can estimate the indirect control, the reaction upon human purposes, of the institutions of property, of urbanisation, of industrialism ? The very presence of the institutions they have themselves created, their magnitude, unity, and permanence, stimulate and unify, confirm and arrest the wills of men.

It is this indirect or reactive controlling function of institutions whose significance is most easily forgotten or misunderstcod, and we must therefore consider it more particularly ; but before doing so we may distinguish it from two more direct forms of institutional control. Of these one is the control self-imposed on every member of an association or community as he understands the necessity of conforming to its institutions if he would attain the ends these institutions serve. This is the necessary discipline involved in all collective action. It is a discipline rendered more complete and imperative with every extension of social organisation, and becomes an ever more important factor in the socialisation of man. The other is a more limited type of control ; it is that imposed, through institutions, by some members of society upon others, imposed upon the rest by those who, from strength of numbers or of prestige, are dominant in the formation and maintenance of institutions. It is not difficult to show, by comparing the religious and political institutions of primitive and advanced peoples, that this other-imposed control grows narrower as the former, the self-imposed control, grows wider.[1] Among primitive peoples political and religious institutions are essentially instruments of coercion. As society advances political obligation ceases to be arbitrary, based on the mere fiat of a governing will. The law comes more and more to be obeyed because the body of citizens identify their good or interest with obedience to the law. The civil code grows immensely in comparison with the bulk of the criminal code. It becomes in some measure realised that law and liberty, instead of being irreconcilable, are cause and

[1] See, *e.g.*, Durkheim, *Division du Travail Social*, I., chaps. v.-vi.

effect ; for though there can be law without liberty there cannot be liberty without law. Control by government becomes more firmly rooted in ethical control, so that the compulsion which it must still bring to bear upon the few is exercised not in the mere name of itself or of the many but in the name of social welfare. The same process is revealed still more fully in the sphere of religion, for though there must always remain some element of compulsion in the political sphere there is no such necessity in the religious sphere. The coercive function of religion has diminished continually, a fact obvious to everyone who knows the part played by religious institutions among primitive peoples of the present and the past, within the tribe, the village-community, and the early city, who knows also and understands the meaning of the world-shaking strife waged for many centuries between the upholders of religious coercion and the champions of religious liberty. In fact, as society develops, it seems driven more and more to the final source of social security, ethical control. The minds of men change from age to age, but the necessity for social control is continuous and unchanging, and if one form grows weaker another must be strengthened. *Here is revealed the immense import-ance of social education* which, becoming now of necessity an education for ethical autonomy, becomes the very basis of communal strength and requires of community its most devoted care and service.

These direct effects of institutions are at least in some degree intended, when men create them, but there are further effects by way of control which lie outside the direct purposes of men. We may express the difference as follows. Men will, as ways of furthering common interests, the two forms of social control just considered, but the third or reactive form of control is in the first place not determined by but determinant of common will. It is one form of that endless reaction of environment, even of the environment we have made. It is a control which may, though unintended, be of profound service to society. It is one of the chief agencies in promoting social solidarity. To illustrate, it is very significant that, though nearly every law issues out of conflict and is carried by a majority in the face of the opposition, often the bitter opposition, of a minority, yet the whole established code of laws comes to have the general support of nearly the whole community. It is not merely that the laws which offended large minorities are repealed—comparatively few of them are ; it is in general because the very fact of establishment reacts on the wills of all, not of a majority alone, creating a common attitude of acceptance, ownership, or even reverence.

On the other hand it is a control to which a grave danger is attached. Its reactive character obscures the original purpose of an institution, and tends to make men cling to it without consideration of the interest which it may serve. The hardening of institutions into a rigid " shell " is in fact, as Bagehot and Maine have strikingly illustrated, the greatest hindrance to the development of life. Doubtless a strong social life can always break the shell, and it may be because the spirit of a people is itself stationary that it stagnates into the institution-ridden life. But new life-movements are at first always small, and are easily controlled out of existence by the rigidity of institutions. In such cases the security afforded by institutions is bought at the cost of progress, life is bought at what may be the unnecessarily high cost of good life. Wherever institutions as such become sacred, wherever the form is reverenced apart from the life it serves and the letter of the law divorced from its social bearing, there institutions become dangerous. This is true not simply of primitive peoples. The history of progressive peoples constantly reveals the danger which arises when institutional forms become ossified, the danger that they may pervert instead of furthering the spirit, tradition, way of life out of which they rose. This is pre-eminently true where the institution is invested with sanctity, as in the case of ecclesiastical institutions. Again and again in the course of history the religious spirit has created institutions by which to express and develop itself, again and again these have petrified and so crushed the religious spirit, for in religion more than anywhere else a free and not a merely formal or constrained attitude is essential, a free attitude of reverence, love, and self-surrender towards a power felt to be infinite and good. No aspect of life is in more urgent need of constant renewal, in none is renewal so difficult. That is because in this more than in any other sphere it is hard to reconcile the flexibility of institutions with their sanctity.

§ 3. Institutions and life.

If we have seen the double necessity of institutions, as means by which social life is both furthered and controlled, we have seen thereby that institutions are not good in themselves but only in the service of life. Institutions are the mechanism of society. That is why an institution may be good at one stage of society, and bad at another. There is perhaps no institution we can name, however rightly detestable to-day, which has not at some time, in some social sphere, become beneficent. Slavery, war, tyranny are all evil in the world of civilisation; can we deny that even these have wrought good in more primitive worlds? Institutions are good or evil according to the ends they serve. They do not exist in their own right, to overpower men, but only to serve them, and when they cease to serve them no antiquity and no sanctity can save them from condemnation. The new wine will at last burst the old bottles, and alas ! both the wine is spilt and the bottles rent. It was so in the French Revolution, the greatest political lesson the world has ever known.

It is impossible to understand the doctrine that the whole can grow otherwise than by the growth of its parts, that the individual can wither while the world grows more and more. Men can indeed transform mechanism from means into an end, exalting mechanism at the expense of life. They may become slaves of the machine as bees or ants seem to become slaves of their social machine, significantly losing the primary life-functions in the process. Men never become slaves of their machines of wood and iron, these remain instruments of liberation. They become slaves only to the mechanism which they create within themselves, when the instituted form of activity becomes master instead of servant. Men can contrive to live in a world of abstract institutions as they sometimes contrive to live in a world of abstract conceptions, conceptions drawn from forgotten realities, institutions created by forgotten needs.

It has been well pointed out that the continuity and permanence of institutions, as contrasted with the short-lived race they serve, gives them often to our eyes a false character, as if they existed for themselves or for some supra-personal end. An excellent illustration of this tendency, in respect of the relations of the family association to the civic institutions which it has brought into being, has been given by Dr. Leslie Mackenzie in Volume I. of the *Sociological Review*. He points out how, " as the individuals whose massed activities have generated the great city all pass away, we are continually obsessed with the illusion that the city has come from some other than a personal source " ; and shows the great dangers of that illusion, on the one side the exaltation of mere officialdom and its divorce from the ideal of service, on the other side the consequent reluctance of those for whom the institution exists to take advantage of its service. The attitude of citizens towards the hospital is a case in point. They cease to realise that this institution exists not for the sake of its doctors and nurses but for the sake of its patients—that in fact it exists for themselves and has no justification save in their service. They cease accordingly to take the best advantage of their institutions.

It is very important that we should realise the true relation of institutions to the life that creates them. Every kind of common life creates appropriate institutions, the life of religion ecclesiastical institutions, the life of trade economic institutions, and so forth. Each form of life must live *by* institutions, never *for* them. The obscuration of this truth leads to two false extremes of theory. It may lead to the principle of regimentation, which makes institutions prior to life, or it may lead to the principle of anarchy which, protesting against the elevation of institutions into ends, fails to allow for their necessity as means.

Now institutions, being objective forms, do not change after the imperceptible manner of the unresting life process. An institution may remain seemingly unchanged while the life which created it has changed entirely, or even when there is behind it no life process any more. Or again, an institution may be created, changed, or destroyed in an hour under the sudden creative or destructive impulse of a life that has moved in silence to new ends. But if institutions are to serve life to the utmost, they must be changed as life changes, transformed as life itself takes new directions.

The lessons of history are notoriously insecure, and men can adduce history, as formerly they were wont to adduce the Bible, in support of any social prejudice whatever; but if history teaches anything at all, it must surely teach us this, that no community can save itself which regards its institutions as unchangeable, which does not subject them continually to the test of the service of the common weal.

In the primitive world a single set of institutions enclosed the life of a people. It was then easy to find a simple external sanction for all conduct. As community develops it unfolds within itself many associations, and these all build their own institutions and call with many voices to many allegiances. Thus the social being can no longer find the unity of his life in the mere acceptance of any single social claim, but only in so far as these various claims have been related and harmonised in the focus of his own responsive personality. That is the ethical realisation, the ethical priority which yet appears last in time. When traditions multiply, the claim of each must cease to be absolute; when and *if* traditions break—and they must break sometime if communities advance—it is vain to lead men straight back to them again. *If* traditions lose their hold, the only security is to lead men from the outer sanctions which they have rejected to the inner sanctions which can renew the world. When a community has rejected the old traditions there *is* no direct way back to them. It must recreate what it cannot restore. For institutions are but means, and the adjustment of institutions to the demands of life constitutes the unceasing social problem.

BOOK III

THE PRIMARY LAWS OF THE DEVELOPMENT OF COMMUNITY

CHAPTER I

THE MEANING OF COMMUNAL DEVELOPMENT

§1. In what sense laws?

In an earlier chapter we attempted to discover the
meaning of social law and its relation to all other kinds
of law. It was unnecessary there to raise the question
of the existence of such laws. No one, I suppose, doubts
to-day that there are social laws, that there are, for
instance, laws of economics as certainly as there are laws
of physics. But when we come to consider, not the
specific laws revealed in definite spheres of association,
but the general laws of that community which unifies all
associations, and especially when we speak of such laws
as laws of development or evolution, we expose ourselves
to the attacks of innumerable critics. Some would distinguish development from evolution, others evolution
from progress, affirming one and denying the other.
Some deny social development *in toto*, others admit it
but deny that it has laws. The only adequate refutation
of the latter criticism must be the demonstration of these
laws themselves, but before entering upon that demonstration we may consider the implications we make when
we assert that there *are* laws of the development of
community.

Here is the issue we must always face when we speak
of developmental laws. Are these merely statements
summing up an actual process of development, historical

or descriptive summaries true of this particular process but not to be regarded as universal principles of development wherever it occurs, true perhaps of the development of western civilisation at a particular epoch but not necessarily true even of communal development as it has taken place almost contemporaneously in the Orient, still less of forms future and unknown ? Or are they principles revealing the real nature of communal development, rules to which every community must necessarily conform in passing from certain stages of its existence to certain higher stages, because these rules are what development at these stages *means* ? The difference is vital : if the former alternative is true, we are still outside any real sociology ; if the latter, we can confidently claim for sociology a place among the sciences. Of the answer I feel no doubt. The term " law " is strictly applicable to the laws of communal development I am about to formulate. Wherever communal development has taken place it has been in accordance with these laws : and whatever communal development will henceforth take place will be in accordance with these laws.

Two assumptions underlie this seemingly bold assertion. We have assumed in the first place that development is something distinct from mere process. The term " evolution " is rather ambiguous in this and some other respects, and may for the moment be left out of the discussion. But the terms " development " and " progress " imply not merely process but process in a certain direction hereafter to be specified. These two terms, though they are sometimes distinguished, I shall (for reasons shortly to appear) use as equivalent, preferring, however, the term " development " because of a certain *narrowed* ethical significance sometimes attached to the term " progress." It will now appear that the assertion set out above is not so vast or bold as it may have sounded. We are concerned, not with the laws of all communal process, but only with the laws of that process which is development. If there are laws of non-progressive communal transformation they do not concern us here. We do not say that all communities or any community must develop, but we do say that those which do develop will conform to the laws to be set out in this book.

The other assumption—an assumption which is the necessary preliminary of every such investigation—is the definition of the nature of community expounded in the preceding books. Community is simply common life, and that common life is more or less adequate according as it more or less completely fulfils in a social harmony the needs and personalities of its members, according as it more or less completely takes up into itself the necessary differences which individuality implies, so that they become differences within a unity and not contradictions of that unity. Common life is thus a question of degrees, and all existent communities realise only in degree the idea of community. The laws to be set forth are laws of the completer realisation of community, and wherever a community moves towards a more perfect communal form, there these laws, some or all, are exemplified. The laws are indeed more than mere inductions from history, for how shall history tell us which is more perfect and which less ? Here we see the nature of the initial assumption, that we know what is meant by community, not merely as exhibited at various historical stages, but in idea. These laws are the explication of the idea of community, they are not simply laws in accordance with which development takes place, they are laws themselves revealing or even constituting the nature of development. History exemplifies them in developing communities, but their necessity follows from the idea of community. So we can say not only that communities at a certain stage of development have actually followed or are actually following these laws, but that if a community is to continue development from a certain stage it *must* follow these laws. They are revealed to us in history, but only because, guided by the idea of community, we know what to look for amid the vast welter of historical vicissitude and contradiction. If it be said that such procedure is arbitrary and circular, that we start with an *a priori* idea of community, and merely select as laws of development those historical changes which conform to it, it may be sufficient to reply—though there is doubtless a deeper answer—that all evolutionary science is faced with the same difficulty. All evolutionary science, however scientists may seek to conceal it, speaks necessarily in terms of development no less than of process—else there would be no system, no hierarchy, no succession, no law. Evolutionary science is concerned not with the history of the world but with the history of selected elements of the world. It is not a kind of history revealing successive stages of life. The amoeba did not disappear when man arose. It is not simply a study of the appearance through time of newer and ever newer forms of life. The facts of reversion and retrogression dispel the idea that we can equate evolution with temporal sequence. Evolution in this connection must mean not change but change in a determinate direction. Take away the idea of development, leave only the idea of process, and evolutionary science would become a mere reflection of the myriad inchoate contradictory processes of nature, no science, but an endless series of inconsequent descriptions with no guiding thread.

It is most worthy of notice that the difficulties which the idea of development introduces into all other evolutionary science, so that scientists with good reason seek to avoid introducing it, do not exist in the sphere of social science. Here and here alone is the idea of development unambiguously present and realised. We are concerned here with the laws in and through which the nature of community is fulfilled, in and through which community attains ever truer forms, purified of alien elements and contradictions through the activities of human beings who increasingly understand its nature, as gold is purified of dross through the activities of men who understand the nature of gold. We are concerned with the unfolding of the nature of community, as a biologist is concerned with the unfolding of the nature of organism : *but* the activities which make and transform community are in their degree purposive activities, the activities of purposive beings. These purposes we know, and we *know* no other purposes in the universe.

Apart from the idea of purpose social development has no meaning. The idea of heterogeneity or complexity is not enough. Is not chaos the very expression of complexity, unordered heterogeneity ? The idea of temporal succession is not enough, else we could not talk of decadence or retrogression. The idea of co-ordination or system is not enough. Do not primitive communities often exhibit a very elaborate order, a sometimes too elaborate system ? If we ask why, for instance, we regard modern western civilisation as more developed than mediæval civilisation, the answer is not simply that it is more complex, but that it satisfies more interests, higher interests. If we ask why it has developed, the answer must be that men have found more interests, higher interests, and have found better ways of satisfying them through social relations. The institutions and customs of community are more developed when they serve life more, community is more developed when it is a greater, better common life. Always in the study of community we are brought back to this ethical ideal, this ideal of completer life which must nevertheless be assumed, never demonstrated. The ethical ideal must remain as rich and concrete and inner *and as inexpressible* as life itself, at whatever cost to the completeness of our theories. The development of community is an aspect of the development of life, the development of institutions means their transformation to the completer service of life. When we study community we are studying a world of values, and in the study of values it is impossible to retain the ideal which perhaps inspires the student of external nature. We must speak of better or worse institutions, of higher or lower stages of development, just because it is values we are concerned about. It is the meaning of values that we should treat them so. It is their essential fact. We must, of course, always beware lest we allow our conceptions of what ought to be to pervert our understanding of what is. We must record existence with the coldest impartiality, but the very meaning of value-existence is lost if we do not treat it as such.

So, alas! we escape one set of difficulties only to be faced with another. We escape the difficulty of the natural sciences which must use the language of development and yet cannot introduce that principle which alone gives clear significance to development, the principle of purpose and value. We are in turn faced with the new difficulty which the idea of value introduces, the difficulty that standards of value vary from man to man, from people to people. This is a real difficulty, but it must not be exaggerated. We have already seen that the conflict here suggested is primarily ethical, not sociological. We must also note that there is after all a general agreement among men in so far as there are certain universal ends which all men seek and thus admit to be good or desirable. The greater divergencies arise over the question how far certain forms of community,

certain institutions, further these ends. When men dispute concerning "socialism," for instance, they dispute
on a basis of agreement in respect of universal ends, they
differ on the question how far a certain organisation of
community would further or retard these ends. Otherwise no argument would be possible. When they dispute
concerning the institution of war, the point on which they
differ is the effect of that institution upon a common weal
in which they alike believe. If, therefore, men apply
contradictory ethical epithets to social institutions ; if
some believe that war is good, others that it is evil ; if
some approve of dominion over alien peoples and others
condemn it ; if some esteem the present worse than the
past, and others the present better than the past ; we
must not assume that here we have an ethical conflict
and one, therefore, insoluble. The effect of institutions
on life is a sociological question, an entirely objective
question, and one absolutely soluble, if not to-day, yet
as a result of more prolonged research into social causes
and effects. It is, indeed, difficult to study with impartiality these relations of cause and effect. It is not
simply because certain institutions have a peculiar significance or value for us that we are so prone to bias,
even against our wills, in the study of them. It is because
we have already made decisions in respect of them, not
merely academic decisions, but decisions engraved in our
very nature, in our emotions and character, decisions felt
and lived, not merely thought. It is these deep-rooted
decisions of the whole being which so easily defeat the
claim and endeavour of impartiality. And yet every
enquiry into the effect of institutions admits of and
demands scientific resolution, and the deeper the effect
upon our whole nature of a way of thinking about them,
the more vital if the more difficult is the knowledge of
its truth. For it is impossible to believe that in a world

bound fast in causality, ignorance and error should in anything profit us in the place of knowledge.

We should note here the necessity to distinguish between the development of communal institutions and the development of communal life. In one aspect associations and institutions are more continuous than life, for a single association may last through millenia and a single institution outlive many generations of life. In another aspect life is more continuous than its created structures. For associations may pass away, institutions may be replaced by totally different institutions, but life is in essence the same wherever it is found, being present in greater or less degree. The will and intelligence which to-day creates the communities of Western Europe is but more of the will and intelligence which integrated the pre-historic horde or clan. Can we not go yet further ? Just as the divine mind may be conceived to comprehend and enjoy the illimitable universe, so the blind worm that feels dimly towards another of its kind is in the measure of its life comprehending and enjoying that much of the universe !

We are to be concerned with the growth of a life as revealed in the structures it has built. In whatever is written about a living developing thing there is almost sure to be some error, but in the study of community there is a peculiar danger. For what we are studying is in process of a development nowhere previously completed before our eyes. We know what a seedling or an embryo will become, for there are previous examples before us of the course of development of individual plant or animal, we know the completed form no less than any present stage of development towards it. But the process of community is as unfulfilled as the process of the universe within which it falls. We know in the early spring what the sprouting lily will become in April, but how shall we know what is spring or summer—if, indeed, we can speak of either—in the history of community ? Life may at any time rise intenser and contradict us. We are studying a force whose strength we do not know, for it is revealed in its effects alone ; whose full character we cannot know, for we cannot certainly say that it is now near or far from fulfilment, and only in its fulfilment—if there be any—is its nature fully discerned ; whose future is at best a probability. What we know is only *direction.* What we can say is only that, if the force be not spent, the maintenance of the present direction will probably lead to such and such results. But we can, it seems, affirm in spite of all uncertainties that certain results are probable. For though at times in the past the force seemed spent, and though at times the direction seemed reversed, the more comprehensive view made possible by anthropology reveals a general direction and a permanent driving force. The intelligence of man may grow feebler, through inner failure or environmental stress, but it has in fact grown stronger ; his plasticity and educability may diminish, but it has in fact increased ; his power of will and control of means may slacken, but they have hitherto in the process been beyond measure reinforced.

Finally, we should understand that it is only *forms* which can in the strict sense be said to evolve, to open out or unfold, powers and energies do not evolve, but increase. We are using the term " development " to denote the whole process in which the forms of life evolve correspondent to the increase of the powers of life in individual and race. And *the laws of community are laws revealing the connection between the evolution of social forms and the increase of human life or personality,* however we care to name that power which we all find within ourselves, more than any forms but for ever formative.

These principles are so vital for the study of community that we must pause to consider more fully their meaning and truth.

§ 2. The kinds of social development and the criteria of communal development.

A thousand social interests are bound up within community, but not in so complete a harmony that the development of one must mean the development of every other. One interest may be pursued to the neglect of or even to the detriment of others. Thus a community may seem to be at once progressive and retrogressive, moving to one social good while it loses another. It may, for instance, attain a high level of external civilisation while its moral standards are abased, as was the case with some Italian cities of the Renaissance. It may reveal a high moral tone (in the narrower sense of the term " moral ") while its culture remains low, as is said to have been the case with the Germanic tribes at the beginning of the Christian era. It may pursue economic-interests to the detriment of the health-interests, as has been the case in the earlier stages of our industrial era. Or it may pursue the health-interests to the neglect of the culture-interests, as in ancient Sparta. What, then, shall we call the development of community ? Is there any unity of forward movement which we can name communal development, any unity of backward movement which we must name communal retrogression ? The complexity of communal life renders this a difficult question, and as a preliminary to its solution we may consider in turn the various kinds of social interest bound up in community, enquiring into the criteria of development within each kind. Thus we shall be better able to seek for that more general development which alone can be named communal.

We may take as basis of enquiry the classification of interests already set out. Specific interests were divided into the two main classes of ultimate and derivative. Now interests which are essentially derivative, although from other points of view of primary importance, are obviously secondary from the point of view of our immediate enquiry. For economic and political systems are but means to the ultimate ends of men. They derive their value from the nature of the ends which they effectively serve, and like all means they may be applied to the service of diverse ends, even of contradictory ends. Hence the only form of development within the sphere of derivative interests which concerns us here is their development as estimated by the service they actually render, *i.e.* as estimated by the development of ultimate ends. The perfection of economic and political systems as pieces of machinery is therefore nothing for our present enquiry and need not be discussed. In no sense could we say that a *community* has developed merely because its economic or political system has become intrinsically more complex or more extensive. This fact is often overlooked and the problem of communal development made to appear even more difficult than it actually is. Take the economic system, together with the system of technical and mechanical appliance on which it largely depends. This is often what we think of when we use the term " civilisation," but it affords no measure whatever of communal development. It would in fact be well if we could restrict the term " civilisation " to this whole system of communal mechanism, and reserve the term " culture " to those interests which are or should be sought for their own sake alone, as ultimate. The importance of marking this distinction is so great as to outweigh our reasonable reluctance to refine on the terms of everyday speech. For " civilisation " so understood, though it is itself a condition of advanced culture, may yet become a substitute for it or even an enemy to it. It has been well said that " nothing probably is more dangerous for the human spirit than science without poetry, civilisation without culture," [1] and the life of the capitals of civilisation, ancient and modern, has often illustrated the truth of that saying. Once the distinction is realised, we realise also the deceptiveness of " civilisation," and are better able to look beyond those trappings of glittering mechanism which so often conceal or even foster an inner primitiveness of life. Or take again the political system. Some look upon the area of a State or its dominions in the same ignorant admiration as leads the rustic to gape at the high buildings and long streets of the city. But who that knows would estimate the worth of the city in these terms, and who that knows would estimate in these terms the worth of a State or nation ? The standard of intelligence and endeavour may be higher in the few square miles of Attica than in the vast expanse of Persia, in the little circle of Florence than in the gross Germanic Empire : if it is, then is the smaller people the greater—and not in any paradoxical sense, for life is then more worth living for the members who compose that people, and any greatness other than that is a mere phantom, *magni nominis umbra*.

Our problem is now reduced to simpler terms, for we need only enquire into the criteria of development in the sphere of ultimate interests and seek there for some correlation or unity which may give meaning to the expression " communal development." We divided ultimate interests into those based on organic and those based on psychical needs. We may for shortness call

[1] Cf. H. S. Chamberlain, *Foundations of the Nineteenth Century* (English translation), Vol. I., p. 36.

these organic and psychical interests respectively, provided we bear in mind that both classes are in the strict sense psychical, and that we in especial are concerned with them only in so far as they create, reveal, or express the interrelations of minds, *i.e.* social relations. We are concerned with development neither from the standpoint of biology nor from that of psychology, and we must employ the conclusions of these sciences only as a basis for our own. It is for this purpose that we now enquire into the criteria of biological and psychological development.

Organic development has an outer and an inner aspect, a structural and a functional aspect, and here again it is important to notice that for the study of development the functional aspect is prior and alone conclusive. If we look at structure alone, we must find development to consist in (1) the increased differentiation of organ from organ and the increased co-ordination of them all into the unity of organic structure, (2) the increased complexity of the separate organs and thus of the whole organism. But these criteria are by themselves totally inadequate. For (1) you may have pathological differentiation of structure, a differentiation harmful to the life of the organism. It may, of course, be said that such differentiations are not co-ordinated in the unity of the organism, but how are we to estimate the co-ordination of organs save as the co-ordination of their functions in the service of the life-function itself ? (2) Complexity within an organ or within the whole organism may also be pathological. A cancerous organism may from the structural point of view be more complex than a healthy one. Mere complexity in organism or in institution is never a good, always an evil. In a healthy organism *useless* complexities atrophy, and it is a sign of organic health that in our human bodies there are many atrophied and atrophying organs.[1] It is a sign that nature creates and supports complexities not for their own sake, but only for the service they render, a lesson that men might well ponder over.

It is very needful to insist on the fact that even organic development cannot be understood in terms of the differentiation, interdependence, complexity, and co-ordination of organic parts. This is especially so in view of the fact that some writers still view the development of community as analogous to that of organism. A perception of the real meaning of organic development would save such writers from falsely mechanical ideals of community. They would no longer think of the members of a community as fulfilling their nature and function when they merely serve as differentiated parts of the social machine or as cells of the social organism. They would no longer exaggerate specialisation and division of labour into intrinsic ends. They would no longer conceive of community as some great Leviathan which in its own inexorable power carries hither and thither the many members of its one body. Finally, they would no longer conceive false views of individuality and individualisation, and so misunderstand the first and greatest of laws, that socialisation and individualisation are one. The development of the organism is the development of its life, and the development of community is the development of the life which exists in its members.

We are thus driven from structure to life in our search for criteria of development. Differentiation that furthers life is development, complexity that increases life-capacity is development. We must mean by an organism either the living creature or the physical vehicle of its life. The

---

[1] " Wiedersheim in his *Der Bau des Menschen* reckons in human beings fifteen organs that are progressing, seventeen that are decaying though still partially useful, and one hundred and seven that are rudimentary and altogether useless." (*Edinburgh Review*, 1912.)

development of a living thing is the development of its life, so that it exhibits greater power, greater vigour, greater mental or spiritual comprehension. Wherever life exists more abundantly it does exhibit signs of differentiation and complexity, but it is always life that creates the structural development. The study of organic development merely leads us on to the study of psychical development, forming a useful guide to what we are seeking but not in itself the object of our search. It is the psyche, the life, which must answer our question : and if we know what psychical development is (taking " psychical " in its widest sense, the adjective corresponding to the substantive " life "), we know already the meaning of communal development ; it is psychical development as fulfilled through common life.

Happily there is a very simple method of tracing psychical development. Every psychical being passes from infancy towards maturity. In the process the whole life develops, not this or that aspect or capacity alone ; develops not indeed equally in all directions but yet as a whole. No lapses in individual instances, no perversions, no instances of arrested precocity or of one-sided growth, can conceal from us the truth that there is a general development, a development of the whole life, in the transition from infancy to adolescence. The psychologist readily devises comprehensive tests of psychical development, and we are all so far psychologists as to be able to trace the general characteristics of development in the multitude of instances that fall within our experience. Further, if we accept the principle that certain adverse influences are " devolutional " in the sense that under them capacities disappear successively in the inverse order of acquirement, the last in acquisition being the first to disappear, we have a means of checking the results obtained by the directer method of study.

It is held both by biologists and psychologists that the
influence of excessive passion, of alcohol and certain
other drugs, of general paralysis of the insane and other
pathological derangements, is devolutional in the sense
described.[1]

It is impossible here to discuss and justify the various
criteria of development which we obtain by the application
of these methods.   We might instance, for example, the
ability to meet new situations, the power to reason or
synthesise, to conceive and express ideals, the power to
control passion by the idea of permanent life-ends and to
control imagination by relevant fact.   But our concern
is with the directly social criteria of development, and of
these the most important discoverable by the application
of these methods are perhaps the following : the power
to understand and estimate the claims of others in comparison with our own, the power to enter into relations
with an ever-wider community, and to enter into more
and more complex relations, the autonomy attained by
the individual in these relations with his fellows, and his
sense of responsibility towards others within these relations.   These are all qualities entirely absent in the
earliest stages and activities of conscious life, and slowly
acquired in some degree by all educable beings.   They
are the social qualities first diminished under the influence
of organic or psychical influences which totally derange
organic and psychical life.   They are also the social
qualities which seem to suffer most when old age mocks
at maturity and declines to second childhood.   For all
these reasons we seem justified in regarding them as
criteria of the general development of the social life of
each.

With these criteria before us, if we have grasped the

---

[1] See, e.g., Ribot, *Psychology of the Emotions*, chap. xiv. ; de Greef,
Le Transformisme Social, Part II., chap. 3.

true relation of individuality to society, the main difficulty of estimating communal development disappears. If these are indeed criteria of individual development, they are by their very nature criteria of communal development, and it must follow that those communities are most developed whose members are most advanced when measured by these standards, and whose institutions are most calculated to promote them. It will be shown in the course of this work that the various criteria we have just mentioned are bound up together and accompany one another. It will also be shown that the development which they measure involves on the whole a correspondent development of the organic basis of life as well.

If we compare the life of communities which we all acknowledge to be at higher and lower stages of development, if we compare, say, the West-European life of to-day with the life of Negritos, Australians, Bushmen, Veddahs, and other most primitive peoples, or if we consider the life of a continuous community at what we all acknowledge to be higher and lower stages of its development, the life, say, of the English people in the thirteenth century with their life to-day, we discover that the stage of living we call higher is one of which this at least is true, that the qualities referred to above are present in it in higher degree.

Let us set out these criteria from the standpoint of community. It will be found that they are reducible under the following heads :

I. (1) The regard or disregard of personality, and of life and health as the basis of personality—the regard or disregard of the personality of the physically weaker, of the poor, of women, of those subject to government, of children, of strangers and aliens. (In Kantian language, the degree in which each counts as end and not merely as means.) Of this criterion the following are corollaries :

(2) The absence or presence of arbitrary control, political, religious, and general, and the absence or presence of the spirit of servitude which accepts or welcomes arbitrary subjection. The form and degree of the exercise of force.

(3) The diversity or uniformity of the members within a community, and the correspondent lightness or heaviness of communal custom.

II. (1) The simplicity or the complexity and the looseness or the strength of the autonomously determined relationship between each member and the whole of any community to which he belongs. (This correlation of simplicity and looseness, complexity and strength, will be justified in Chapter III. It will also be shown that II. (1) is simply the reverse of I. (1), so that we shall have finally attained a single criterion of communal development.) Of this criterion the following are corollaries :

(2) The multiplicity or paucity of associations within community.

(3) The breadth or narrowness of the largest community of which each individual is a member, the breadth or narrowness of the bounds within which social life is enclosed.

What we have been seeking and now seem to have found, though subject to confirmation by our further study, is a simple criterion whereby to estimate the development of community. But we must not suppose that all our difficulty is thereby solved.

For we must remember that a community, even a close and near community, remains but a more or less imperfect co-ordination of the various aspects of life and of the lives of its various members. The action and reaction of interest upon interest or will upon will, the processes of imitation and assimilation, the adaptation of all its members to one physical environment, these influences do ensure a certain general standard of life and thought for all within it. But the various portions of a community, whether we divide it in terms of locality or of class, cannot be said even roughly to present a uniform degree of development. Further, it may so happen that one portion attains its completer development through means, say slavery, war, the exclusive possession of land or capital, which depress the development of another and perhaps greater portion. Lastly, changes constantly occur and loosen the existing co-ordination of community, so that even if the change be progressive there is a certain loss beside the gain. Such loss is often in fact the debt which the changing present owes to the evil and the good of the still active but irrevocable past. For example, when the wandering barbarian learned to take the great step from nomadic to settled life, a step on which all further development depended, he probably suffered a certain loss—though one which I believe may easily be exaggerated [1]—of the sense of comradeship. The few gained at the expense of the many, so that for a time it would have been hard to equate the profit and the loss. The first settled possession of land brought, in a kind of necessity, the institutions of forced labour, serfdom and slavery, dividing the community into castes, determining the many as the chattels of the few ; and men have had to redeem slowly and painfully the loss involved in the very means of gain.

Since community is not wholly integral, and since our criteria refer not to those institutions which are its common forms of organisation but in the first place to the lives which its several members and portions live under the different conditions created for them by common institutions, our problem remains as yet in part unsolved. We have discovered the criteria of development, we have yet

[1] Cf. Wallis, *Sociological Study of the Bible*, p. xxvii.

to show that there is at any period or on the whole a *unity* of communal movement in one or other direction. We have in particular to consider more fully the nature of retrogression, decadence, and kindred phenomena ; and in the light of that investigation we have to discuss the *reality* of communal development.

§ 3. The meaning of stagnation, reaction, retrogression, and decadence.

There are, we have seen, certain social phenomena which forbid the most optimistic to regard community as pursuing one continuous process of development. These phenomena can be classed under the heads of stagnation, reaction, retrogression and decadence. These terms are not at all synonymous, but stand for various forms of non-progressive movement, and the consideration of these forms serves as a useful introduction to the study of communal development.

I have called them forms of movement, and it may be objected that *stagnation* is a form of inertia, not of movement. Yet of one thing we may be sure—life never stands still, life is activity, and all activity, physical and psychical, leaves its world inexorably changed. For a time the sun may seem stationary in the sky, for a time the life-conditions of a people may seem unchanging. If the people be a primitive one, the period of seeming changelessness may be considerable. Their life-conditions are simpler, their life-activities less intense, and the life-movements therefore slower. Again, such peoples are remote from ourselves, if not in place yet always in spirit, while their history remains largely unwritten and unknown, and so we are the less ready to discern the changes actually occurring within them. But closer observation reveals everywhere under seeming immobility the processes of change, the transitions that all life must welcome or undergo. Occasionally a people whom we have regarded as belonging to the category of stagnant communities seems to change in a day before our eyes, revealing the hitherto hidden processes of its changing life.

The incessant changes of human life are obvious to every eye, but it is sometimes held that they are insignificant and leave the essential nature of men unchanged. This also is inadmissible. It is only the misunderstanding of history and the ignorance of anthropology that make possible such a dictum as this of Schopenhauer's : " The true philosophy of history consists of the insight that throughout the jumble of all these ceaseless changes we have ever before our eyes just the same unchanging being, pursuing to-day the same course as yesterday and always."[1] It is open to any one to argue, though the argument would involve a curious reversal of all accepted ethical and intellectual standards, that the essential changes of human nature in the course of the more universal history have been changes for the worse and not for the better ; it is possible to argue that they have now elevated, now lowered human nature : it is entirely foolish to argue that there have been no essential changes. There are principles of conduct active in the world to-day, there are modes of thought familiar to the least intellectual of ordinary men, which would have been utterly unintelligible to any members of any people within a quite measurable past.

What then must be the meaning of stagnation if our conception is to correspond to social reality ? If life always changes, what remains unchanged ? It is the system of institutions by which life is both served and controlled. Not that these can remain absolutely unchanged, but they may be so much more rigid than life that they crush its new impulses. Hence there exists

[1] Schopenhauer, *Welt als Wille und Vorstellung*, II., chap. 38.

for any community a grave danger whenever it rests so confidently on an existing system as to exclude new forces. Every institution that makes an absolute claim brings danger. For an institution is merely a social vessel created by the human spirit, and it must age. The necessity by which the form always ages is the reverse side of the liberty by which the spirit always recreates. To deny all need for social reparation and reconstruction is to deny the necessity that the form must age, and involves the yet vaster denial, of the liberty wherein the spirit can create. The resistance to the beneficent recreative force is most visible in communities where seniority serves as the special qualification for social office, where the elders of the people, grey in traditions and spiritually ossified, strive with all the unreason of age to suppress the new life-movements that would preserve society itself from greyness and ossification. A state of stagnation exists wherever the slow and tender beginnings of social movement are continually repressed by the weight of social control. Doubtless, if that control remains very rigid, it remains so *because* the life-movement is slow within the community; so that the state of society in which rigid control is enforced is the very state in which rigid control is most dangerous. (It may, at the same time, be true that it is the very state in which rigid control is most necessary, since the outward control requires to be strongest where the inner control is weakest—but necessities are often dangerous.)

In a state of communal stagnation there is an unreflecting insistence on inherited custom and tradition. The community holds passionately to its past, seeking to make the present conform to it. In reality they seek an impossibility. The present refuses to be an enforced and thus unreal copy of its past. We must change, whether we will or not: if we refuse or are unable to go forward we must slide backward. If the present is conformed to the past it loses the spontaneity, freshness, reality of that past. Institutional stagnation, if it does not provoke that violence of revolution which is simply the bursting of suppressed and accumulated life, leads either to retrogression or to decadence. The spirit of adaptability is the essential principle not simply of progress but of life itself. " The prolonged continuance of a race under the same social conditions is generally fatal to the life of that race." (Guyau, *Education and Heredity*, c. viii.)

When a community seems to return to an earlier stage of development, we may call its movement *retrogression*.[1] When a community consciously endeavours to return to an earlier stage, we may speak of the movement as *reaction*. Reaction is thus a special kind of retrogression, one in which the community directly wills the return, setting forward the idea of it as an end. Retrogression may take place apart from such conscious endeavour, through unfavourable changes of environment, or through evil forms of social selection. It should be remembered that reaction and retrogression indicate not simply a return to a prior social condition—for a prior social condition may have been better than the existent one—but a return to a state that as measured by our criteria is itself less developed. Man so fears the new that he often tries to smuggle it in under the aegis of the old, and the greater the revolution the farther back does he go to find its justification. So the Japanese statesmen who abolished the feudal system in 1871 looked back eleven or twelve centuries, to the time of Fujiwara Kamatari, for the model of their new administration,[2] while the intellectuals of the French Revolution, scorners of tradition more than most

[1] The term " reversion " has a definite biological meaning, and should not be used as equivalent to retrogression.

[2] Cf. Murdoch, *History of Japan*, Vol. I., p. 21.

men, must needs call this revolt a return to primitive simplicity. It is perhaps fortunate that there is always somewhere in the past the memory of a tradition to which any new spirit may claim affinity.

The life-histories of individuals often provide us with instances of reaction. Often men in their old age resort to principles opposed to those on which their whole development was built. A formidable array of names could be set out illustrating this tendency of old age and showing unfortunately that old age and wisdom are not such inseparable companions as men have often supposed. One instance may here suffice, the case of David Hume. Every intelligent student of his life must have been struck by the growth of the spirit of reaction upon him in his latest years, slowly overcoming his powerful mind, transforming his most characteristic opinions, leading him, for instance, to modify a work originally written to vindicate " The Liberty of the Press," so that he declared this liberty to be " one of the evils attending mixed forms of government," a declaration totally contradictory of its central plea. It is needless to illustrate further,[1] because our own world constantly presents instances of men forsaking the lines of their development and returning, like Plato's Cephalus, to the superstitions of their childhood. Some men seem to retain to the end the principle of their growth, and the very greatest men, such as Shakespeare, Kant, and Goethe, are shining instances of this truth. (This is in keeping with the general principle that the highest *peoples* are those whose members are slowest to *attain* their full maturity.) But there are sufficient instances to establish the reality of reaction and to enable us to observe its characteristics.

It must be clearly understood that communal reaction,

---

[1] Various instances, including that of Hume, are given in Mr. J. M. Robertson's *Essays in Sociology*, in the essay on *Culture and Reaction*.

the reaction revealed at times in the life of peoples, is not to be explained on the simple ground that peoples too grow old. The individual life is bound to an ageing organism, whereas a community consists of lives young and old, and is not bound to the organic wheel that turns full circle at the last. We may call a community reactionary when its members are predominantly reactionary, or when those members who most determine its policy and direction are reactionary ; in other words, when so far as it acts as a unity it exhibits those characteristics of reaction which we so often find associated with the old age of men.

Communal reaction manifests itself in many ways. Sometimes it appears as a kind of tiredness which falls upon men, when they have not the elasticity to meet the incessantly new demands of life. Sometimes it is the rebound from a good custom whose very excess seems to be corrupting the world so that men realise no longer even its intrinsic goodness. Sometimes it is a kind of revulsion which seizes men when they have prized overmuch some in itself to be desired end ; when they have built new institutions in the vain hope that these alone can renew the world and have discovered the vanity of that hope ; when they have in any way or for any cause expected too much of the world and pass from the illusion of easy progress to the denial of progress altogether.[1] Sometimes it is men's unreasoned fear that what is new

[1] The educational principle of suggesting to children that social and political institutions are perfect in wisdom and goodness, that their country is beyond compare, that their city is all a city should be, is very dangerous for that reason. Would it not be wiser as well as more honest if we taught children from the beginning that they live in a world which may be bettered, but which is bettered only in so far as men will to better it, and that they too will have a share in that great and difficult task, no easy entrance into an inheritance fully prepared ? Would it not save something of the disillusionment and cynicism which in certain cases is the rebound from the placid lessons of perfection too often learned in early youth ?

will disrupt the social world as it disrupts the world of their own thoughts, and the belief that security can be attained only by shutting out every disturbing element. But in every form it involves a cessation of that difficult open-mindedness and sympathy which sees other men not as mere masses or mere types, or mere instances of a type, but as real striving personalities. A group is reactionary when it sets a lower value upon personality and upon the autonomy through which alone it can be realised ; when it narrows down its world and sets up nearer frontiers to its thoughts ; when it becomes more completely self-enclosed, like the old German gilds that sought vainly to save themselves from a widening civilisation by making their own doors more fast.

All retrogression is not reaction. Life is bound fast to physical and organic conditions, and these may change, whether through man's activity or not, in directions hostile to his progress. Again, the ordering of a community may create conditions of social selection which operate to the detriment of the race, lowering the life of the successive generations. In various ways men may fall to lower stages of development, apart from that turning of their faces backward which is reaction. Only we should note that retrogression is never *simply* a return to an earlier stage. It is something worse and something different, as certainly as " second childhood " is something more pitiable than the first ; it is something pathological and evil. For those beings who have once entered upon the way of development there is, strictly speaking, no return. They are like men who have begun cultivating a garden (except that they and the garden are one) : if they stop, the last state is worse than the first. The cultivated plant never returns simply to its less developed form ; it has become dependent upon cultivation. So in the world of men. What intelligence has begun to construct, intelligence must maintain and develop. The forces of nature renew the external world, the forces of intelligent life must renew the world it has conquered— or its failure is disastrous in the degree of its earlier success.

Hence the failure of life may manifest itself in a way of life which bears no close resemblance to that of the more primitive stages of development. It is then to be named *decadence*, the decay of community revealed rather as a slackening of its life than as a return to more simple forms of life. Again we must bear in mind that such decadence is not equivalent to the "natural" process of decay which awaits organic being, the process of crumbling change through which time leads all that is organic, but is a psychical or spiritual declension (doubtless correlated to *some* form of organic failure), a declension not after but in place of fulfilment. In the light of what has been already said, the signs of such decadence are easily set forth. They are briefly a lack of thoroughness in endeavour, an engrossment in the mere ornamental fringes of life, a search after subtle and often perverted satisfactions, organic and spiritual (satisfactions that in Spencerian language do not subserve but hinder life), an intellectual childishness that always seeks distraction in some new thing, a flippantly cynical philosophy of life, a detached and goal-less "individualism" that denies the deeper responsibilities of each to his society, and to the race which lives only in its members and whose immortality its living members hold in fee.

Decadence is thus a failure of life. Historians are fond of giving reasons for the decline of peoples and the fall of States. These reasons, if our account is true, are at best secondary conditions, results of a lowering of the spiritual activity rather than its causes. Mr. Balfour in his essay on *Decadence* is right in refusing to admit that mere historical circumstances, external events, the defeat of armies, the mistakes of statesmen, constitute the full explanation of the waning of social life, the social enfeeblement that is made catastrophic when it involves the dissolution of a State. " It is vain that historians enumerate the public calamities which preceded and no doubt contributed to the final catastrophe. Civil dissensions, military disasters, famines, pestilences, tyrants, taxgatherers, growing burdens, and waning wealth—the gloomy catalogue is unrolled before our eyes, yet somehow it does not in all cases fully satisfy us. We feel that some of these diseases are of a kind which a vigorous body politic should easily be able to survive, that others are secondary symptoms of some obscurer malady, and that in neither case do they supply us with the full explanations of which we are in search." Defeat, pestilence, and famine may decimate a people and not crush its spirit or its vitality. It is the strength and character of its spiritual unity that makes or unmakes a people. Not decimation of numbers, a loss speedily reparable, but the narrowing or enfeeblement of its spirit, however conditioned and however explained, is the ultimate social misfortune and the cause of social disaster.

§ 4. The reality of communal development.

Is it true that in spite of reaction, retrogression, aberration, decadence, we can trace in the life of community a process of development even as we can trace a process of development in the individual life ? The question can be answered on no *a priori* grounds. We cannot infer that because an organism or a mind undergoes a process of development, therefore the succession of organically-conditioned minds which make the successive life of community must also reveal development. We can answer our question only in the study of the history of mankind.

There are moments in the history of nearly all men when the selective imagination, spurred by some experienced stroke of fate, masses all the evil contingencies of life, bereavement, the blasting of promise, the malevolence of men, the ruthlessness of the world's wheels guided by no ethical charioteer, the inevitable onset of organic decay, all the indignities that the spirit suffers, and, under a sky black with the clouds of human sorrow, sees vanity of vanities written over the world. It is not with that mood or that mode of thought, whether temporary or in rare cases permanent, that we are concerned, but with the reasoned judgment that strives to see impartially the actual process of human history.

Again, the social phenomena we have just been considering may easily lead the impatient thinker to a doctrine either of the unchangeableness of human nature or of its present decadence. Often the impatient thinker, seeing liberty become licence, half believes that tyranny is itself a good; seeing democracy become corrupt bureaucracy, prefers—in the distance—the unqualified government of the unelected few; seeing a world renouncing the bondage of hereditary and caste determination only to give itself over to the worship of wealth, applauds imaginative reconstructions of *anciens régimes*. The inference of a present decadence or a permanent tendency to decadence in human nature is one dear to a certain type of mind in every age. The earliest records of the world are full of stories of man's declension from the standards of a yet further past, full of stories of the undegenerate days of the great dead, " mighty men which were of old, men of renown " ; and not an age since but has found voices to echo that complaint. It is as prominent in the literature of the ages we now regard as " golden " as in those which we call " silvern " or " leaden." It is, therefore, obvious that there are sources of this doctrine other than the comparative study of past and present. As old age is inconceivable to the young, so youth becomes inconceivable to the old ; and people often think their community is growing old merely because they are growing old themselves ! On the other hand, it is a curious fact that a common incentive to reflections of man's decadence is the actual progress of the reflecting mind, which makes it the more conscious of the evils that exist. These suggestions also we must seek to discount if we are to estimate the reality of communal development.

It is also a common habit of mind to condemn social developments because of incidental evils, to condemn blindly, without considering the necessity of the development or the incidentalness of the evil—to condemn the city, for example, because it tends to lower vitality, or industrialism, because of the evils of excessive competition, or democratic liberty, because of the power it gives to the ignorant. It may be wiser to accept the city, and show that it can be made healthy ; the industrial system, and reveal the truth that it need not involve excessive competition ; democracy, and strive to make it enlightened.

Sometimes the impatient thinker concludes that human nature changes little after all, or merely abandons one form of error to embrace another equally grave. He sees reaction after progress, extreme succeeded by extreme, high ends degenerated into the means of ignoble ends, the vision of the few transformed into the blind dogma of the many, and confident schemes and prophecies of social regeneration proved to be illusions ; so he concludes with Machiavelli [1] and Schopenhauer that under all the changes of customs, laws, and governments men remain unchanged in nature, unchanged in the good and evil of their hearts, in the wisdom and folly of their

[1] *Discorsi, passim.*

thoughts. But this too may be reaction, reaction from the unqualified dream of easy progress which seems the natural outlook of youth.

A true view of human development in community is possible only if we survey the great secular movements of human life, counting the changes within a single age or within the limits of a single interest as of little moment ; and it is possible only if we can read behind the more salient and picturesque-seeming events which the historian loves (massed as they are for us into a drama unwitnessed by the agents and contemporaries of them) the life of real men and women, so understanding the falseness of the enchantment which distance lends to outgrown institutions. When we rid ourselves of our false conceptions of the " noble savage," and learn from anthropology what a mean and miserable creature he really was, when we dispel the glamour of retrospective romance that hides from us the social and economic wretchedness of our forefathers, and forget the narrow and dubious glory of king and warrior to remember the dismal subjection of the peasant, then we may understand how the endless activity of man does not after all go for nothing, but indeed in great things no less than in small is painfully creating a world nearer to his desire. In a word, if we take all the life-conditions together, and take large enough periods of time for comparison, community is revealed beyond any doubt as having already undergone, within the era bounded by the limits of our knowledge, a vast process of development.

The only complete proof of this statement would be a history of society in which the criteria of development were rigorously applied to the conditions of every age and every community. Such a work is far beyond our present purpose, since we are concerned not with the history of development but with its meaning and laws,

laws revealed in that history but not constituted by it. We can merely assert that a social history so written would modify considerably our conventional estimates of the relative advance of different ages and peoples, and show that the line of development, though very far from straight, is clearer than has generally been supposed. To take an illustration. In the history of England we often think of the Elizabethan Age as a very peak of progress. We think of Shakespeare and the Armada, and forget— how much ! Applying our tests of communal development we discover a community essentially less developed than our own to-day. Personality was held of less account, as is witnessed by the degree of actual coercion, religious, economic, civil, personal, which characterised that age. An age which believed in religious persecution and tortured innocent human beings for " witchcraft," an age which suffered a thousand arbitrary restraints on personal liberty, an age whose methods of government first fostered economic misery and then attempted to coerce it by making liable to severe punishment the unemployed poor, an age which counted the peasant as a chattel attached to the land—such an age must be regarded as exhibiting a distinctly lower stage of development than our own.[1] A similar analysis would reduce many of the seeming-glorious ages of history to lower levels.

The essential progress of men, discontinuous and apparently capricious, but, if we make the periods large enough, certain and verifiable, is made clearer if we remember our distinction of external civilisation and inner culture. As

---

[1] One might here refer to the attitude of Shakespeare himself, in whose plays " the commons " are characterised as " rude unpolished hinds," " the sweaty mob," and so forth. It is true these are the words of patricians, but the characteristic treatment of the masses in the plays, merely as uncivilised and gullible animals, and of their units merely as comic foils, suggests little of that wider understanding which is one of the criteria of social development. If it were the case that Shakespeare portrayed these classes as they were in reality, it would merely strengthen our conclusion.

archaeology uncovers for us the vast ribs of ancient
civilisations, and shows us skill and art in places where
we never suspected its presence, we are apt again to
think that the world has gone backward and not forward.
The men of to-day, we think, cannot equal the men of
forgotten pasts in moving mountains of stone or in fitting
stone to stone with scrupulous nicety, or in building
age-enduring roads and aqueducts, or in mixing unfading
colours, or in carving marble. If this be true—and there
is a vast deal to set against the contention—it is but
the lesser side of the truth. Look away from the stone
and the marble to the life and spirit which built and
carved. So we learn, for example, that those Egyptians
whose vast temples demand our admiration built them
in a spirit of abject barbarism, in the degraded worship
of ibises or cats or jackals, in the worship of primitive
priest or king, or in the worship of a sun and stars so
little glorified that their kings are conceived to spend
an after-life in consuming them. The land of these vast
temples is revealed as indeed the land of bondage, of
spiritual bondage. Or again we learn that the Greeks,
certainly a far stage advanced beyond the Egyptians,
were yet, for all the marvel of their poets, artists, sculptors,
and philosophers, at no high level *as communities*. Resting on the insecure and degrading basis of slavery, alter-
nately tyrannising and being tyrannised over, divided
city against city no less than every city against itself,
finding no reproach in infanticide or in the subjection of
women, openly addicted to the most anti-social of vices,
exposed to the sudden ravage of disease and pestilence,
they are found wanting by every criterion of development.

It is not to be assumed that in seeming to deprecate
the past we wish to exalt the present. It is a question
of comparative estimate. Judged by even the standards
of the present, our communal life is in many respects

rudimentary. We are at best on the verge of civilisation in its larger meaning. A world full of prejudices, exclusivenesses, and dogmatisms, a world in which only the few even among the most civilised peoples understand the wider interests and only the few care, in which worth is largely estimated in terms of wealth, in which nearly a third of our European population are on the verge of hunger—such a world will fill no impartial thinker with complacency. Nor, again, do we for a moment imply that the development revealed in history must continue. This is a subject on which it is impossible ever to prophesy.

Yet we may point out that the *conditions* of physical and organic life indicate possibilities of completer development. Life is dependent on these conditions, though we must never regard them as constituting life. Under unfavourable conditions life cannot develop, under favourable conditions it can—if the life-force is there to seize them. Now human control over the conditions of life has grown amazingly, and is still growing. Over many forms of disease scientific genius has proved triumphant, and has revealed the possibility of completer triumph. Already, thanks to investigators like Jenner, Pasteur, Lister, Ehrlich and the Curies, we have that knowledge which is gradually becoming power over organic evil. In like manner we have gained and are beginning to utilise immense power over the physical resources of the earth. We are becoming masters of our world. Doubtless there are even in our mastery some elements of danger, some possibilities of unknown disaster. But to those who suggest unknown perils we may well reply that there are also unknown powers of control. The forces of the present will never meet the problems of the future, but there are forces in the womb of the present of which the present does not dream.

Another ground of hope is revealed by biological science.

The invisible processes of our bodies, the inscrutable wonders of the organic maintenance, and above all of the reproduction, of life, reveal a wisdom and power infinitely greater than is ever manifested in our conscious activities. The conscious operation of the finest intelligence is but a blind fumbling compared with the sure and delicate operation of minute organic cells. " Even the amoeba is no fool," say the authors of a little book on Evolution.[1] It is true, but it is also true that even the most successful functioning of the highest human intelligence is incomparably clumsy beside the elaborate exactitude of organic adaptations. May not this knowledge of wisdom and power within us but not yet ours be, as it were, a glimpse of the long road of conscious development yet to be trodden—if only we have the strength to pursue it ? Always there remains that *if*. We cannot determine it in the affirmative, but neither can we, as the next chapter will show, determine it in the negative.

[1] Thomson and Geddes.

CHAPTER II

THE SUPPOSED LAW OF COMMUNAL MORTALITY

§1. **A false analogy between individual and communal life.**

It is often supposed, even by those who admit no other laws of communal development, that every community is subject to this one law at least, that it comes into being, runs its course, and passes away, fulfilling thus the curve of life traced by the individual life. This is a mistake which we must disprove before we can reveal the true principles of development. We are here to show that community is in its nature non-mortal, that it is subject to no *law* of mortality. If it were so subject, it would have of necessity certain positive characters, like those of the mortal organism, which would make its development merely an episode in its career. Such a law would not only narrow the meaning and interest of that development, it would be contradictory to the main principles we are seeking to establish. Hence the necessity of proving in the first place the fallacy of all reasoning on which the doctrine of communal mortality has been based.

Nothing has more impressed the mind of men in all ages than the fate which has overtaken great nations and empires. The mortality of the individual we can take for granted, we know the conditions of life ; to decline and die is part and conclusion of the sequence that begins with birth. We see and accept the end in the beginning.

But it is surely different with a community, where generation succeeds generation, and new lives in endless succession replace the old ? The decline and fall of a nation is an instance of mortality beyond our reckoning. It is catastrophic. It is a failure of the source of life, a failure in the natural process of society. For social rejuvenation would seem as much a natural law as individual senescence. It seems as natural that life should renew itself in succeeding generations as that it grows old in each. The dissolution of a nation seems therefore a catastrophe of nature, not, like the death of an individual, a fulfilment of nature. Though every individual dies, life may go on unabated, but if a people die, a whole area of life is lost.

Yet, if catastrophes these be, we tend to look upon the whole of history as a record of such catastrophes. " Assyria, Greece, Rome, Carthage, what are they ? " If social dissolution is catastrophic and not natural, why should all the empires of the past have disappeared ? Is there any hope that we in our turn shall escape from what seems the operation of a mysterious law ? The Greek moralised on the fall of Persia ; the Roman on the fall of Greece ; as to-day we moralise over Rome, will not some future nation moralise over us ? We may remember how, in one of the most touching and human letters preserved to us from the ancient world, " the Roman friend of Rome's least mortal mind " sought to console that mind in its sorrow for the loss of an only daughter, pointing out the insignificance of individual loss in the face of the more universal catastrophe that overtakes a people. " As I was returning from Asia, on the voyage from Assyria to Megara, I cast my eyes on the surrounding lands. Behind me lay Aegina, before me Megara, on the right, Piraeus, on the left, Corinth. These cities at one time flourished exceedingly, and there

they stood to view dismantled and in ruins. I began
to reason thus with myself, Good cause forsooth have we
mannikins for repining when any of us, short in comparison as our lives must be, dies or is slain, seeing a
single region can show the lifeless forms of so many
cities." Nor have there been wanting men like Byron
to apply the moral to ourselves. Indeed it requires little
imagination to conjure up, with Macaulay, the picture
of a future age, when our country too will show only
the ruins of a vanished glory. It is a commonplace of
reflection, the thought that our time is coming, that
perhaps even now the hour is struck which numbers us
also with the past. We are possessed by the idea that
the same law of mortality holds for communities as for
men. The seeming universality of the fate which has
overtaken all the greatest nations of history has led us
to regard that fate as inevitably awaiting those that now
exist, to believe that for the community as for the single
life there is no escape from an immutable law of mortality.
On such a view, the downfall of nations is only catastrophic when untimely, like the death of a young man,
the hastening of a consummation that might have been
delayed—for a time. I hope to show that this common
view is superficial and false, and that, if ever a nation
is wiped out or dissolved, such a disaster is no necessary
fulfilment of the law of its existence. Because a community lives, it does *not* follow that it shall die.

The chief scientific support of the popular idea is found
in the vicious " social organism " theory. If we regard
community as an organism, we are ready to attribute
to the larger unity the qualities that distinguish the
smaller. An organism is born, develops, reaches maturity,
declines and dies. It comes into being and passes out
of being. Within these limits of appearance and disappearance, its life may be represented as a simple curve

slowly mounting up and more suddenly declining. If
the supposed analogy holds, a community too is born
into being and passes out of being, a community too may
be represented as following a gradual upward curve till,
having reached a culminating point, it descends quickly
through decline into extinction. Such an idea is undoubtedly at the back of our minds when we speak of
the " decline and fall " of nations or even of the
" maturity " which preceded the decline, maturity being
the culminating point of the simple curve of life. But
all the time we are thinking on the lines of a most inapt
analogy. A community is not born, and a community
does not necessarily die. A community has no maturity,
no predestined culminating point. We know of maturity
only in beings who are but members in the chain of
generations, and we know nothing of maturity apart
from such succession. We speak of civilisations " flower-
ing " when they have reached some highest point of
attainment, but again the analogy cannot be pressed.
Humanity itself is the chain, the stock which " flowers "
through sucessive generations, and the relation of flower
to plant is in no sense the relation of the highest reach
of civilisation in any given period to the preceding and
succeeding levels of civilisation. It is not time that makes
us old, but the limits of our organism. If the limits are
removed, as in the healthy succession of the generations,
time, so far, counts for nothing. Mankind is incalculably
old, but the eyes of a child are no less bright to-day ;
nature is incalculably older, but her garment of green is
as fresh and young to-day as in her past infinitude.

It may seem a hard saying this, that a community is
not born and does not die. Has every community existed
before time was ? Does not history tell us of the beginning of some communities, even modern history ? Did
the communities of America have no beginning ? Can

we not name the very year of their birth ? And if they have had a beginning, must they not too have an end ? Can a community be an exception to the general law that time devours all his children ?

The answer is simple. In a community, the generations of life are integrally bound together, young life with old life, parents with youth. Now life is a process of evolution, and evolution knows nothing of beginning or end. It knows nothing of a time when life sprang out of lifelessness, and nothing of a time when life shall be resolved in lifelessness. Evolutionary science cannot say whether there has been a beginning or will be an end. It knows an intermediate space only. It has the vision of a traveller on a road who can trace backwards the path he has trodden and foresee a very little of the path to come, but cannot even conceive a beginning to the road or to his travelling. A living thing cannot by its very nature conceive a beginning to life. But life is essentially and always communal life. Every living thing is born into community and owes its life to community. Wherever there is life, there is a community, however rudimentary. Science knowing nothing of the birth of life, knows therefore nothing of the birth of community. And the same is true of its end. It is only that which is born that must die, and unless we show that a community has been born, we can never show that it must die. Individuals, generations, succeed each other in a chain of life. But community is always there, not successive like the generations but continuous, changing incessantly but never dying. Every individual presupposes precedent individuals, but a community does not in like manner presuppose precedent communities. Every living thing is born into a community of which he in time becomes a member, and so the community itself, its spirit constantly renewed by its successive members, the inheritors of the traditions and thoughts and usages of their fathers, lives on. It is like a flame that never dies because it is constantly fed. So long as a single human being endures, that is sufficient evidence for the non-mortality of communal life, for he is an inheritor of that life. Every living being is thus a member of a community which has endured. The very existence of a single community to-day is the last proof that communities do not necessarily follow a simple curve of life, up to maturity and thence down to extinction. The law of evolution reveals direction alone, not beginning nor end, the pathway of life and neither its entrance nor its goal. It reveals an up or a down, a progress or a retrogression. It reveals no law of mortality. Therefore to understand the progress or the decline of a community, we must remember that we have no right to make it subject to that law of mortality which inexorably governs the living body, the organism.

Communities develop, they do not begin. The new life of America did not begin when English adventurers settled in Virginia, or English Puritans in New England. Alike they brought their social life into the new land. There are no new communities save in the division or extension or reformation or development of pre-existent communities.

§ 2. An appeal to history.

If we appeal to history, we find instant confirmation of this view. Were the social-organism theory true, every community must have a time of birth, a time of development, a culmination, a time of decline, and an hour of death. That is the process of the organic life. Every present community would be at some stage in that process of growing old, whether young, adult, or senescent. And the last stage would mean an inevitable process

towards dissolution, without hope of recovery, to be
evaded by no effort its members could make. And there
would be on record many instances of past communities
which had run their course and disappeared out of life.

History shatters that illusion. History indeed shows
that communities are not necessarily immortal. Peoples
have perished of violence and of pestilence—and of
" civilisation." Caribs, Fuegians, American Indians, and
Polynesian peoples are dead or almost dead. There are
to-day on the earth communities of human beings which
are undoubtedly in process of extinction, where no new
life in equal quantity and vigour is united to the old to
continue the community. There are aboriginal peoples
who are dying out under the conditions of life brought
to them by superior races. Therefore a community is
certainly exposed to the danger of mortality ; it may
die, but yet it is not its nature to fulfil a cycle of life
that ends in death. The wrecks of history are like the
fossils of prehistoric animals, they tell us that some types
of living creature have disappeared, leaving no successors ;
they do not tell us that all types must so disappear, for
we know in fact that many types have survived, some
with no discernible change, others changing under changing conditions. We do not predict the death of mankind
of racial old age because we have discovered the bones
of saurians. Some types must have lived on or there
would be no life to-day.

We may now take some historical instances, those that
most readily occur when we talk of the fall of nations,
and show that, whatever their decline and fall may mean,
it does not mean the passing out of existence of a community. Let us take first the community or communities
that made ancient Greece, as we know it from the time
depicted in the Homeric poems. We may say that
Homeric Greece passed away, that the Greece of Hero-

dotus and Thucydides passed away, that the Greece of
the Macedonian supremacy passed away ; we may take
broader periods, and speak of ancient and mediæval and
modern Greece.   But make the periods what we please,
there is never a point at which the community dies, as
there is an hour in which the organism dies.   There has
been a continuous Greek community from the beginning
of history until to-day, a community whose level of
civilisation and vigour has risen and fallen and risen
again.   What we find is never the death of a body, but
always the transformation of a spirit.   The former is
momentary, determinate, final ; the latter is gradual,
continuous, infinite.   Here there is no body that as it
ages at last subdues the spirit.   For a community is
neither old nor young, and need not grow older or younger.
Hence its life is not subject to the rhythm of organic life
or to the law of organic mortality.   The organic life
appears at a definite point out of the unknown and,
fulfilling its simple curve, disappears at a definite point
into the unknown.   But for the curve of communal life
there is no base-line whence it arises and into which it
falls.   This is evident if we trace the course of the Greek
communities, from the days of Homeric barbarism,
barbarism half hidden by the splendour of the poet, up
to the height of fifth century achievement, down through
Macedonian and Roman domination, and lastly Turkish
oppression, and up again after it all, not indeed to its
former distinction, but at least to the higher level revealed
in new national unity and consciousness of liberty.
Customs and manners and institutions and forms of
civilisation pass away, but the communal life, of which
these are merely expressions, may persist throughout it
all.   To that life we can assign neither beginning nor
end.

   We may take as a further illustration the case of that

community whose downfall has more than that of any other impressed the historian with a sense of the mortality of all things human. It is an illustration which brings out clearly the need for distinguishing the passing institutions from the undying life of community. At a certain period of history, the communal life centring round the city of Rome had extended so far as to make of Italy a communal unity. The decline of that community is the most momentous in history, but its life has survived every historical disaster. Through all the history of Rome there has lived a continuous community, sometimes threatened with destruction, at the hands of Gauls or Carthaginians or Goths, but never destroyed, rising and falling to social heights and depths alike almost unparalleled, sometimes torn and disunited, sometimes almost overwhelmed by the wave of barbaric immigration, but in the end revealing in rediscovered unity the immortal integrity of communal life. The Roman empire passed away, but the communal life of Rome and Italy never failed altogether. The life changed just as the language changed in which it found expression, but both life and language remained. States come into being and are dissolved, but community which creates them is greater than they. The Roman *empire* was not a community, not a living thing, but an imposed system, an institution. When the communal life of Italy slackened, it could no longer enforce that system over the communal life of its subject-communities. The system collapsed, the life survived. It may even be that the growing life of these subject-communities—" the bursting of the ripe seed," as one recent writer has expressed it—was as much responsible for the collapse of empire as the weakening life of Italy. As a community grows strong it refuses to accept institutions imposed from without, institutions it has not itself created for the furtherance of its own

life.   At any rate we must distinguish the fall of a State
from the death of a community.   The State and its
institutions collapse, it may be in an hour, the community
lives on and creates new institutions, a new State.   The
fall of a State is a commonplace of history, the death
of a community is an event rare and abnormal.   Most
of the communities that have figured in history have
indeed suffered eclipse, but none of these have perished,
and some have risen again and are even now rising, a
witness to the eternal possibility of communal rejuvenes-
cence.

We talk of young peoples, of new nations.   Let us
remember that no nation is younger than another, except
in spirit, except in the strength of communal purpose.
The peoples of America are no younger than the peoples
of Europe ; the new nations of our colonies, of Canada,
Australia, New Zealand, are the children of an older
England only in the same sense that we ourselves are
its offspring.   If their spirit is younger, it is because
new conditions of life stimulate old energies, because
new opportunities and new freedom renew the spirit.
But let us not for one moment suppose that a new country
is the only or the surest stimulus of the spirit of society.
Far more potent forces exist stored in every community,
the challenge of the ideal still so imperfectly realised,
the vision of present attainment which past attainment
has made possible.   When that challenge and that vision
enter the hearts of the members of a community, uniting
them more closely in common effort, in social solidarity,
its life is already renewed.   " Here or nowhere is our
America."

Even to the individual, bound as he is to the wheel of
organic change, there comes at intervals, longer or shorter,
a period of renewal, a sense of greater good, of greater
worth in existence, as if fresh oil had been poured on

the flame of life. So there seem to be times when the
breath of a new spirit wakens within an age. To the
unageing community that breath may come at any time.
Our organic bodies refuse at last to respond to the call
of the spirit. They lose that power of response which
is the very principle of life. But a community can always
renew its body, the shell of institutions and customs it
has created for the protection of its spirit. If these grow
old it can cast them off like an outworn garment, it can
replace them, as it has done before, by new and better
institutions and customs. Our will at last avails not,
for all our vision of health and strength, to stay the
oncoming of decay, but the will of a community avails ;
if only it sees the vision, if only it hears the challenge.
It is therefore absurd to talk, as men have talked in
every age, of the *inevitable* decadence which must sometime at the last befall our country. For indeed community is a spiritual thing to which there belongs no
natural destiny of decay or death. Into that ever re-
juvenated life each of us is taken up, in spite of our mere
organic fate. If that life fail, it is a failure of the spirit
unpredictable as the coming and the going of the wind.
And if it fail, it may be renewed ; for the failure is not
the inexorable failure of old age preceding dissolution,
but like the falling of the wind, the abating of a power
which again may spring into rediscovered life.

§ 3. The conditions of communal non-mortality.

The " law " of communal mortality has turned out to
be an illusion. In truth communities grow in experience,
in knowledge, and in power, in so far as each generation
hands down its gains. They do not grow in age, for each
generation is new, new as was the inconceivable beginning
of life, indeed with an increased capacity of life in so far
as past generations have striven to improve it. Com-

munity alone is granted that rare and inestimable possession, the advantage of experience without its penalty of
powerlessness. To grow wiser without growing older is
perhaps the highest boon a man could ask of the gods.
That boon is granted to community.

But it is granted at a price. It is literally true that
a community to save itself must lose itself. The immortality which it may attain is an immortality of
continuity, not of self-sameness, continuity secured
through the surrender of self-sameness. It becomes, in
fact, immortal in so far as the constituents of its life lose
their self-sameness through intermixture. By this, it
must be clearly understood, we do not for a moment
mean that a community is other than its members, or
that it is made immortal through the sacrifice of the
personality of its members. On the contrary, in its continuity the personality of its members is fulfilled. Yet
it remains true that only as each enters into relationships
with others does he contribute to the continuity and
immortality of communal life. It remains true, both
biologically and socially, that the greater the life the
wider must be the intermixture of its units in order that
it may survive.

The earliest life is asexual. The beginning of the
increase of life was the development of sexual reproduction. The attainment of this first form of intermixture meant a mechanism elaborate beyond our power
of understanding, a rebuilding of the first foundations
of life, and a transformation of all its modes. This was
not necessary for the mere continuance of life but for
its advance alone. Life might have continued for ever
by the simple way of monogony, without advance, without pain or toil or death, but because increase of life
necessitated intermixture, nature undertook (if we may
use anthropomorphic language to cover our ignorance)

the vast labour and the prodigal expenditure and the endless problem of sex. Life was reconstituted so that it should henceforth be born out of essential intermixture.

The process of intermixture widened with the increase of life and consciousness. Community as it became more intensive became more extensive also. The family group gained an intenser life by breaking down its bounds, by losing its self-sameness. We have in the preceding sections of this chapter spoken of communities as though they were absolutely and not relatively integral wholes ; it is necessary here to insist again that community is a matter of degree. Its non-mortality is bound to that principle.

From the biological standpoint, families no less than individuals are successive and not continuous. If they abide centuries, they abide only in name. With every new marriage a new family comes into being, and it is only the custom of agnatic nomenclature which deceives us into supposing that it merely carries on an original family. If we take family in the wider sense of a kin-group, the general statement still holds true. We might suppose that where close intermarriage is a rule within a group the larger family remains permanent. If it is a large group, it may well so abide for a time—though at last it is sure to have the alternative of fusion or extinction. If it is a small group, the more it retains its family-identity, the more surely it decays.

The community to which we ascribe non-mortality is a common life of individuals and of families, successive in themselves ; and the only community which we can so isolate as to call it integral and immortal is the largest area of common life within which individuals and families enter, have entered, or shall enter into living relations. Perhaps in the fullest sense, over a wider period of time than our minds can grasp, the only community which owns an absolute and unconditioned immortality, as it is the only community which can be absolutely integral, is the widest potential community of all mankind. The others, the smaller areas of common life, are only relatively or in some cases even nominally immortal. This does not mean that the smaller communities must pass away. It means that in the course of the ages they receive elements of life from a greater whole to which they belong, as they give of their life to it in return. They are for ever continuous, but they are for ever changing. Relating themselves to one another, they form portions of a never-ending and ever-new-born community, since it is only from within humanity that human regeneration can proceed.

CHAPTER III

THE FUNDAMENTAL LAW OF COMMUNAL DEVELOPMENT

§ 1. Some definitions.

The law we are to set out in this chapter is the first and greatest of all the laws of community, and all its other laws are, in fact, but corollaries or implications of this law. It is the key to the whole process of communal development. It is a law whose significance most of the greater writers [1] on society have felt, though, perhaps from its very obviousness, it has rarely been formulated in any precise manner or given its true place in the communal scheme. It may be expressed as follows : *Socialisation and individualisation are the two sides of a single process.*

In this brief statement we have used two terms which require careful definition. When we say that a being has become more individualised, we mean tnat he has become more an autonomous being, more a distinct personality self-directed and self-determining, recognising and recognised as having in himself a worth or value of his own. When again we speak of socialisation we mean the process in which a being strikes deeper root in society, in which his social relations grow more complex and

---

[1] Among more recent writers who have realised its significance, in general or in particular aspects, one might instance J. S. Mill, Bain, Leslie Stephen, T. H. Green, Herbert Spencer, Professor Alexander, and Professor Hobhouse.

more extensive, in which he finds the fulfilment of his life in and through the increase and development of his relations with his fellows.   We can thus express the law as follows :   *Sociality and individuality develop pari passu,* sociality and individuality being the qualities corresponding to the processes of socialisation and individualisation.

It must be noted that we are here using the terms " sociality " and " socialisation " in a somewhat wider sense than they often bear.   A man is sometimes said to be " socialised " when he adopts the current usages, ideas, standards, of a given social milieu.   But we are using the term to indicate adaptation to social life in any form and any degree, so that to be completely socialised would mean to have one's nature brought into complete harmony not simply to the ends of a specific association or community, but to the ends of the widest community to which the individual is capable of responding, ends deep enough and wide enough to fulfil every potentiality of his being.   Socialisation does not mean reduction to any given social type.   It would be absurd, for instance, to regard the man who carelessly accepts and reflects the existent social order as more socialised than the man who spends his life in an earnest endeavour to improve social conditions ;   or again, to regard the completest pirate in a community of pirates as not less socialised than the completest patriot in a community of patriots.   The latter has his being rooted far more profoundly in society.   And we shall see as we proceed that the profounder his socialisation the wider the *potential* community to which an individual belongs.   The roots that strike deepest will, if they are allowed, extend also furthest.

We must also hedge round the terms " individuality " and " individualisation " from possible misinterpretations. By individuality we mean not the whole nature of the

individual, but a certain aspect of it. It was pointed
out at the beginning of this work that every man's character or self is personality woven of individuality and
sociality. When we speak of individuality we mean that
quality and power of self-determination and self-expres-
sion which is as necessary to the growth of personality
as is the social environment. Individuality does not
therefore mean mere difference, still less mere eccentricity.
Certain philosophies have spurned individuality because
they have conceived it in this abstract and unreal form,
but that self-determination which is the core of individuality need not and perhaps should not be based on
the difference of man from man. Personality is the substantial reality and end which individuality and sociality
together determine, and any doctrine which exalts either
of these aspects at the expense of the other, or either of
them at the expense of their unity in personality, is
partial and untrue to the facts of life. To understand
how individuality and sociality have revealed their con-
sentaneous growth in the concrete personalities of men,
as these have emerged out of the meagre group-controlled
uniformities of primitive life into the richer and more
autonomous natures which even the most ordinary members of our own civilisation possess, that is the key to
the understanding of the whole process of communal
development.

For community, let us insist once more, holds nothing
but its related members, nothing but those actual socialised
men and women in whose likenesses and differences, in
whose interrelations and interactivities, type and difference, nationality and race, individuality and sociality,
find their sole realisation. Community is the common
life of persons, and its vitality depends on the individuality and sociality of these persons. These are the tests
of all community, not one alone, but both together. For

as each of us makes his society, so does our society make each of us.   Our individuality, if it is strong, goes out to strengthen—if it is weak, to weaken—our society ; and to our society we owe in turn the measure of our individuality.   The opposition of sociality and individuality is accidental, in essentials they develop out of one another ; and as a true society seeks to develop individuality, so the most gifted individuality finds its expression and fulfilment in society.   The more the members of a community enter into the life of that community, the richer by the amount of what they themselves have brought becomes that life.   Its quality is the quality of the social units whose common life it is—if the fuel is poor, how can the flame be bright ?   Its intensity is the degree in which these members are united in that common life,—scatter the coals and what once glowed in a radiant focus will flicker feebly in dispersed and meagre fires.   It is this spiritual activity we call society, this conscious co-operation in a great common life, that sustains within it the life of every contributor, as the energy of its ardent centre keeps every coal in the fire aglow.   To fall away from that fire is to pale and grow cold like a cinder, to lose the communion of society is to lose the community in which each life is quickened.

There are two other antithetical terms which we must define in order to prevent misconception of our fundamental law.   These are the terms " individualism " and " socialism," coins worn and almost indecipherable through long circulation in the market-place.   It must at the outset be noted that our law is in no sense concerned with the principles we call individualism and socialism.   For while individuality and sociality are qualities and individualisation and socialisation processes, individualism and socialism are ideals or theories.   Our law expresses a *de facto* relation between two actual processes, it is not concerned with any theory as to how individuals *ought* to be related within society. Individualism and socialism are in all their variants theories of that character. Socialism in its narrower sense is the theory that the means of production, distribution, and exchange *should* be owned collectively; in its broader sense it is any theory which insists on the importance of collective action and control. Individualism means sometimes the opposing theory which insists on the importance of private ownership and control, sometimes the theory that each individual is essentially independent of his society, sometimes the claim that any individual should be allowed to express and practise his own ideas when they are opposed to those of the majority, and sometimes is a mere euphemistic expression for the claim of egoism. All these theories must be judged by their results ; the only justification of any individualism or any socialism is the furtherance of personality which its adoption would ensure.

We may note in passing that when the interest of one individual is opposed to the interest of his fellows it is strictly an opposition between private and common, or between particular and general, not between individual and social interest. Nor again should we speak of individual *versus* social action when we really mean distributive *versus* collective action. We have always to remember that every individual is a social individual, and that his activity as an individual may still be for the sake of social ends. The terms " individual " and " social " are scandalously and most unnecessarily overworked. So men fall more readily into that gross confusion which sets the end or good of *the* individual (not some individuals) over against the end or good of society. Even if, as the old theory declared, every individual had to suffer some loss for the sake of the whole, he is

yet a member of the whole so benefited ; or even if, as
a newer theory may insist, every present individual has
to make some sacrifice that the race, the successive generations, may prosper, it is always a succession of social
individuals for whose welfare we thus toil and make
sacrifices.

Lastly, let us note that we are not at all concerned
here with the metaphysical problems of individuality.
What ultimate unity holds individuals within itself, how
they may all be but " moments " or elements or " indi-
viduations " of universal being, concerns us not. It is
enough that in the world of social experience men grow
in individuality as they grow in sociality.

§ 2. General explanation of the law.

We have now seen that individuality and sociality are
aspects of the unity of personality. The living whole
is the individual person or the union of persons as community, to both of which we attribute individuality and
sociality. Our thesis, therefore, takes the form that *as
personality develops, for each and for all, it reveals the
twofold development of individuality and sociality.*

If we reflect for only a moment, it becomes obvious
that all values are personal values, that all social development is the development of some kind and degree of
personality, or secondarily of that system of mechanisms
and institutions which are the means of personality. All
art, all science, all progress consists in the free expression
of creative personality, stimulated into activity by the
union of its opportunity and its need, its need of trans-
lating idea into reality, its opportunity of an outer environment which provides the means of translation, and
of a social environment which permits the translation
because its constituent personalities can receive the idea.
All religion is but the apotheosis of personality, stimu-

lating the finite life by the effective conception of more infinite personality. In all our life, that which gives interest both to work and play, to living in short, is the exercise of personality, at the least the witnessing of the revelation of personality afforded by social intercourse, by novel and drama, at the highest the furtherance of personality within the greatest social milieu to which our influence extends. The power of an institution or an association is measured by its hold and influence upon the persons whom it serves. When it makes a deep effective claim on personality it is strong and lasting. The strength of State or church is proportioned to the degree of the devotion of its members, which is the degree in which their personalities are identified with its existence. Conversely, when an association stands for the fulfilment of fundamental needs, it demands a permanent devotion. Thus the marriage-association, rooted in the depths of personality and making the greatest demands upon it, requires for its fulfilment complete permanence and complete devotion. Finally, community itself is strongest in the measure in which the claim of every association is proportioned to the service it can render to personality, so that each member, obeying all claims harmoniously, attains the fullest harmony and completion of life.

It follows, if we are right in regarding personality as a unity whose factors are individuality and sociality, that where personality most exists, there will individuality be most advanced and there too will the social relations of men be most extensive and most profound. This principle is revealed wherever social life exists. We shall therefore in the present section explain and illustrate its universality, proceeding thereafter to the specific application of the principle within our own present social world.

Let us take first the aspect of individuality. Individuality is least in the lowest. In plant life (propagated by suckers, buds, layers, grafts, etc.) and in the lower forms of animal life (Polyps, Infusorians) even that first form of individuation, the physical demarcation of individual from individual, is often very incomplete. Greater individuation, first organic, then psychical, is characteristic of whatever life we call higher, and it is by the aid of this individuality that still higher stages are attained. " It is essentially the free-living and self-supporting creatures that really get on, that evolve in the best sense." (*Evolution*, Thomson and Geddes.) If we turn to human society we find that all anthropologists, though they may differ in their explanation of the fact,[1] are agreed as to the relative insignificance of individuality in primitive life. In the primitive clan or tribe we find an almost complete uniformity of custom correlated to a very great uniformity of character. Where interests are non-individualised, race-interest, sex-interest, social interest of any kind, the interests are in fact undeveloped. When the type is uniformly realised in each, the value of the type is in fact low. When custom is all-comprehensive and coercive, the custom is in fact primitive.

As personality grows, non-individualised social interests are transformed into individualised social interests. The race-interest, as pursued by a primitive tribe or clan or nation, was undifferentiated. The great image of his victorious type, the principle of the excellence of his race (itself the primitive form of a high moral principle),

[1] For instance, no writers have more insisted on the correlation between individuality and civilisation than Herbert Spencer and M. Durkheim, but they differ very profoundly in their respective attempts to account for it. See Durkheim, *Division du Travail Social*, Book I., chap. v. It may be suggested that no such incidental fact as the primitive necessity of militarism (Spencer), or the absence of centralisation and of division of labour (Durkheim), can be adequate to account for a law so fundamental as that we are considering.

formed the semi-altruistic motive which inspired the noblest efforts and sacrifices of the kinsman for his kin. The value of the type was realised, but the nature of the type was of necessity misunderstood. It was thought to stand in mere contrast to all other types, and it was thought to be endangered by its own variety. Men sought for the social fact, of course after the obscure primitive way of seeking, in a highest common factor rather than in a lowest common denominator. Their social discipline repressed individuality, insisting on the customs conformed to the identity of type in the many and endeavouring to suppress the variation of type in the few. In such a society the shibboleth, the taboo, the proverb, the fixed epithet are dominant. But as personality (in spite of the attempted repression of individuality) grows slowly greater, as the more comprehensive mind attains the knowledge of wider values the differentiations revealed in personality become more prized and protected. A wider liberty is realised, the condition of the revelation of the infinitely variant personalities who are indeed the completer expressions of the type.

For the interests of individuality are not properly opposed to those of type, whether expressed a race or sex or class, but are a development of these interests. Our organic or racial interests do not disappear when they become individualised. Through individualisation they may be limited, but through individualisation they are at once shaped and realised. The organic need, the racial interest, the type factor remains. The civilised being feels no less the driving of the sex-interest and the family-interest, but the satisfaction of these is no longer simple, for the interest is no longer a *mere* sex-interest, a *mere* family-interest. It is complex and differentiated. Sex means more—and less. Its satisfaction requires ultimate and peculiar conditions ; it necessitates individually-determined choice, for it is (apart from the mere momentary eruptions of suppressed desire) not any man but this man (or, at least, this kind of man), not any woman but this woman. So our instincts widen out into complex and wonderful interests, no longer isolated impulses independently satisfied but interwoven life-principles springing from the unity of personality and demanding harmonious realisation.

The growth of individuality within society involves a transition from abstract to concrete values, from the obscure estimation of the mere type to the clarified estimation of the type-realities, from the belief that the type is best preserved and realised in the suppression and subordination of the individuals who represent it to the discovery that the fulfilment of the members is the realisation of the type also. It is said that abstract ideas are a late growth of intelligence, but in truth abstract ideas dominate the human mind from the beginning, and only by slow degrees is it liberated in the understanding of the ever more concretely comprehended fact. In the earliest stages the idea of the group is so abstract that it must be *symbolised* by totem or *incarnated* in a tribal god. The first comprehensive effort to think out the meaning of the social world, the marvellous work of Plato, was based on a similar abstract notion to that which permeated the whole thought not of the Greek cities alone but of every tribal community, every village community, every empire of antiquity, the notion of the race, the stock, the breed, in a word the type, abstracted from the living individualised members who more and more resist definition in such terms. The philosopher, when philosophy took a " surer hold on him," [1] came to see that the differences are no less real and

[1] Cf. *Parmenides*, 130.

significant than the identity, that the type or form is realised in every detail of sense, down even to those things " of which the very mention may provoke a smile, things like hair, mud, dirt, and whatever is paltry and of no account." So to the social consciousness in its own sphere those early notions of race or tribe or nation appear abstract and inadequate as the living and growing complexity of civil or national life, the increasing differentiation of the members of a people or a nation, is realised. The abstractness disappears together with the exclusiveness of early views, and race and nationality are revealed as indeed permeating and decisive factors, but factors alone, not moulds from which the individual members issue.

Let us turn next to the aspect of sociality and show that the growth of personality involves the correspondent growth of this factor as well. It is this correlation which is most easily misunderstood. Sometimes it is even thought that as personality grows men become more independent of society, but this false conception disappears when we understand that society is a life and not a mechanism or mere system of order.

Sociality is least in the lowest and increases with every increase of life. Whatever form of life we consider we find that the degree of sociality, the degree in which the individual is rooted in and dependent upon social life, corresponds to the capacity of growth in each. The greater that capacity the greater the benefit an organised and co-operative community can confer on its members as they grow up to maturity within it. The greater that capacity for growth the more do the growing members *need* the service of society. For such capacity implies that the individual no longer moves in the deep narrow secure grooves of instinct, it means a greater initial helplessness and uncertainty, a greater need to learn as well as a greater facility for learning, a greater dependence on society as well as a greater fulfilment through society. The less a being depends on instinct the more it depends upon society.

In the lowest stages of life the young animal is thrown freely at birth into the hazards of its environment, aided not at all by the services of parental or other social care. As we ascend the scale we see the young, less equipped in decisive instincts, fostered by the care of parents while the more elaborate structure of their intelligence is being formed—socially formed. So the horse, the dog, the monkey emerge into an intelligent life proportionate at once to their initial helplessness and to the care of the older generation. In the highest type of all not the family alone but also the wider community serve the increased helplessness of the young. Human beings are of all beings the most helpless at birth, of all beings the most plastic and potential, the most able to profit by the stored experience of community. The better a community is organised, the more it serves the needs not only of its adult individualities but also of its potential members. When a community is so organised that not the family alone but all associations within the community contribute their full respective shares to the formation of new individualities no less than to the expression of those already formed, then socialisation may be said to be complete and individualisation advanced to the highest capacity of its members.

It is a serious mistake to regard primitive peoples as more socialised than the peoples of civilisation. The member of a primitive people seems more socialised only because his social relations are more simple. He owes one allegiance instead of many—but he owes it in a more mechanical way. The more primitive the community, the less has each a unique place within it, a place of his own. Society is more homogeneous—take any member away, and there is no gap in the social structure. Civilised society is *in this respect* more organic.[1] The social relations of the civilised man ramify further. Community grows more complex and differentiated as it responds to the demands of autonomous personality for social fulfilment, and the member of the differentiated community is of necessity more and not less socialised than the member of the undifferentiated.

We are now able to express our law as follows : *The differentiation of community is relative to the growth of personality in social individuals*. Under this form we shall consider more concretely its fundamental character and significance.

§ 3. The differentiation of community as relative to the growth of personality.

Looked at externally, the differentiation of community is the process in which its various associations emerge in their distinctness, each with its proper place and claims, in which community ceases to be identified with or wholly subject to any single form of social life, in which the circle of social relationships becomes more extensive and reveals within it, as it widens, grade beyond grade of common life, in which each social relation grows more complex and each social being more closely bound to each in the interdependence of the whole. In this section these essential characters of communal differentiation will be examined, and shown to be determined by, as they in turn determine, that growing personality of men which seeks fulfilment by the double way of sociality and individuality.

" In the beginning " community was without form. Family was State and State was family, church was

[1] See Durkheim, *Division du Travail Social, passim*.

State and State was church. The isolated primitive
community held together inchoately, without distinction
of principles or separation of associations, all the elements,
not yet become forms, of social life. The ostensible basis
of community might be common kin or common worship,
but the real basis is homogeneous tradition extending to
every relationship of life. For kin itself is not yet a
demarcated principle, nor is worship. There is no family,
no State, no church as we to-day understand these terms.
Law, custom, and morality were undifferentiated, and
therefore none of these were realised in their present
significance.[1] Even in the age depicted in the Homeric
poems, morality and religion were regarded as nearly
equivalent.[2] Even in classical Greece and republican
Rome, the civic grouping was not clearly distinguished
from the kinship grouping. Even in the eighteenth
century in England, political unity was confused with
religious unity. The history of society is on the whole
the history of the slow, and even in the most advanced
communities still very incomplete process in which the
various social forms emerge in their distinctness, and as
they emerge become co-ordinated, strengthened, and
purified within the widened unity of communal life.

It is obviously impossible here to trace even in outline
this vast process of differentiation. Our object is to
show that the differentiation of community corresponds
in general to the growth of personality and is determined
by its double claim. To this end we shall briefly consider
the significance of certain primary forms of differentiation.

(a) *The demarcation of the political life.*

No other process in human history has been so slow
and none is still so far from finality as that whereby

---

[1] This is illustrated by the history of such terms as *dharma*, θέμις,
δίκη, *fas*, *mishpat*, *recht*, *right*.

[2] Cf., *e.g.*, Grote, *History of Greece*, Pt. I., chap. xx. ; De Coulanges,
La Cité Antique, passim.

community and State have grown not separate but distinct. Let us, as we have hitherto done, take law as the criterion of the existence and character of the State. We can then regard the process in which law emerges out of custom, in which unwritten or customary law becomes the written law of code and legal precedent, as revealing the slow development of the State proper within community. Or we can trace the same process in the obscure evolution of the law-giver, judge, or king out of the patriarch or tribal chief, or again in the transition from communal to legal punishment. The endless details and obscurities of these processes cannot detain us here. What alone is clear and what alone concerns us is the immensely significant result (and at least partial cause) of that differentiation. It is the recognition of the many-sidedness of human nature, the fact of personality destroying the homogeneity of custom, so that the tide of communal life no longer moves as a complete consentience of the members of community. Law emerges from custom, because distinctions in the rigour and necessity of social relationships are being revealed. Patriarch and law-giver cease to be identical, because the claim of family is becoming distinguished from the claim of State. Many loyalties are revealed, each with its own limits, where formerly only one seemed to exist. When the State comes to distinguish breach of custom from breach of law, when it assumes the sole right of punishment, suppressing vendetta and private war, when it distinguishes criminal from civil offence and thus limits its own right of punishment, it is shaping itself for the greatest of all social functions, it is emerging out of community as a vast organ for the universal protection and furtherance of community.

A comparison of the great States of antiquity (and especially the Greek States) with the great States of

to-day offers an excellent illustration of this process. In
the strictest sense there was no Greek State, just as
there was no Greek church. There was no term to distinguish community or city from its State-form. The
πόλις was undifferentiated, it meant more than the term
State by which it is so often rendered. This lack of
differentiation is revealed in the inclusive character
of the ancient " State," in the all-comprehensiveness of
citizenship, with its " moral-religious " no less than
" legal-political " character ; [1] it is revealed in every
communal institution, military service, marriage-regu-
lations, system of land-tenure, administration of law and
administration of rights. The πόλις was in truth a
" partnership in all science, a partnership in all art, a
partnership in every virtue." But an unlimited partnership of that kind, involving as it must unlimited control,
meant endless enforcement or endless division. It has
often been pointed out that liberty meant something
quite different in ancient Athens or Rome from what it
means for us to-day.[2] It was rather the liberty of the
city regarded as a unity over against other cities than
the liberty of its citizens. But in truth the city hardly
ever was a moral-religious and legal-political unity, and
the attempt of each division to determine that fictitious
unity was disastrous to the whole civilisation of Greece.
Demarcation of State and community was a profound
necessity for the development of social life. Itself
stimulated by the claims of individuality it was also
the condition of the deepening and strengthening of
sociality.

---

[1] Cf. Mommsen, *History of Rome* (tr. Dickson), I., 246.

[2] This was noted even by Hobbes (*Leviathan*, c. 21). Renan (*La
Réforme Intellectuelle et Morale*) remarks, *qu'on le regrette ou qu'on
s'en réjouisse, la liberté moderne n'est nullement la liberté antique ni
celle des républiques du moyen âge. Elle est bien plus réelle, mais beau-
coup moins brillante.*

The earlier life and custom of the city-communities of Greece and Rome, in the absence of distinction between community and State, rested on the principle which regards the city, and not the citizen, as the unit of personality. The principle worked well for a time. It is a principle that gives to a community a vast effectiveness in the primitive operations of war, conquest, and domination. But a time comes when it no longer meets the expanding spiritual necessities of personality. The danger then is that in its revolt against traditional social claims it will deny the validity of every social claim. So arose the false "individualism" of the Stoic, the Epicurean, the creedless cosmopolite, aye, and of the early Christian too, an individualism which indeed makes the person the focus of his own personality, but makes him focus and circumference as well. The individual finds his individuality within his social relations, but they sought to find it by stripping him of social relationships. In thus making him all they emptied him of all. The true relation of sociality to individuality is realised as men find both the necessity and the limits of the State, as it becomes demarcated within community.

(b) *The demarcation of the religious life.*

Originally religion is simply an aspect of the undifferentiated communal life. When first the gods become conceived as persons and not as mere nature-forms—for until then there is strictly speaking no religion—they are conceived as members of or powers within the community. The circle of community and the circle of religious worship are coincident.

In the primitive world the gods are conceived first as nature-powers, the causes behind natural phenomena. Some of these nature-powers are local, the gods of streams and mountains, others are more universal, powers of the sky and sea and earth. As men's conceptions of per-

sonality grow stronger, the nature-powers are transformed from mere elemental beings vaguely anthropomorphic into the definitely personal if superhuman
guardians, judges, and lawgivers of men. The process
might take either of two forms. Sometimes men came
to conceive more personally the already local powers,
the geographical gods of the fatherland, while the more
universal powers remained distant and insubstantial.
Or else the universal powers themselves might be narrowed
to local habitations and names, as Zeus the rain-god
became the god of the Achaeans, and Yahweh, also a
god of the thunder and rain, became the god of Israel.
In either case it is the limited deity who becomes the
centre of worship, the real and effective god to whom
prayer is made and who answers prayer, for whom men
fight and who aids men in battle. Thus the Attic ephebos
swears to uphold and honour, not the Olympian hierarchy
in the due order of their majesty, but " the gods of the
fatherland, Agraulos, Enyalios, Ares, Zeus, Thallo, Auxo,
Hegemone." The position of Zeus and Ares in this list
of obscure deities shows that the Zeus reverenced here
is not conceived as the mighty " father of gods and
men," but as a nearer local power, that Ares is not the
universal god of war, but a special deity of Attica. It
is significant, as Professor Gilbert Murray has said, that
the temple of Olympian Zeus begun by Peisistratus remained unfinished throughout the whole period of Greek
history while the temples of the localised Athena and
Poseidon, " the native Earth-maiden and the native sea,"
received all the treasures of Athenian genius and Athenian
wealth.[1] The Greeks, indeed, were generally too reasonable ever completely to confine their religion to the
worship of local or tribal gods, and their religious history
illustrated the conflict between the claims of the nearer

[1] See Murray, *Four Stages of Greek Religion.*

and the farther gods. Many a similar conflict must lie unrecorded behind the scanty history of ancient peoples, but one, the issue which transformed the god of Israel into the deity of western civilisation, has become a supreme factor in the world's development.

Yahweh, first conceived as an elemental power, became the god of Israel, and even if the Israelite considered him the maker of heaven and earth, it was because their god must be mightier than other gods—he still guided only the Israelite, his chosen people. Their land is his " inheritance," within whose frontiers alone is his law proclaimed. To enter into the land was to come within the place of his worship. When the Moabite Ruth follows her Israelitish mother-in-law Naomi out of Moab into Judah, she cries to Naomi, " Thy people shall be my people, and thy God my God." (*Ruth* i. 10.) To be cast out of the land was to be exiled from the presence and worship of Yahweh. When Saul pursues David from the land, David declares that his enemies have driven him out " from abiding in the inheritance of the Lord, saying, Go, serve other Gods." (1 *Sam.* xxvi. 19.) Doubtless in later days the Jews learned to carry their religion with them through the world, to serve as essential bond uniting the scattered people, but in these and like passages we have the earlier conception. Yahweh reigned in Israel as Chemosh reigned in Moab, as Milcom reigned in Ammon and Dagon in Philistia. So every nomadic tribe and every settled community had its own god or gods who had no care for any other tribe or community. Every settled land was the inheritance of its proper divinity who, like a human ruler, had no jurisdiction beyond its bounds, but within them was named supreme judge and lawgiver, the god of their hosts, strong to aid them in battle.

In our world to-day the wider and ultra-social character of religion is so clearly realised that we can scarcely understand this original undifferentiation, this communal limitation of deity. It is for that reason I have insisted at greater length on the primitive fact. To trace the process of the emergence of the religious life would be to summarise the history of both philosophy and religion, and in particular to explain the significance of the transition from Hebraism to Christianity. One aspect of that transition will be considered in a further chapter. Here we must again limit ourselves to pointing out its inspiration and result. It is the purification and deepening of religious life as it becomes self-determined and free from alien claims and limitations. Religion becomes infinitely deeper and richer as it reveals itself to the free reverence of social beings, in their free union as members not simply of one community but of one church.

(c) *The demarcation of the family life.*

It may seem at first glance curious to assert that the family-association itself becomes strengthened and purified as it becomes differentiated within community. We think of the fierce insistence of early peoples on the blood-bond and assume that with the advance of culture the family loses rather than gains. In reality, it is only as the family comes to limit itself within a wider life that it comes to realise itself. To establish this principle let us in the briefest fashion trace the stages of the evolution of the family within community.

The earliest forms of "family" which we know are almost self-sufficient, for then family is itself almost or altogether identical with community. We need not go back to the fabled Cyclopes [1] for instances of this condition, nor is it peculiar to such isolated peoples as Ved-

[1] Among the Cyclopes,

$$\theta\epsilon\mu\iota\sigma\tau\epsilon\acute{\upsilon}\epsilon\iota \ \delta\grave{\epsilon} \ \acute{\epsilon}\kappa\alpha\sigma\tau\sigma\varsigma$$
$$\pi\alpha\acute{\iota}\delta\omega\nu \ \mathring{\eta}\delta' \ \mathring{\alpha}\lambda\acute{o}\chi\omega\nu, \ \sigma\mathring{\upsilon}\delta' \ \mathring{\alpha}\lambda\lambda\mathring{\eta}\lambda\omega\nu \ \mathring{\alpha}\lambda\acute{\epsilon}\gamma\sigma\upsilon\sigma\iota. \quad Od.\ \text{ix. 114-5.}$$
Cf. Plato, *Laws*, iii. 680, and Aristotle, *Politics*, I. 2.7.

dahs, Eskimos, or Australian Blackfellows. Nearly everywhere in primitive life kinship determines status, assigns
rights and duties. The whole community is held together
by family tradition, the spirit of "clannishness." The
family protects, aids, and avenges its members. Each
is then literally his brother's keeper. In Anglo-Saxon
England an outcast was a "kin-shattered" man. The
levirate of the Hebrews (*Deut.* xxv. 5) and the niyoga
of the Hindus are crystallised forms of this principle.
In China *public opinion* still compels the son-in-law to
support his parents-in-law. In ancient Athens, on the
other hand, a brother had become *legally* responsible for
his deceased brother's wife and daughters. It is of importance to note that here the kin-obligation, in becoming
crystallised into a legal form, has lost its primitive character.

Such survivals point back to a still less differentiated
form of community, and our point is that in this primitive
form the family means less not more. The first form of
community may be called a larger family, but it is a
confused family. The meaning of the family life is
obscured. We see extreme forms of this obscuration
among the peoples who adopt the "classificatory system"
of kinship, in accordance with which a man calls all the
men who belong to a certain exogamous group his fathers,
all the women of a certain group his mothers, making
no distinction of name between his actual mother and all
those women whom his actual father or any male of the
same group might have married, and so for all other
relationships.[1] Here it is obvious that no true family
exists at all. The family as we understand it is a small
intimate unity. The more it appears as a large kin-group,
the less it can possess that intimacy and unity. It is

[1] Frazer, *Totemism and Exogamy*, Vol. IV., "Summary and Conclusion," § 3.

significant that a single term is generally used by a primitive people for family proper and for the wider kindred.[1]

As community advances, the family loses its former self-sufficiency. Communal custom grows wider than family-custom. New economic conditions break down the economic autonomy of the family-group, wider political laws abrogate the supreme control of the head of the family over its members and the right of the family to avenge itself, and a profounder religion can no longer find its centre of worship in the family-altar, among the Lares and Penates of the family. Yet through the process of limitation the family attains a completeness impossible before. Its members may now realise within it what is in truth the life of the family, for it now retains alone within its limits that principle of mutual affection of husband, wife, and children which alone is its *exclusive* possession.

Let us illustrate by the extreme case of delimitation, that of the family in the dense competitive city.[2] Here exist in their highest power all those conditions which break up the old family, the cluster of relatives with their corporate responsibility, and reduce it to the essential family-form, the parents-children group. Here the self-sufficiency of the family is least, for the parents cannot within its narrowed bounds fit the child to succeed, even to live, within the wider community. They cannot directly clothe or educate him or cure his ailments. Yet the child is better clothed, better educated, better attended to than before. In abandoning its self-sufficiency the family has achieved the greater fulfilment of its members. The wider community which the members of many

---

[1] So even in Anglo-Saxon. Cf. Phillpotts, *Kindred and Clan*, p. 216.

[2] Cf. Dr. Leslie Mackenzie, *The Family and the City* (*Sociological Review*, Vol. I.).

families have built (though not as families alone) limits, emphasises, and strengthens the family. It reveals the essential nature and the essential basis of the family and enables it the better to perform its own most distinctive service in the fulfilment of its members.

We have taken these primary forms of differentiation simply as illustrations of the universal principle. It might similarly be shown that as university, trade-union, professional associations, and so forth, differentiate the more within community each comes to fulfil better its essential function. Now this differentiation of communal forms means that community has become a far greater and profounder unity ; in other words, that its members have revealed more clearly the many aspects of their sociality. The individualising impulse is fulfilled in socialisation. The differentiation of community, which looked at formally means the demarcation within a social unity of the specific aspects and functions of society, means intrinsically the double and correspondent development of the sociality and the individuality of its members.

It must not be supposed that the process of communal differentiation which we have illustrated in this section has followed any straight or simple course, or any clear order of succession. Each stage in the process has everywhere contained factors adverse to any further stage— which is but a way of saying that no external form is of avail apart from the continuous energy of the life which created it, that no social attainment is of avail save for those who have themselves the capacity to attain. Some delays and obstacles of the process will be illustrated in the succeeding chapter.

§ 4. General conclusion.

Society is not prior to its members, as Aristotle declared, for society exists only within its members. For the same reason the members of society cannot be prior to their society, as the social-contract theorists imagined. All such theories of priority and posteriority are due to the false abstractions we have already analysed.

It is true that partial oppositions constantly arise between individuals and the social forms within which they live—between, that is, some members of society and the prevailing social conditions which express the mind of a majority or dominant portion. It is also true that there are forms of society which may be adverse to the interests not of a few only but of a majority within the society. If we say that the welfare of men is realised only under social forms, we do not say that it is realisable under any social forms, or that men are always so enlightened as to build such social forms as best realise their social needs. It is conversely true that differentiations, forms of individuality, do occur which are most certainly adverse to the unity of society, the individualities for instance of the hermit, the sexual pervert, the unsocial mystic, the anchorless cosmopolite. In such cases we have a sundering of the two necessary elements of life, individuality and sociality, but it is a pathological condition, it is adverse to personality. Examine carefully any instance where individuality breaks away, not from perverted social forms, but from society altogether, and you find that such individuality is evil and frustrate, involving the loss of one or other of the essential elements of personality.

The claim of individuality and the claim of sociality are in the last resort not two but one. The claim of individuality is autonomy, that self-direction through which personality may be fulfilled, that social opportunity by which capacity emerges into expression and service, the release of personality from subjection to mere status itself unacquired by personality and from that subordination to mere media of personality, to mere possessions, which creates in every stage of community one of the most serious problems of communal life. But autonomy is empty except within society, self-fulfilment is meaningless except in social relations, and deliverance from servitude is vain unless it means also deliverance for service. Liberty in the void is valueless. It demands equipment of many kinds to be of any avail, in a word, it demands society.

It is well to note that by the claim of individuality we do not mean the claim of every individual for liberty of action over other individuals. The claim of egotism is self-contradictory because in the name of the individuality of one it seeks to constrain the individuality of others. It is only because the essential claim of individuality is also the claim of sociality that it is free from this contradiction. Within a society where all men alike claim individuality, the common claim, if realised, destroys the contradictions which may lie in separate claims ; it becomes a claim for such a social order as will most further the individuality of each in its degree. This is the true claim of individuality, and it is part of our contention that it can be realised only by extending and perfecting social order.

Liberty, let us admit, is undoubtedly liberty to go wrong no less than liberty to go right, to be self-seeking no less than to be altruistic. Liberty is a condition and not a kind of life. Until it is defined within a definite situation it is an abstract thing which cannot be adjudged. The claim of individuality is not a claim for absolute liberty, but for an ordered liberty, subject to all *needful* compulsion. The acceptance of its claim makes social order so much the stronger. For realised liberty narrows and determines the place of the individual no less than does extreme tyranny. Only in the former case the narrower place is that determined by the nature of the individual, his own place in the complex structure, his not by external appointment but by inner quality. Surely the whole structure is strengthened thereby.

If we take a broad enough survey of the development of community we see that more and more the power of selection, of direction, falls to the individual. Direction in such matters as religion, marriage, occupation, decided in the past according to general communal traditions, more and more comes to depend on individual choice. The opportunity for capacity to reveal itself extends, so that it need not be lost as before in predetermined tasks. Men are not tied in the same way to the grosser necessities of labour. As the machine develops, the value of the man and his autonomy grow together. With the growth of knowledge, and especially of the knowledge of the power of association, the few are less able to exploit the many.[1] Whatever forms of the repression of individuality may remain, however gloomy the " industrial serfdom " of the present may appear, relatively there has been a remarkable release of individuality, to the enrichment of personality, to the enrichment of community. How far more intricate, intensive, and extensive do social relations grow where men grow more autonomous !

A good illustration may be found in the changing position of women in modern life. The " woman's question " arises out of the increasing differentiation of women, on the whole the less differentiated sex, having remained closer to type in thought and activity than men. This differentiation reveals itself not merely in increased initiative or individuality, but also in a deepened sociality, a wider interest in social matters, a fuller entry into social relations. We are not here concerned with the special problems thereby raised. What concerns us is

[1] Cf. de Maday, *Revue Internationale de Sociologie*, June, 1913.

that the movement illustrates the correlation on which we have insisted. Women too, like all beings who come to self-knowledge, are claiming to be regarded as values in themselves, as ends not less than as means. For longer than men women have been regarded, and have regarded themselves, as means alone, to husbands, to families, and to the race. If our contention holds they will serve husband, family, and the race the better as they grow more themselves. And certainly it is apparent that their growth in individuality means also, if we neglect the perversions which accompany every change in human life, a deepening of social relations. One indication is the number of women who have done notable social service in recent times.

Nature scorns our doctrines of " natural " limits. The wisest of the Greeks held that the barbarian, the non-Hellene, was " by nature " a slave. The wise men of every people have taught that woman is " by nature " the subject and the servant of man. And to-day many wise men among ourselves still declare that woman is " by nature " unfitted for citizenship. To nature they appeal, and by nature, by human nature, they must be justified. If nature destroys the frontier lines which we presume to set up, if women so grow as to seek a wider life, on what grounds can it be denied them ? We may perceive the deep problems which such a claim must raise, we must perceive also the impossibility of any solution which does not admit them. Those who fear the dangers attached to such a movement should find comfort in the knowledge that the process of individual-isation, though it may break some established institutions, proves, over any wide period of history, to be a process of socialisation as well.

For type and difference, sociality and individuality, are as warp and woof of the personality of men and of communities, personality shaped under the stimulus of individual need and ideal, individual situation and endowment on the one hand, and on the other under the pressure of common race-impulse, common temper and fate, and the common control and necessity and law of social environment. And yet warp and woof proves an insufficient analogy, for in this case the strength of the warp and the strength of the woof are interdependent. On the same wheel by the same unknown power the thread of both is spun.

Why should this law of reciprocity (and more than reciprocity) characterise communal life ? Why personal values should essentially harmonise and not essentially conflict, why the activity which furthers each distinct personality should not only be made possible within community, but should on the whole and essentially further and be furthered by the corresponding activities of other personalities—this is the deepest question of social philosophy, part of the great integral wonder of the unity of the cosmos, of the fact whose completer understanding is the aim and result of all our knowing, that we do in truth live in a *universe*.

CHAPTER IV

PROBLEMS CONNECTED WITH THE FOREGOING
LAW: (1) THE CO-ORDINATION OF COMMUNITY

§ 1. Statement of the problems.

We have already attempted to reveal the principle of
the co-ordination of communal life, but our general account
took little heed of the problems which the incessant process
of differentiation is always raising afresh. We must now
seek to understand more particularly the adjustment to
one another, and to the whole, of the multitudinous
differentiated associations, localities, classes, and nations,
which become revealed as factors or elements within the
widened and differentiated community. The fierce activity
of social development is always dissolving past forms of
co-ordination and seeking after new ones. What we have
to show is the application, under the incessant changes
within community, of the principle of co-ordination we
have already discovered. This subject is so vast that it
can be treated in the merest outline alone.

There are two aspects of this supreme problem of
co-ordination. If we look at the enormous number of
associations which emerge within the differentiated community ; if we observe that these associations cut across
the lines of other groupings, locality- and class-groupings ;
if we observe also that the only unity within which these
associations, localities, and classes are organised, that of
the country-community acting through the State, is itself

not large enough to circumscribe their various interests ; we realise at once the problem of the relative places and claims of all these intersecting *forms* of society. If, again, we remember that every association, every class, every nation consists of persons, each of whom in the multitude of his relationships has somehow to find a reconciling unity of life and end, a second form of problem emerges. The first will be considered in the present chapter, the second, whose solution will but complete the solution of the first, will be treated in the succeeding chapter.

§ 2. The co-ordination of associations.

When the forms of association grew first distinct within community, there was born a problem of co-ordination which worked itself out through the strife of many centuries. The lessons of that strife, in respect of the true co-ordination of associations, seem to the writer to be these.

(1) *Each form of association has its distinctive place and character which cannot without social loss be usurped by any other association.*

Each of the greater forms of association has sought to make its own peculiar bond the bond of all community. Most generally it is kinship or race. Among primitive peoples the range of this one social factor, real or assumed, as a rule determines the limits of all others. Sometimes the dominating bond is religion. Then the believer in one dogma can have no social dealings with the " infidel " who believes in any other. Difference in respect of one social factor means exclusion from, likeness in that respect means inclusion within, the circle of community. Other forms of association have made more partial attempts at domination, for instance, the guilds of the middle ages sought to identify civil rights with guild-rights, and thus to usurp the place of the city proper. Finally, the

State, to which alone is given the power and right to defend for each association its due place in the whole, has instead sought at times to make itself the whole which it should protect and further, not only making its own limits the limits of other associations but also dominating the internal character of these. In the extreme case it abolished them altogether.[1]

This domination of associations over community, as they emerge within it, checks the process of development of which the emergence of associations is itself a sign. It represses for a time the spontaneity of social relations. It sacrifices in the name of a wrong conception of social unity the many-sidedness of social life. For when one association makes its single principle the rule of all, the true character and service of all other associations is obscured. Hence the necessity for the corollary which follows.

(2) *The more each kind of association devotes itself to a single appropriate type of interest, the better its service to community.*

There are two ways in which associations have violated this principle. They have, as we have just seen, attempted to include more than rightly belongs to their sphere, they have at the same time imposed arbitrary limitations on that sphere. The sins of commission and omission have generally been concomitants here. For example, the university, before it learned its true and universal function, used to impose irrelevant conditions upon its membership, thus at once arbitrarily extending

---

[1] " The abolition of every kind of corporation formed among citizens of the same State is a fundamental basis of the French constitution." (Declaration of the French Revolutionary Assembly, 1791.) We might compare the English Combination Law of 1800. To-day, on the contrary, in the most civilised States there is practically complete liberty on the part of the citizens to form, subject to the ordinary laws, unions or associations. In truth, the greater the State is, and the more " democratic " it is, the more chaotic also must it remain, a mere jumble of undistinguished interests, unless it permit the distinct organisation of interests by association.

and arbitrarily limiting its sphere.[1] If community is to find its true co-ordination, *every* association must have its limits of interest in, of right over, its members, its limits also of exclusiveness. It is a general principle that with all individualisation the exclusiveness of some association is broken, and with all socialisation the limits of some association are widened.

Where exclusion from an association is determined by considerations irrelevant to the proper end of the association, where, for example, plebeians are excluded from government not because of their lack of governing capacity, the poor excluded from higher education not because of their inability to receive it—there is from the standpoint of community this evil consequence, the essential waste of elements of personality and service, insomuch as not only are the excluded themselves prevented from developing their powers, but they are prevented also from rendering the social services which they are willing and would, if liberated, have been enabled to render. The distinctions between men are essential in some regards, accidental

[1] For example, the mediæval university of Bologna denied the right of membership to those who had attained the civil rights of Bologna. In this way it usurped a privilege of the city, and it denied the universal function of the university. Oxford and Cambridge until 1871 excluded non-conformists from their degrees, fellowships, and offices, and still exclude women. Yet in respect of the end of a university proper, religion and sex are equally irrelevant. It is not, of course, implied that the members of one religion or of one sex may not legitimately create a university for themselves, although it is probable that a university so limited will fulfil less completely the function of a university ; but it is implied that all who have the requisite capacity and desire should be eligible for the corresponding instruction and its privileges. Thus in this particular instance, where women or nonconformists have enjoyed all the teaching and proper training of a university, to deny them on the ground of sex or religion alone the degree equivalent to their training is to impose an irrelevant condition. A recent instance may be added. It has been proposed by certain members of the University of Cambridge that military training should with certain exceptions be a condition in respect of its baccalaureate. This also is a confusion of spheres. It is for the State and not for the university to exact this kind of service. These confusions do harm to the national life.

in others. In so far as the accidental is confused with the essential, community remains undifferentiated. Thus rank and wealth and religion are properly accidental in respect of the rights of citizenship, and where they determine citizenship, the community is incomplete ; nationality is properly accidental in respect of justice, and where it limits justice the community is incomplete. The evil consequences of the domination or exclusiveness of associations, as they resist the claims of developing sociality and individuality, were never so well revealed as during the tragic confusion of the spheres of church and State.[1]

A moment's comparison of the associations of the Middle Ages with those of to-day makes the advantage of due limitation clear. The mediæval association— State, church, corporation, or gild—was complex and intrusive, its hierarchy controlled not one but many kinds of interest. Neither State or church set limits to its sphere, the " art " or gild was a jumble of political and social no less than industrial interests.[2] These old associations were complex and inadequate, they pursued no single end, they were involved in the contradictions and disruptions of conflicting aims, such as must attend all associations devoted to interests not intrinsically unified. The efficiency of the new industrial associations

---

[1] Note in passing the special gain of the State when it admits the process of social differentiation. It is thus enabled to retain the undivided allegiance of its members. Could an English Catholic before 1829 have worked as whole-heartedly for his State as he can to-day ? Could England and Scotland have formed an effective political union if that had meant also a unity of religion ?

[2] It might be said that the modern trade-union also seeks political as well as industrial ends. But the trade-union seeks political power for one definite purpose, the advantage of an industrial class. Its members, unlike those of the " art," are clearly differentiated as employees. For the hierarchy of the " art," involving difference of interest, is substituted the equality of those who meet on the ground of identical interest. It may be added that the proposal of a new " Guild System," which has recently found an able advocacy, is in no sense a proposal to restore the ancient gilds. Such a proposal would to-day be meaningless.

is due to their self-imposed limitations. Each pursues
a unified interest, its members are members only because
they share that interest, and each wisely endeavours to
include, so far as is compatible with common action, all
to whom the interest itself is common. This process of
inclusion and clarification is made possible by the extension of the area of effective community. The smaller
the circle of community, the less easy it is to keep interests
simple and pure. As in the small workshop many personal and social complications influence both employer
and worker which are unknown in the large factory, so
in the small community as compared with the greater.
Associations as they transcend *accidental* limits of locality,
class, or even nationality, attain to purer forms. This
is illustrated by the progress of the modern trade-union,
at first local, gradually becoming national, and finally
endeavouring in some respects to transcend even the
limit of nationality. As it has so grown, its interest
has become more specific and clear. Wherever like
interests extend they call for a unity of association to
promote them. Like calls to like everywhere, but in
the past like has generally called in vain to like across
boundaries of class or locality or country, because a
certain primary and instinctive form of likeness was
supposed to be determinative or at least indicative of
all likenesses. The development of associations has
meant the making common of like interests hitherto
kept apart within confusedly exclusive circles. As the
exclusiveness breaks, a great federal system comes into
being, each degree and kind of likeness finding associational form.[1] This phenomenon will be explained more
fully in the succeeding sections.

[1] In the economic sphere, in especial, this growing federalism is
manifest. Each trade or craft is subdivided according to locality
and specific function (*e.g.*, the railway-men into signalmen, shunters,
etc., organised both locally and nationally) and yet forms a unified

Family, church, economic association, State, each has its proper function and value which none other can possibly fulfil. If an association has any right to exist at all, it is in virtue of its peculiar function alone, and it cannot properly fulfil that function unless it has learned to distinguish it from every other.

Let us take by way of illustration the much-debated question of the relation of ecclesiastical to political divisions. The tendency of these to correspond so that one church is identified with one political party, another with another, is a dangerous thing to community. For men of one political creed come to regard the church identified with another as a mere party-instrument. Its universal meaning is obscured, its universal message is subtly vitiated. It is true that the earnest church leader is in a difficult position when he believes that one party is right and another wrong. But he must realise the peril of advocating a party's programme. The religious spirit is the subtlest and most easily perverted of all spirits. If it is not first of all an attitude of worship and reverence towards the conception of the universal being, it loses all its distinctness, its apartness, its value. It is merely taking the place or sharing the work of other associations which profess their ends with greater candour. Certainly the religion of a man permeates his whole character, and affects his opinions on every social question (just as his social outlook affects his religion).

or " amalgamated " association (*e.g.* the Amalgamated Society of Railway Servants). This whole association in turn forms part of the vaster association of the unions. Hitherto isolated common interests are constantly revealing themselves and finding a common rubric for association, witness the coming together of clerks, or government employees, or shop-assistants, and so forth. These new associations are greatly aided by the growth of economic legislation, involving specific enactments for the special conditions of every form of occupation. In the United Kingdom the " Shops Act " and still more the " National Health Insurance Act " have recently stimulated this movement.

But the church which is convinced that the principles of its religion involve this or that social application, when the application is one on which political opinion is divided, should trust to the power of the principles themselves acting on the minds of its members. If the application is valid, the principles will themselves persuade in that direction those who believe them. For example, the Christian churches worship a God conceived as of perfect justice and uprightness. They cannot honestly so worship unless they believe in justice within society. They believe in a God before whom all men are equal. They cannot honestly worship such a God unless they believe also in the greatest possible equality of opportunity for all men. They profess belief in a God who abhors oppression and the lawless use of force. If their profession is not vain they must abjure the principle that might is right in the relations of men and of States. Now there are certain clear social applications of the ethical principles involved in such a religion. Others, again, violently divide political parties. In regard to these latter the church should simply insist on the principles involved and the necessity of following them. As a church it so fulfils its duty. Its members, as citizens and not as churchmen, must be left to decide all questionable political issues. , This is the only safe course for a church, the only way in which it can keep religion pure, and avoid the miserable results which all through history have followed the confusion of church and State. Religion is an attitude of spirit, a recognition of essential values derived from, reflected in, and contributing to the conception of God. Social institutions are forms, means towards values, in Carlyle's language clothes of the spirit, without which it could not live in a world where spirit discovers itself only as incorporated, incarnated, vestured. As we conceive values we shape institutions. As the church conceives values, so will its members, animated by the stimulus of its conception, work in every sphere of social activity for the establishment of consonant institutions.

Whatever type of association we take, it can be similarly shown that before it can do its proper work it must find and guard its proper place within community.

(3) *The different types of association do not form a hierarchy within community but a co-ordinate series under the organisation of the State.*

Since each type of association has its proper and unique function, no one, at least of those which pursue intrinsic and not derivative interests, can be made directly subordinate to any other. Associations certainly differ in their service to community. In particular, the family, as nearly every sociologist since Le Play has insisted (in striking contrast to its comparative neglect by the thinkers of the ancient world), has a fundamental importance as the primary mould of life, no less than as the most intimate condition of human happiness. Yet the family has not on that account any hierarchical relation towards other associations, for the others have also after their kind their own unique and exclusive places.

The position of the State might seem an exception to this rule, but on the contrary it is the position of the State which makes the rule possible. For the State has its own unique function, that of protecting and organising all the others, protecting each in the fulfilment of its essential service, co-ordinating them all under its common law, lending to each the aid of its central organisation. The State has in its own political way to adjust the respective claims and further the respective ends of all the associations, groups, and smaller communities whose single common instrument it is.

§3. The co-ordination of localities.

The extension of the area of community, no less than the differentiation of its associations within any given area, is a necessary aspect of the process of development. Under this aspect also very serious problems arise. The extension of community intensifies, where it does not create, the problem of the relation of localities to the widened community.

The extension of community is generally at the first a more or less mechanical thing. The simplest form is created by conquest, being the rude imperial relation of victorious to subject people. Another form is voluntary aggregation or " synoecism " for defensive or other purposes. In both we have, apart from governmental centralisation or the privilege of superiority on the one side and the necessities of subordination on the other, a mere juxtaposition of communities. We find instances of this aggregation or juxtaposition not only in all the empires of the past but even in the small communal units, the small primitive city-community or the smaller and more primitive village-community. The ancient city of Teheran, for instance, was divided into twelve districts, almost totally isolated from one another and permanently at variance with one another, so that the resident of one district never entered into another.[1]   In early Rome we witness the spectacle of a not yet co-ordinated city which is in fact two externally related communities, that of the patricians and that of the plebeians. There is some evidence that the English village-community represented " the tribe with a village-community in serfdom." [2]   These instances could be multiplied endlessly. Without doubt, everywhere in early times the extension of community is very external

[1] Cf. René Maunier, *L'Origine et la Fonction Économique des Villes.*
[2] Cf. Gomme, *The Sociological Review,* Vol. II.

and mechanical, as is witnessed by the relation of clans to totem-groups within the tribe, of demes within the city (as in Hellas), of towns within the league (as in the Hansa), of districts within the country (as in Saxon England), of fiefs within the feudal community. It is a compartmental system only slightly disturbed by the necessities of military or governmental centralisation. Every primitive community of any size is more an agglomeration than a unity.

But to aggregation there succeeds a unifying process, that endless social process wherein like calls to like across the barriers which have isolated them, abolishing irrelevant oppositions, making their like interests a common interest and thereby ensuring a greater fulfilment. The increase of efficiency ensured by community of interest is sooner or later realised, in one aspect or in many, by all intelligent peoples. Associations intersect the boundaries of localities, and unity succeeds agglomeration.

It must not be supposed that such a unity, say the unity of a nation, has been anywhere attained, so far as it is attained, without endless historical vicissitude. Excess of centralisation succeeds defect of centralisation. The true co-ordination of localities is hard to attain, and will always present fresh problems for solution.

But there is one universal problem which presents itself wherever localities—villages, cities, counties or greater areas—form part of a larger community. For the unity which the large community attains is not the unity which the smaller community had previously attained. The former pays a price for its greater universality and efficiency. If needs essentially universal find their purer form in the large community, there are more intimate needs, needs more deeply rooted in the emotional nature, which it cannot satisfy. It cannot take the place of the near community, but can only supplement it. In so far as it becomes a substitute for the near community, men have but found one good at the cost of another.

The service of the large community is to fulfil and not to destroy the smaller. Our life is realised within not one but many communities, circling us round, grade beyond grade. The near community demands intimate loyalties and personal relationships, the concrete traditions and memories of everyday life. But where the near community is all community, its exclusiveness rests on ignorance and narrowness of thought, its emotional strength is accompanied by intellectual weakness. Its member becomes the slave of its traditions, the prisoner of his own affections. Without the widening of gates—nay, without the breaking down of walls—there is no progress. Here is the service of the wider community, not only a completer " civilisation," but also the freedom of a broader culture. Often historically it has been the incorporation of small communities in a wider that has broken down the petty tyrannies of the former.[1] The forces moving in a great community take the edge off all dogmatisms and break the compulsion of many uniformities. In the large community every interest new awakened can search and find a like interest and thus become socialised and strong. In the small community an isolated independent spirit can rarely assert its independence in face of the overwhelming forces of conformity, and its peculiar value, its peculiar contribution to community, is lost ; in the large community it may easily be saved.

Again, let us insist that the larger community gains these advantages at a price. Often at the cost of emotional warmth, of the effective moving force of near affections, of the intimate unity where the whole folk is bound up in personal relationships. The centre of the great com-

---

[1] One might illustrate by the case of the German free towns.

munity is further removed from most of its members. The relations binding men to the whole become more partial, more impersonal, more distant. For the near personalities which direct the small community there seem to be substituted either distant personalities or even abstract principles. Associations and institutions grown great seem to become remote from humanity in the process, and greatness itself proves no true substitute for intimacy. This is well illustrated by the modern devotion to the nation. That devotion is itself the highest emotional achievement of the widened community, but how difficult it proves to comprehend properly the object of our attachment ! How partial is the ideal of national greatness which inspires the most of men, mere greatness without content ! And how often, unable to realise the meaning of this vast community, do we have recourse to personal loyalties *instead*, devotion to some mere representative of it, to some mere symbol of it !

The claims of the smaller and of the greater community have been in antagonism all through history, for history is in large part the record of the widening of community. In every case the widening of community has involved conflict. Generally the rude means of conquest has settled the question whether men shall belong to smaller or larger communities. But underneath the conflict of arms, and asserting itself when that noisier conflict is stilled, there has always been the spiritual conflict, the conflict between the spiritual claims of the small and of the large community. Men have found it most difficult to realise the necessity of both, to realise that their claims are antagonistic only through a false exclusiveness on either side, and that intrinsically they are not opposed but complementary.

When we see that the widening of community need

not and should not mean the abolition of the small community for the sake of the greater, since the small community fulfils a service which the greater cannot fulfil, we have begun to understand the true co-ordination of localities in the national or wider communal life.   Some definite aspects of this co-ordination may now be pointed out.

(1) *The true relation of localities to the whole community may be described as federal.*

I use the term "federal" for want of a better, to describe the general relation of local to national autonomy, though this term is generally and more properly limited to the relation of part-states to a greater inclusive State. It is the same principle in both cases.   Some needs being universal are more fully maintained and more purely organised directly by the more universal community. Others, being local or sectional, are narrowed in their degree to more intimate circles.   All men have a direct interest in equity, justice, freedom of communication or travel, and freedom of thought, and therefore the widest community possible should directly establish these.   But all men have not a direct interest in, say, the water-supply or the road-system of a particular town. The locality, through its local associations, has to apply the universal principle within its area.   Because the principle is universal, the autonomy of the locality must be limited ;   because the application of the principle within a locality has a special interest for its inhabitants, the autonomy of the locality should be real.   This is the wider meaning of federalism, the reconciliation of the nearer specialised claim with the more universal claim.

It follows also that the local should be connected as directly as possible with the national.   It is impossible here to enter into any detail, but the following applications are obvious. There should be a direct relation between local and national councils of every kind, so that, for example, the former may serve as a stepping-stone to the latter. In this way not only does the dignity of the former acquire a much needed enhancement but also its significance for the wider community is made more manifest. Again, national projects should as far as is compatible with efficiency be executed through local councils. It is well to have the wider social responsibilities made real by the nearer obligation of each locality, for, as we shall see in the next chapter, neither official nor layman can feel the significance of his action as a member of a vast whole in the way that he may learn to feel it as a member of a closer circle.

(2) *Under such a "federal" system there is no contradiction between the completest activity of the smaller and the completest activity of the greater community.*

Local activities demand central activity, central activity is fulfilled through local activities. In this point the simile of the organism is relevant, in respect that there is no opposition but rather a necessary harmony between the smooth and free functioning of each organ and of the central system. Where opposition exists, a true co-ordination has not been attained. If the activity of the organ of the great community, the central State-government, depresses rather than stimulates the activities of the local areas, it is a sign of excessive centralisation. If, on the other hand, the activities of the part-communities impede the united activity of the whole, we have the opposite condition. What is wrong in either case is not the amount of activity undertaken by one or the other, nor even to a large extent its kind, it is mainly the method, the failure to apportion to each its due share of responsibility and co-operation within a common service.

We may illustrate the general argument as follows.

The city of Cologne is perhaps the most enterprising municipality in Europe, exceeding in both the range and thoroughness of its services the usual progressive city, making fuller provision for the sick, the crippled, the out-of-work, and the destitute, holding itself responsible for the greater municipal institutions of university, opera-house, theatre, library, picture-gallery, controlling the planning and building of the city and the land necessary for both housing and recreation. Now, supposing all cities emulated Cologne in the completeness of their services, these municipal activities, properly undertaken, would certainly enhance the central activity of the State, since they require in some way the support and sanction of a central organisation, and since they inevitably increase the supreme task of State co-ordination. It might on the other hand be shown that the greater legislative activity displayed by West-European States in recent years has added greatly to the dignities and responsibilities of localities, even though rarely has the fullest possible advantage been taken of their services.

It may be noted in passing that the conditions which favour the extension of community may also make the nearer community more intensive. Thus facility of communication not only brings a wider area into community, it may also increase the solidarity of the smaller. A local press may stimulate local unity just as a national press stimulates national unity. At the same time it must be remembered that in the realisation of the wider unity many interests formerly localised are revealed to be broader than locality and cease to be identified with its range. Thus locality both loses and gains in the process of the extension of community.

(3) *Where localities have built, for the furtherance of a specific common interest, a central association, that central association should be no longer organised according to local*

R

divisions but according to the intrinsic divisions of the specific interest concerned.

A simple illustration will make this point clear. At the Universities of Aberdeen and Glasgow the students still vote by "nations" or localities, a relic of the times when universities, in the poverty and uniformity of their studies, were organised according to local divisions. Of course such an external grouping has in all other respects long since given place to the essential organisation of a university, that according to faculties or branches of study. This brief illustration is significant of many wider cases. Localities do not stand for specific interests, being areas of community which circumscribe only a very limited and, with the extension of community, less and less definite exclusiveness of social type and interest. It is in very great measure the mere convenience of contiguity rather than the intrinsic distinctiveness of local interests which makes the locality an effective social unit. But in the central association that convenience no longer counts, and here organisation by local divisions is, except under special circumstances, a mere impediment to the activity of the association. The case of representative government has interest in this connection. While the unit of election remains locality, the division of interests within the central legislature scarcely ever follows the lines of locality. Consequently it becomes very difficult to attain any form of true representation on the basis of local election. Members ostensibly elected to represent a locality often in fact represent, though inadequately on account of the mode of election, not merely the broad policy of a party, but the special interest of some association, some trade or profession or church or other grouping. This cross-representation is creating one of the most difficult problems within the sphere of political science.

§4. The co-ordination of classes.

We have seen that the extension of community often means at the first the accentuation of class differences. What has hitherto been an independent community often sinks into the inferior and exploited caste of the enlarged community, and class stands external to class as locality stands external to locality. Such a relation means continual oppression and division, the double waste of energy always involved in the opposed standpoints of tyrant and of slave. Such an extreme cleavage is, as a rule, only temporary. The barrier of caste, like the barrier of locality, is broken across by new or widened associations, established to further interests that have proved more universal than that of caste. So there comes a true community into being, that of the nation or people, which feels and knows itself one. But however intense this feeling of unity it can never dissolve the distinctions between classes. Some inequalities of birth, fortune, ability, opportunity, and power must always remain as class-determinants in any social world which we can at present conceive, and the practical issue comes to be the relative priority of these various determinants in the formation and maintenance of classes.

We have already pointed out that the interests of community are best served when classes rest as far as possible on intrinsic differences, as little as possible on mere privilege or status not acquired by the personal qualities of their possessors. The degree in which extrinsic differences determine classes represents the degree in which community loses the intrinsic qualities thereby subordinated. It is, therefore, an evil to the whole community when the members of any class feel themselves cut off, apart from any ability they may possess, from a share in the direction of the community, from a

share in the completest life or the highest culture of the
community. This feeling of irrelevant exclusion is the
true basis of " class-war."

The check given to socialisation by irrelevant social
barriers is, of course, at the same time a check to individualisation. Men can realise their individualities only
within the appropriate social relations. In the light of
our general law it is therefore easy to state the conditions
of class-relationship which would best serve the welfare
of the whole. They should be such as would both give
every kind of capacity the opportunity to reveal itself
and permit revealed capacity to function at the highest
level of service for which it is adapted, not debarred from
that service by any consideration of social status otherwise determined. No forms of social service, least of all
the highest, should be the privilege of any pre-determined
class. In Plato's metaphor, no social function—and all
human activity is also social function—should be either
inaccessible to the golden offspring of, it may be, silvern
parents or pre-allotted to the silvern offspring of, it may
be, golden parents.

In the greater democracies of our day these conditions
are, on the whole, more adequately fulfilled than perhaps
in any community of the past. With the ever-increased
accessibility of both general education and specific training there is scarcely a form of service which remains
wholly closed to any who reveal a high and early aptitude
for it. Even military rank ceases to be wholly the privilege of a class, and the companion career of diplomacy
alone retains almost intact, together with its ancient
rubrics and often antiquated ideals, its ancient class-
exclusiveness. Everywhere the conditions of social service have become clarified, if we compare them with past
conditions, by the increased recognition of the importance
of personal capacity. It is true that in this as in every

other respect we have to strike a balance between the gain and the loss due to the more complicated conditions of modern service. Thus in the wide world of industry the division of labour has brought both loss and gain, loss in so far as the increased necessity for specialised ability has narrowed its scope and its chances of promotion, gain because the expansion of the industrial unit, workshop or factory, has made more possible the revelation of organising ability, which, being less specific and restricted than technical ability, can be transferred from grade to grade, from department to department, and even from occupation to occupation.

For the further development of community there is necessary such an organisation of social function as would give every qualified aspirant direct access to the next higher grade within his sphere of service. The more that ideal is realised the more will classes come to be based on considerations of intrinsic quality, for social function always in the long run gives significance to social class. Here we must point out the chief obstacle in the way of that further fulfilment. It is the power which inherited property retains as a determinant of social function, forming part of that vast problem of property which every social thinker is compelled to face. Its significance will be considered in a later chapter.

§ 5. The co-ordination of nations or peoples.

When the barriers of locality and class are broken across by the recognition and establishment of wider common interests, the nation or people emerges as an integral community. This attainment of nationality represents a vast step on the way of development. It is the complete affirmation of the superiority of common interest over the differences determined by locality and class. When the nation learns its unity, its ministering association, the State, definitely sets itself the task of co-ordinating all social groupings within its limits, associations, localities, classes. Thus the whole community is closely knit together, so that the imaginations of men can ignore the differences that remain and credit the nation with being a single " soul." But there is, in truth, no end to the process, no national unity of soul such as can stand conclusive of all common interests. The nation is a profoundly significant circle of community, it does not reach its outermost circumference. Like calls to like across the boundaries of nations as across the boundaries of classes, and nations with their territorial limits stand in need of co-ordination no less than their component localities. The nature of this co-ordination concerns us here, but in order to appreciate it we must clearly realise the meaning, the service, and the limits of nationality.

(1) Let us in the first place understand that we are here concerned with the relationships of nations and not at all with those of *races*. Distinctions of race, particularly as between civilised peoples, are at best partial and always largely hypothetical, so that they are never the true determinants of communal areas. Community can be nowhere identified with race, and that for two reasons. First, there are no pure races, no races whose blood is free from admixture with that which flows in other races. In the endless vicissitude of human migrations and conquests all the streams of human life, parted from some unknown and doubtless single source, have met and mingled and parted again. The races of men are not species or subspecies of the genus man.[1] Even if we could regard the peoples which appear distinct at the beginnings of our historical knowledge as themselves pure races, a most hazardous hypothesis, successions of

[1] Cf., *e.g.*, Deniker, *The Races of Man*, chaps. i. and viii.

invasions along the great routes of peoples have destroyed that original distinctness. The so-called great families of peoples, Aryan, Caucasian, Semitic, and so forth, represent unities or similarities of language, from which there is no true inference to common racial origin. Many specific branches of these putative families have intermingled again and again. All the great peoples of the ancient and the modern world are known to have resulted from intermixture, the Egyptians, the Greeks, the Romans, even the Hebrews, as well as the Teutons, the Latin peoples, the Chinese and the Japanese. It would, indeed, seem as if appropriate intermixture were a very condition of national greatness, as if racial fusion, like spiritual contact, were a stimulus to development.

Anthropology confirms the conclusion derived from history. Whatever criterion of race we consider most decisive, colour of skin, eyes, or hair, texture of hair, cephalic, orbital, gnathic, or nasal index,[1] it is impossible to regard the somatic character so chosen as an adequate criterion of psychological or social type as well. The attempts of such writers as Taine, Renan, Gobineau, Lapouge, Kossinna, and Stewart Chamberlain to explain national character or literature or history purely in terms of race have come to shipwreck over facts to which their theories rendered these writers blind. In particular they all belong to that great order of theorists who fail to realise the *resultant* character of all social phenomena, born as these are out of the incessant action of their varying and multiple environments upon the native capacities of men.

[1] It is significant that the different somatic indices give very different classifications of racial types. It has been pointed out, for instance, that there is no correlation between the cephalic index (the relation of the antero-posterior to the transverse diameter of the head or cranium) and the colour of the skin, and that there is no complete correspondence between the nasal and the cephalic indices. For a critical discussion of these indices see Mariano-H. Cornejo, *Revue Internationale de Sociologie*, March, 1911.

Here we are brought to the second reason why the race can never be identified with the nation. When a once homogeneous people expands so that different portions of it become exposed to different geographical conditions, or when a portion is brought into contact with the influence of another civilisation, the former homogeneity disappears, so much so that the portions thus differentiated may become distinct peoples. The Greek of the plain differed greatly from the Greek of the mountain; the English Canadian or Australian feels himself different from the Englishman at home. All who have observed how readily the children of one people when educated in the home-life of another assimilate the new atmosphere and come to find that of their parents alien, how readily, for instance, English children educated in France or Germany develop French or German traits, realise that national characteristics are in great measure due to physical influences emanating from individual points or developed under the specific conditions and opportunities of a common environment. Men become in all literalness " naturalised " to their social surroundings. It may be that environment modifies the physical character,[1] it is beyond all doubt that environment has

---

[1] The evidence of the United States Immigration Commission shows that the children of European immigrants to America tend to approximate to the American type, the extreme head-formations, represented by the Jews on the one hand and by the Sicilians on the other, being modified in opposite directions towards an intermediate and characteristically American form. Dr. Lomer (*Bulletin Mensuel de l'Institut de Sociologie Solvay*, 1910) corroborates this view from personal observation, and believes also that in Japan and China children of pure European origin approximate to the native facial type. Ridgeway holds that the inhabitants of mountain countries become round-headed in the course of a few generations, just as the long-headed Boer horse becomes round-headed when reared in the Basutoland mountains. Again, the investigations of Lapouge and Ammon lead to the conclusion that, within certain regions, the long-headed type prevails more in the city than in the surrounding country, but here, as in so many cases, an alternative *explanation* is possible. See Ripley, *The Races of Europe*, chaps. xix. and xx.

a powerful influence on the social type. The unity of the American nation, built out of the fragments of many and diverse peoples, and under the diverse conditions of a broad continent, is the most signal proof of the reality of social assimilation.[1] Common life is a factor in the formation of national like-mindedness, and common origin cannot therefore be more than a factor. In view of the deep interactions of environmental and native influences it is mere blindness to equate community and race.

(2) But the nation *is* a community, it is the resultant of these factors, not a hypothetical structure like race, but a concrete living reality. It means a certain community of nature, however brought into being, the like-mindedness that by the laws of our psychical being develops in any group associated into common life, that congeniality of a people which as culture advances seems to support itself less and less on the *idea* of consanguinity.[2] The idea of race is abstract and can give no concrete purposes to the community it binds. It can suggest no further ideal than the continuance, propagation, and dominance of the kin. It is but the expression of the undifferentiated

---

[1] Of course men differ as to the relative efficacy of assimilation in particular instances, as to how far, for example, the United States to-day assimilates its constant stream of immigrants. Thus M. Jean Finot (*Contemporary Review*, 1911) believes in the almost unlimited assimilative power of the United States, while Mr. A. E. Zimmern (*Sociological Review*, 1912) strenuously denies that America to-day is a " melting-pot " of the nations. But all writers assume that there is an American nation and an American character to which aliens are or are not assimilated. It is noteworthy that writers tend to differ as to the efficacy of assimilation according as they think it *desirable* or not, those who think it undesirable tending to deny it.

Of course where aliens form a small compact community within a greater, such as the foreign quarters in large cities, the process of assimilation is necessarily retarded.

[2] This is insisted on by Durkheim, *Division du Travail Social*, Book II., chap. iv., who, however, speaks, not quite correctly, in terms of " heredity," and by Ratzenhofer, who sums up the matter in these words, *Für die wichtigen Culturvölker ist, dem Wesen nach, das Blutband ein überwundenes Interesse* (*Die Sociologische Erkenntniss*, 1898, p. 217).

life-force which has not yet discovered definite forms of activity, and while a group inspires itself with that abstract ideal, it too remains primitive and undifferentiated, its consciousness the mere vehicle of blind desires. A community that finds its unity and its inspiration in the blood-bond alone, and not on any intrinsic interests this may be held to involve, can scarcely have any definite object beyond mere aggrandisement and the reduction of rival communities. A community must transcend the ideal of race or remain limited, thwarted, and irrational.

Nationality too, as we must see, proves but a limited social inspiration, but the nation, unlike the race, is nevertheless a true community, revealing that degree of likemindedness which makes it a strong and definite unit of common activity. Even in primitive communities the need for this concreter unity was felt, and the blood-bond was often the simplified popular representation of nationality. This is witnessed to by the primitive custom of " adopting " individuals or groups from beyond the supposed limits of the kin,[1] whereby the aegis of race was cast over them to bring them into community.

The intense consciousness of nationality, like the intense consciousness of race with which it is so easily confused, represents a stage in social development, and is the means by which a widened form of social unity is maintained. It fulfils a double service. Negatively, it is an important protest against *false* universal claims, the claim, for instance, of political Rome over the world, or, again, the claim of ecclesiastical Rome over the world. It was largely through the spirit of nationality that these claims were overthrown. Positively, it provides a ground for the union of localities and for the reconciliation of classes, often in the past so widely separated in interests,

[1] Cf. Maine, *Ancient Law*, chap. v.

giving a somewhat vague though often very effective sentimental community to those divided by hard distinctions of class, station, and culture. The idea of nationality is thus, on the other hand, an expression of the widened social thoughts of men. Again, and in consequence, the principle of nationality enables those who share it to unite effectively for the common pursuit of the concrete interests which also they share. It is the basis on which men build the association of the State, on which, through its aid, they realise in harmony that community of human interests which is deeper than all the differences of men.

Here it is necessary to draw an important distinction, that between nationality as fact and nationality as ideal. The fact of common nationality is definite and determinative, not to be denied or renounced, a real basis of unity and condition of common action. Whether the ideal of nationality grows stronger or weaker in the future, the fact of nationality, though of constantly changing nationality, will always remain. All the laws of life conspire to give a common and distinctive character to every area of community, and especially to those areas bounded by the frontiers of States. The great currents of culture that sweep over continents and even over the world along the increasing channels of communication will never obliterate but rather will enrich that character of national individuality. Nevertheless the *ideal* of nationality is vague and confused, and, save in one respect, can give little or no true guidance to the spirit. It is one of the greatest errors of our time to confuse the significance of the fact of nationality and the significance of the ideal of nationality.

Nationality, in a word, is properly the ground and not the inspiration of common action. Let us illustrate from one of the most important forms of modern national

activity, that of economic legislation. Do we pass these
Acts, say the Factory Acts, because we are thinking of
the national characteristics of Englishmen (while, at the
same time, the Germans pass similar Acts because they
are thinking of the peculiar needs of Germans), because
we regard cleanliness and fresh air as good for the *English*
physique, because we think *English* children are in-
jured by long hours in factories, because we think *English*
workers require security against accident ? Is the stress
laid on the nationality of the worker or on the fact that
the worker as such requires protection ? Is nationality
the inspiration of the common activity or rather the
basis of the association which achieves it ? The answer
is plain. Nationality is, as it were, the colour of community, not a name for the whole complex of communal
interests. The distinction is manifest again if we ask
how far nationality is the inspiration of national literature. How thin and lifeless are those dramas and tales
which set out to portray national differences, supposed
national characteristics, how inevitably they run into
broad caricature or foolish laudation ! Take any national
literature or other art, and you perceive that its great
works are concerned with essentially human problems,
the creators of them revealing their nationality in their
very attempt to reveal humanity. Nationality is a way
of being human, a communal individuality. Just as no
individual can find inspiration if he looks to his own
individuality instead of realising it in intrinsic interests,
so no nation can find true inspiration if its eyes are turned
to its own distinctive nationality.

The one respect in which nationality can serve as the
ideal no less than as the basis of community is here
revealed. It is simply when men seek this basis of community. It is simply the ideal that the nation should
govern itself, should form an autonomous unit for the

achievement, through the State, of intrinsic interests.[1]
That inspiration has been one of the most vital and
effective ideals in modern history.   It is also, let us add,
the most imperative, since the achievement of an adequate
basis for common action is prior in claim to any further
common end.   But when the ideal is achieved, it is vain
to regard it as any longer an ideal.   When the principle
of national liberty has been achieved, the true inspiration
of nationality is fulfilled, and nationality having become
the basis of community must cease to be also its
ideal.

In all higher stages of culture most of the interests
pursued by any people are, in respect of any other people,
either complementary or common or both.   They are
complementary in so far as relative opportunities for the
pursuit of interests leads to exchange of services, not
only in the economic, but in every sphere of activity.
They are common in being intrinsic universal interests,
of value not to a particular people alone.   In barbarism,
interests are discrete—the interests of the Bushman or
Basuto are his alone, what concern are they of the Fiji
or Eskimo, what of any people besides themselves except
as they may affect their relative strength should they
meet in antagonism ?   If the peoples are too remote for
contact, their interests are wholly exclusive.   But the
interests which the Japanese pursues to-day are of moment
also to the German and the Englishman because alike,
as civilised peoples, their concern is with intrinsic values
which are values for all men.   Whoever seeks knowledge

[1] Of course this ideal can be realised only where a nation exclusively
occupies a determinate area, or in other words is itself a determinate
community.   Wherever different peoples, at or near the same cultural
stage, are through any historical vicissitude *intermingled* upon a common territory while yet retaining their national distinctness, a situation
of great difficulty exists, and the only hope of peaceful development
lies in the further operation of that process of social assimilation which
we have already seen to be the principle determining the formation of
nationality.

or practises an art, whoever subdues the human environment or interprets human nature, whoever speculates on human destiny or divine existence, however coloured his views may be by national prejudices, however determined by national temperament, is engaged in a work that is contradictory or futile unless the results achieved stand as an achievement not of the individual, not of his nation alone, but of humanity.

This is not the denial of intermediate interests nor the advancement of any claim of cosmopolitanism. As a work of art gains, in place of losing, in value for other men because of the individuality of the artist—and all work at the level of intrinsic interests is served by the individuality of the worker—so the work of a people is of greater and not less value to other peoples because of its nationality, because it reveals the individuality of a people, because it enables those others to look from standpoints not their own, with eyes not their own, at their own indisputable world. It is true that as culture advances communities, becoming more differentiated as to their members, become less differentiated from one another. Savage peoples, though they may stand on a common level of ignorance, superstition, and narrow-mindedness, reveal, as a result of the exclusiveness of their interests, very great contrasts in customs and institutions and beliefs. But the advance in culture involves the discovery of intrinsic interests and is therefore inconsistent with a complete difference of character between communities. However widely separated two primitive peoples may be in form and custom, the process of differentiation is much the same for both, the division of labour creating like specialised faculties, the growth of competition creating like habits of mind, like unities of group against group ; while over against these unconscious forms of rapprochement there is at work the

conscious unifying thought born of the increasing knowledge alike of the common elements and conditions of
our humanity and of the common world in which we
live.   Ignorance separates and knowledge unites.   In the
process of development communities grow in essential
likenesses because they reveal their essential characters.
As in the intercourse of men, so in the intercourse of
peoples, what cannot stand contact with others is either
weakness or folly or mere eccentricity.   If in the multitude of offerings which intercommunity brings some are
universally seized upon and utilised, we need feel no
surprise, it merely tells us again that the likenesses of
men lie deeper in their nature than do their differences.

The current of social intercourse brings psychical stimulus to individual and nation ; contact with other peoples,
as with other men, brings new ideas, the salt of society
without which one way of custom good or bad, one
standard growing more rigid as its spontaneity wears
away, inevitably corrupts the world.   The growing difference between the newer and the older ways of nationality-
contact forms one of the best reasons for the hope that
our world of to-day may not, like the world in other
ages, harden in tradition while it weakens in character,
until the institutions its younger spirit built become mere
vessels to contain its decay.

(3) Understanding the service and limits of nationality,
we are now in a position to consider how nations both
are and can be co-ordinated within the wider community
which they build.   Such co-ordination can be directly
achieved only through the State, which is the primary
association corresponding to the nation.   It is true that
the limits of nations and States are still far from being
coincident, but the great historical movements have been
leading towards that ideal.   In any case it must be the
co-operation of States, whether they do or do not coin-

cide with nations, which will bring order into the still existing chaos of the nations.

Our distinction between the fact and the ideal of nationality is here applicable. The State should be, as it in fact tends to be, based on nationality, which seems to represent the degree of community requisite for effective political activity. But since the interests of any nation are wider than its nationality, being so largely interests complementary to and common with those of other nations, the State is more than the mere protector of nationality, it is the protector and maintainer of each concrete nation, the community of which nationality is, as it were, the colour, and all interests within that sphere, those which unite no less than those which separate the community from others, are its great and ever-deepening responsibility. For the protection of the wider common interests inter-State action is necessary and inevitable. This is becoming more and more apparent in the modern world, for, with the development of the means of communication, there has come a great development of common interests, a great transformation of like interests into common interests. Wherever an interest is realised as common, the corresponding common will organises it under an associational form. Hence the numerous international associations which have sprung up in recent years, associations of commerce and industry, of scientific research, of art, religion, music, letters. Like calls to like across the boundaries of States as surely as across the boundaries of localities and classes. But no single State can give sanction and protection to associations which outpass its bounds, for the State, unlike community, has rigid frontiers. So come the agreements of States which have already created elementary international organisation for the civilised world, witnessed for instance by the International Postal Union, the Universal Telegraph Union, and the Universal Wireless Telegraph Union, by international agreements for passenger and freight transportation by sea and land, international maritime codes and shipping regulations, international rules of patent and copyright, international rules of war itself.

But mere rules of this character, and the spasmodic conventions which have established them, are wholly inadequate for the co-ordination rendered necessary by the growth of common interests. The protection of the vast extent of common interests formed and forming, no less than the settlement of the differences which are incidental to all community, necessitates some permanent form of international federation and some not yet established sanction of international agreements. Such a federation has indeed been forming almost against the will of States, but the sanction must wait for the unity of will.[1]

With the growth of this international organisation and of the consequent interdependence of nations, there has developed a clearer recognition of the nature and sphere of the State. It has been well said that ever since the beginning of the modern era two opposing views of the State have been struggling for predominance.[2] These are (1) the "Machiavellian," as it is popularly though perhaps not rightly called, the view that States are wholly unlimited powers owing no responsibility to one another, bound to one another by no rights and obligations save those they choose to establish, and by these only so long as they do not choose to repudiate them, and (2) the Grotian or Althusian, the view that States exist for the establishment and maintenance of rights, that therefore their powers are limited and that they have duties towards

[1] See Appendix B.

[2] See Hon. D. Jaynes Hill, *World Organisation and the Modern State.*

S

one another, being themselves members of a society of
States. At various times and in different States one or
other view has prevailed, but the growth of intercommunity is turning the scale generally in the most civilised
States in favour of the Grotian doctrine. It would, in
fact, be the only scientific doctrine, the only one consistent with an understanding of the essential nature of
the State, even if States were self-sufficient and not
united by common interests. For it is law that assigns
the sphere, and reveals the meaning and limitations of
the State. The State exists first of all as the upholder
of law, its first business is therefore justice, the meting
out of what is fair and the repressing of lawless might.
It is therefore a " juristic person," and a " juristic person " cannot claim arbitrary right in respect of another
" juristic person " without denying the very nature of
both.

The absence of settled juristic relations between States
works in its degree the same effect as the absence of
settled juristic relations between individual men. Just
as surely as for individual men, in the degree of their
approach to a " state of nature " where no established
law civilises their relations one to another, life remains,
in Hobbes' famous phrase, " solitary, poor, nasty, brutish,
and short," just as surely does it hold that States, in so
far as they remain irresponsible, unsocialised, political
leviathans beyond the greater law, must also be poorer,
more unhappy, and more brutish in their kind. Poorer
because of the economic insufficiency of each, more unhappy because of the all-round insecurity of men's lives
and wealth, more brutish because public policy reflects
and reacts upon every standard of life.

The gradual recognition of this truth is leading slowly
to settled juristic relations between States, as distinct
from mere congresses and agreements on particular

questions.   One important step in the process has been
made as a result of the Hague conferences of 1899 and
1907, the establishment of an international arbitral court.
But there is needed a far completer international judicature than has yet been called into existence, as well
as—what does not exist at all—some form of international legislature.   Such a legislature, following in due
historical order the establishment of a judicature, would
give international " law," at length based on the common
will of States, the full sanction and force of intranational
law.   It is reasonably probable that the necessities involved in the remarkable development of intercommunity
will in course of time overcome the existing obstacles to
such a consummation.[1]

(4) The development of common interests is making
the institution of war between nations irrational and
vain.   War is a relation of hostility between peoples as
organised by States.   Its method of mere destruction
implies that there is a complete antagonism of interest
between the warring peoples.   But the interests of
civilised nations are no longer isolable, one civilised
people cannot hurt the interests of another without
hurting its own as well.   It is only when communities
are essentially isolated, or when the relation between
them is that of dominant to subject peoples, that the
hurt of one can be the good of the other.   Therefore,
as intercommunity extends, war becomes more and more
irrational.   This is most obvious in the economic sphere,
owing especially to the internationalisation of capital,
so that one civilised community, in destroying the commerce and capital of another, is destroying or injuring
the investments of its own members.   Again, as international trade grows, more and more members of each
community live by the commercial prosperity of other

[1] See Appendix B.

communities, and are necessarily ruined when that suffers.[1] Commerce affords the clearest case of the indissolubility of intercommunity, because the effects of war on commerce are measurable.[2] But the kinds of intercommunity which we cannot measure are no less significant.

War is a means by which *States* settle their differences, and if the differences are real, they are differences in respect of such interests as are bounded by State-frontiers. These are at most interests of nationality. But war destroys other interests than these. The State does not determine all community, nor does nationality sum up all communal interests. There are many interests which divide the citizens of one State, there are many interests which unite associations, groups, and classes across the frontiers of States. A State which initiates war destroys, in the name of at best some national interest, those further unities of interests in which the members of nationalities are joined. Civilised men have come to realise the irrationality of war instituted by non-political associations, the fatuity of the religious wars in which churches involved communities ; they have abjured also the resort to war by groups or classes within a community, stigmatising it as ' civil war " ; and to-day the same reasons which are the condemnation of war as between churches or classes are in operation to condemn warfare between nationalities. The spirit of militarism still seeks to isolate the interests of civilised peoples, in this way to exalt one at the expense of the other ; but the growth

[1] Consider the significance of such a fact as the following : The trade of Germany with the British Empire " has more than doubled since 1902, and has now reached the enormous total, in 1911, of 185 millions sterling. In fact, so far as our people live by trade, one-tenth of our population are absolutely dependent upon German trade." (P. A. Molteno, *Contemporary Review*, Feb., 1914.)

[2] See Angell, *The Great Illusion*, Part I., and *The Foundations of International Polity*, chap. iii.

of intercommunity renders its efforts vain, it can no longer dissolve the interdependence of nations, it can only ruin the nations which are interdependent.

(5) We have been hitherto concerned with the relations of peoples standing on similar levels of culture, but there is another problem of co-ordination, and one more difficult to solve. When peoples representing very different stages of development are brought into contact, their relations cannot be adjusted on the simple lines we have just indicated. Relations of superiority and subordination inevitably take the place of relations of equality. There can be no equal interchange of services, no free adjustment of differences through the agreement of wills. This is clearly seen in the economic sphere. The higher people, from the very fact of their higher culture, cannot meet on equal terms, even if otherwise they were willing to do so, the economic competition, in respect of the less skilled forms of labour, of the lower people who can live more cheaply. The superior people, owning that predominance of power which higher intelligence can nearly always command, inevitably subordinate the interests of the lower people to their own.

Yet it must be admitted that relations of predominance and subordination involve danger for both the lower and the higher people. For then the higher, if in close contact with the lower, tend to harden into a stubborn conservatism. In resisting the influence of a lower social environment they easily shut out progressive influences as well : they must deaden on one side their social suggestibility and thus tend to deaden it on every side, thereby retarding the whole social process. This has nearly always been a characteristic of white populations who live surrounded by blacks. Again, the lower rarely gain by such contact, for in general they are merely exploited as a servile race, and often, losing traditions and not gaining responsibilities, they fall victims to the stock-destroying vices which flourish in the absence of these prophylactics. (Even the attempt to enforce higher customs may be prejudicial to the lower people, since it is easier to destroy the old than to construct the new.) Thus the common danger of the ordinary relations of predominance and subordination suggests that here too the common interests may be profounder than the oppositions which create these relations. For these dangers are minimised in so far as the superior people, while retaining their necessary predominance, learn to adopt the attitude of tutelage in place of the attitude of exploitation. We may contrast in this respect the comparative success of the American nation in their dealings with inferior peoples and the complete failure of the older Spanish colonists of the New World, whose methods were disastrous at once to the natives and to themselves.

No empire, in the ancient sense of the term, can be enduring, for empire of such a kind means the direct subjection of people to people. This subjection is no longer possible if, as so often has happened, the subject-peoples attain a level of culture near to that of the dominant people. The successive granting of autonomy to its parts, as these attain political insight and the desire for self-government, is the only possible way in which such an empire can, if only in name, remain entire. For when, of two peoples not remote in culture, one holds the other beneath the political yoke, there is no acquiescence, no assimilation, no peace, until the subject-people is either liberated or destroyed.

In the modern world the sphere of empire, in the ancient sense of a centralised, military, tax-collecting system, is becoming more and more circumscribed. Modern States have been interested chiefly in the industrial exploitation of their colonies, but in course of time the colonies come to safeguard their industrial interests as autonomous units. An excellent illustration of the disappearance of the ancient colony or " dependency " is afforded by the history of the American continent, where State after State in a long succession, the United States (1774-5), the Argentine (1810-16), Chile (1810-17), Paraguay (1811), Colombia (1819), later divided into the independent republics of Venezuela, New Granada, and Ecuador (1829-30), Mexico (1821), Brazil (1822), Bolivia and Peru (1824), and of course, though by a more gradual process, Canada, passed from subordination to autonomy. It is no mere accident that all the empires of the ancient world have passed away, nor is it mere accident that the empires of the modern world are being transformed, where empire means the political subordination of peoples not remote in cultural stage from the governing people, into loose federal unities.[1]

§ 6. General survey of the problem of co-ordination.

All community is a matter of degree. Our life falls within not one but many communities, and these stretch around us grade beyond grade, building associations of every kind. They make diverse claims upon their members, claims which historically have been in fierce opposition, but which in the advance of society we more and more perceive to be reconcilable. The revelation of the likeness which is deeper than difference is the revelation of the meaning of difference also. The widening of the social consciousness is the deepening of the social consciousness, not the making of it shallow, as some suppose. Immanent in men, and gradually manifested in the growth of intelligence, is the capacity of many devotions, to

[1] An interesting short discussion of these and some further international questions, such as that of exclusive national rights of fishing and navigation, is to be found in an article by G. Olphe Galliard, *La Morale des Nations Contemporaines*, in *La Science Sociale*, March, 1912.

family, to city, to nation, to the world of civilisation, to the world of humanity itself. There remains much confusion within this growing hierarchy of communal life, and there are infinite partial attractions and repulsions within every area of community. But the map of community is already, we may hope, sufficiently unfolded to enable us to perceive the general principles of its co-ordination.

Every great civilisation has in its course brought to birth the conception of a community extending far beyond the exclusive limits of any one people or State. Indeed, this conception is a necessary consequence of the growth of intelligence, and the modes and places of its emergence, seen in their historical setting, are most significant, for they reveal to us the central drama of all history, the thousand-times renewed conflict between the nearer and the wider social claim. The nearer claim, the claim of kindred or city or nationality, is always at the first exclusive and complete. Such exclusiveness is a necessary safeguard of the narrower mind which, unless it find one simple allegiance to which it can cling, must drift in helplessness. But in time the peril of exclusiveness becomes greater than its security. If the spirit of exclusiveness remains triumphant, the exclusive community must yield before its wiser neighbours, for its exclusiveness means not only inferiority of wisdom but also inferiority of power. How often might a community have been saved from submergence or decay if its members had been wise enough to know the wisdom of its greatest minds !

" And who is my neighbour ? " asked the Jewish lawyer who would justify himself. The answer had been clear enough to the Jew of the Pentateuch. Did not Yahweh command him to have no dealings with " the Gentiles " ? " Thou shalt smite them, and utterly destroy them ;

thou shalt make no covenant with them, nor show mercy unto them." (*Deut.* vii. 2.) With scarce a protest, this spirit rules throughout Jewish history. Bound to this exclusive creed, and yet blindly seeking the Messiah who would save him from the impotence and failure it ensured, the Jew heard in vain the message of Jesus, bidding him see in every man his neighbour. That any salvation should come with the breaking down of exclusiveness seemed foolishness to him. So the message passed to his more universal-minded neighbours. " Seeing ye put it from you," cried Paul—who himself had lived " after the most straitest sect of our religion "—" lo, we turn to the Gentiles." (*Acts* xiii. 46.) So while Paul preached the more universal law " where there is neither Greek nor Jew, circumcision nor uncircumcision, Barbarian, Scythian, bond nor free " (*Col.* iii. 11), the Jews pursued that stubborn principle of exclusiveness, which brought upon them the destruction of their temple and city, and ended in their dispersal throughout the world, to be the homeless dependents of all other nations. Never was the nemesis of unyielding exclusiveness more complete.

The problem of the wider and the narrower community was set for the Greeks in a still acuter form, while their failure to solve it, despite the teaching of their greatest men, was no less striking. Here it was in the first place civic and not national allegiance which men failed to reconcile with the idea of a wider community. Not even the fact of participation in common nationality, culture, religion, and speech, not even the experience of common danger scarce outlived and the knowledge of common danger still impending, not even the recognition of the endless disaster of intranational division could break the exclusiveness of the city-community. Leagues and confederacies and common festivals there were by the score, but every attempt to create the sentiment and establish the reality of the wider community was frustrate or partial or momentary or perverted by the spirit of domination. In vain their poets and artists revealed the common mind of Greece. In vain Thucydides pictured the ravages of intra-Hellenic divisions, in vain Demosthenes pled for intra-Hellenic unity, in vain Plato declared that the strife of Greek with Greek was " civil discord " ($\sigma\tau\acute{a}\sigma\iota\varsigma$) and not " war," and conceived a more ideal Hellenic community whose members, all " philhellenes," would regard Hellas as their country, share its temples in common, and " never bring themselves to tear in pieces their own nurse and mother." (*Republic*, pp. 470-1.) Too late the Greek cities laid aside their enmities, seeking the remedy of federation only when already the yoke of strangers was laid upon them. Too late they learned as subjects of a seemingly universal empire the claims of the wider community which they had rejected as free citizens—and even so learned them in one-sided fashion, never reconciling the " community of man " with the nearer community of the city. It may be that, as a recent historian has claimed, the city has a better chance than the nation of extending its particular freedoms and gifts to the wider world ; the Greek city, at any rate, never learned to reconcile its life with the life beyond its gates.

We shall indeed misconceive the problem if we regard the solution as the throwing open to the whole world of the proper liberties and privileges of the small community or city. This, the Roman solution, was in its turn equally extreme. It is a problem of the co-ordination of communities, not of the proper way to extend to the greater the privileges and rights of the smaller. It is a problem of the reconciliation of allegiances, not of the reduction of all allegiances to one. The Romans

who extended the citizenship of Rome to the conquered
peoples were wiser than the Greeks, who knew no third
course beside local independence and mere empire, but
they still were far from realising the meaning of the
wider community. They extended to the world a citizenship that grew more unmeaning with each extension.
They had nothing but citizenship, admission to the privileges and rights of the one city, to offer the world : they
would make the world a greater city, instead of the city
part of the greater community of their world. They
achieved no political co-ordination of the smaller and
the greater community ; they found no middle terms
between " citizen of Rome," to the last the badge of
political right through the vast empire, and " citizen
of the world," the equally extreme watchword and re-
joinder of the philosophers. The idea (like the name)
of humanity, unknown to Greece, was discovered in the
Roman world, but was regarded as in mere contrast
to the idea and the name of Rome, and so remained
barren and abstract. It was only in the sphere of law
that any real reconciliation and harmony was made
between the interests, claims, and necessities of the city
and those of the empire.

Certainly as intelligence grows there is an increased
recognition of the preponderance of uniting over dividing
interests. The primitive and the superficial intelligence
see only difference where the widened mind sees the
vaster likeness. It was in the name of the essential
likeness of Jew and Christian that Shylock is represented
as protesting against the persecution of his people.
" Hath not a Jew eyes ? hath not a Jew hands, organs,
dimensions, senses, affections, passions ? " It was no
wonder, therefore, that men passed from the narrow
doctrines of the city-state to an extreme of cosmopolitanism. In that extreme form was expressed the greater

enlightenment of both the Stoic and the Christian. So
Paul had demanded for the Gentile from the Jew the
same toleration which in the revolution of the ages the
Jew was driven to demand from the Gentile. " For
there is no difference between the Jew and the Greek."
(*Romans* x. 12.) So Marcus Aurelius insisted on the
oneness of reason or spirit in all peoples. For every
man's nature is " kindred to my own, not because he
shares the same flesh and blood and is sprung from
the same seed, but because he partakes of the same
reason and the same spark of divinity." (*Meditations*,
II. 1.) As men grow wiser, as they realise their own
world the more, they see more the depth and potentiality
of their like natures, the community of their hopes and
fates.

But the necessities of social life cannot be satisfied
in a single vast community of all men. Within the
widened community there must always remain the
numerous likenesses and differences of social groups.
The character of a people is not obliterated by intercommunity with others, any more than the character
of an individual is obliterated by his social intercourse.
In both cases intercommunity is a psychical stimulus, a
stimulus to the development of *character*. These likenesses and differences necessitate nearer centres of social
activity, nearer unities. Further, the activities of men
are determined by the necessities and limitations of
locality, so that each area of community requires its
own autonomy. Decentralisation is as necessary as centralisation. If Greece erred in one direction, Rome erred
as grievously in the other. The true principle is federal,
a common organisation for common interests, special
organisations for special interests, centralisation for universal order and security, decentralisation for the fulfilment of life.

The true principle of the co-ordination of community began to be realised at the dawn of the modern world. The co-ordination of the universal mediæval church suggested the co-ordination of universal community. This conception is already clear in the mind of Aquinas,[1] and finds later a remarkable expression in the *De Monarchia* of Dante. Each area of community, Dante pointed out, has its proper place and end in the fulfilment of the whole ; each is partial in some respects, integral in others. Beyond the household extends the village and the city, beyond the city the kingdom, beyond the kingdom the world of men (*universitas humana*), not as a mere conception but as a reality necessitating a single government after its kind, just as each smaller area requires its own unity of government after its kind.[2] But many barriers had to be removed before even the beginning of such an order could appear. In particular the disintegration of mediæval society made a decisive centralisation a necessary preliminary. Centralised and exclusive nations arose in strength out of the chaos of empire, and for a time each of these great areas, unified under the form of the State, seemed to satisfy within itself all the needs of community.

But there remained everywhere at least one association, the church, which crossed the now so exclusive frontiers, and there arose many associations whose activities came to undermine the basis of centralisation. From this confusion community is even now emerging. Speaking broadly, we may say that the greatest social and political movement of the eighteenth century in the west was concerned with the overthrow of smaller associations which had taken despotic and arbitrary and narrowing

[1] Cf. Gierke, *Political Theories of the Middle Age* (tr. Maitland), §§ I.-IV.

[2] *De Monarchia*, I., chap. v., ff.

forms, in favour of the claim of the greater State. The nineteenth, on the other hand, we may say in the same broad fashion, has been concerned in building up the smaller associations on a new basis, not in their old arbitrary independence, but in their due relation to wider claims. From the standpoint of community, the result has been the development of the principle of federation. In this way the small community regains what it loses in its first submergence in the great community. And our social world assumes the form of community beyond community, from village or parish or town-ward out to the greatest area of federated territory whose common interests we have the intelligence to discern and the wisdom to unite. For the final law revealed in federation is this, that so far as common interest extends, so far and in so far ought community also to extend. Not isolation and not absorption, not parochialism and not cosmopolitanism—but narrower and wider circles of community in due correspondence to narrower and wider needs. Not parochialism and not cosmopolitanism—for if we justly condemn cosmopolitanism in the light of the history of Rome, shall we the less condemn parochialism in the light of the history of Greece? Not isolation and not absorption—for strength without liberty is blind, and justice without affection is empty.

From the point of view of the sociologist the internal progress of any particular group or community is necessarily partial in so far as it does not bring that group or community into completer harmony with others. This is a necessary implication of our fundamental law of development. Since the widening of community is itself one result of the growth of personality, we cannot regard the ideal of progress as attained apart from the completest possible harmony of all men, all interests, and all groups. In the light of this law he is not a sociologist, but a partisan, who refuses to construct the ideal of progress from the standpoint of humanity itself. The sociologist can no more retain the primitive though still predominant attitude of men towards their respective nations than the scientist could retain the primitive idea of the universe. Men found the earth to be the whole meaning of the universe just as men still find their country to be the whole meaning of community. These theories are very comfortable and come very easy to our egoisms. But when men comprehended the truth about the earth, all the broken fragments of their physical knowledge were pieced together as parts of a hitherto undreamed-of harmony of science. In like manner when men realise that their own country is but a part of the meaning of community, all the broken social interests of to-day will be revealed as co-ordinated within the *universitas humana*. And men will despise the lesser if more comfortable thoughts of our age, as we despise the ignorance of the Pre-Copernicans.

CHAPTER V

PROBLEMS CONNECTED WITH THE FOREGOING
LAW: (2) THE UNITY OF THE INDIVIDUAL
LIFE

§ 1. The problem.

In the primitive world where community is undifferentiated, the members of society find the unity of their lives in an easy fashion, for a single system of sanctions, customs, and traditions hedges them round. There is no opposition of standards or ideals, no conflict of duties necessitating the search for an inner principle. The uniformity of the social environment determines the rule of conduct as simple devotion to one allegiance. This conformity gives its security and stability to primitive life.

But when associations within community differentiate and when society reveals itself as no longer one enclosing circle but a graded series of communities, a problem of great significance arises. As associations multiply, each acquires its own distinctive customs and traditions, its own distinctive morality, in respect of the life-conditions with which it is especially concerned. Thus each acquires its average or characteristic form of honour, as, for instance, the honour of the soldier, of the lawyer, of the tradesman, of the doctor, down even to the honour among thieves. A man, as a rule, follows a single profession, and therefore the differences of standard between these may involve no direct conflict of ideals ; but every man belongs also to various associations, family, club, church, economic associations, and so forth, the variety and uncertainty of whose standards, unless he find a principle of harmony, may well bring confusion into his life. Again, as the life of men becomes involved in nearer and farther circles of community, it becomes more and more difficult to find any general or communal traditions such as can comprehend all their activities. The differentiation of community, we have seen, stimulates both the sociality and the individuality of men. We now see that it raises perhaps the ultimate practical question in life, that of the unity of life for each individual as an active member of society. As community differentiates and individuality grows men lose the security, the comfort of conformity, and are driven to seek, through perils and negations, a profounder source of unity. This is a necessary episode in all transition from tutelage to manhood. The social being who formerly accepted a principle of unity has henceforth to attain it.

A man is more than a soldier or a lawyer or a merchant or a mechanic, wrought as his occupation is upon his character ; he is more than a member of a family or a church or a city or a nation, nay, he is more than a member of a family *and* a church *and* a profession *and* a city *and* a nation. For a man's character seeks to be a unity. Not only does the personality of man refuse to be summed up under a single social relationship, it is not wholly revealed as the total of a series of social relationships. Historically it was seen that a social individual was more than a citizen because he was also a kinsman and a churchman, but finally he is more than a citizen because he is a *person*. The increase of the social relationships of men, as their individuality grows, more and more fulfils, but it never exhausts, the personality of men. Some-

T

times men seem to contract into the mere type of a profession or class, becoming, say, professionalised into mere official or mere ecclesiastic. Yet, however conformed a man may be to the tradition of profession or class, in his highest moments he will rise above that conformity, as in his lowest he may sink beneath it.

We think too much in types. The idea we form of another's personality is always generalised and imperfect, because we cannot fully conceive the elements of unlikeness to ourselves which it contains. How often do we dismiss a man as the member of a social type, especially if his activities lie in social spheres remote from our own, as a grocer or a priest or a concierge or a member of parliament or whatever it may be, who, if we knew him better, would appear less and less the type, the mere member of an occupation or a class, more and more the person, a being with the richness and elusiveness and incompleteness—and seeming contradictoriness—of personality. Simmel has well remarked that, even when we apply no definite category to a man to sum up his personality, we yet characterise him *nach einem wortlosen Typus, mit dem sein reines Fürsichsein nicht zusammenfällt.* (*Soziologie,* p. 33.) Finally, we can never form a completely true idea of a personality because its revelation is itself fragmentary, not integral. " We are all fragments, not only of humanity, but of ourselves."

The growth of personality renders the acceptance of traditional standards less easy, it also obscures these standards themselves. Associations and circles of community are not isolated, so that men can retain clear and distinct principles within each. If, therefore, men seek merely to follow in each sphere of social activity whatever ruling traditions they can still find within it, they lose the unity of life. This is generally realised to-day. As Professor Small says : " Speaking generally, our ethical capital consists of a heterogeneous collection of provincial moralities. . . . By means of them society keeps in motion, but in spite of enormous waste consumed upon the frictions which retard the motion. We have no universal ethical standard to which one class may appeal against another class and get a verdict which the defeated litigant feels bound to accept." (*General Sociology*, p. 657.) It is right that there should be a specific code of ethics for every situation, but the specific code should be an application of the universal code. If the code is limited to securing the interests of the specific class or profession, without consideration of the part that class or profession plays in the whole community, does not the principle come dangerously near to that of " honour among thieves " ?   " What do we more than these ? "

Professor Small uses the following illustration. " Suppose, for example, we are in the midst of a labour conflict. It is proposed to arbitrate the difficulty. Representatives of the conflicting parties meet. A looker-on, if he happen to be a philosopher, soon discovers that the issue cannot be decided on ethical grounds, for the conflicting parties, and perhaps the arbitrating board, have each a different standard of ethics. The employers' ethics are founded upon conceptions of the rights of property. The employees' ethics take as their standard certain conceptions of the rights of labour. The arbitrators' ethics may vary from the lawyer's interpretation of the civil code to the speculative philosopher's conception of the ideal rights of the generic man. There is no common ethical appeal. Neither litigants nor referees can convince the others that they must recognise a paramount standard of right. The decision has to be reached either by resort to force or by a compromise of claims, each of which continues to assert its full title in spite of the pressure of circumstances." (P. 659.)

It is not to be supposed that the codes of different classes or types will ever fully agree, or that the situation dramatised by the author of *Strife* will ever disappear. But the chaos of our ethical standards might well be reduced to some degree of order if we were taught to think in terms of community, if we were taught to realise the universal meaning of the ethical claim upon us, calling to us not merely as members of a class or profession but as finally responsible personalities. Our specific codes are like little land-locked harbours whose mouths have been silted up in the process of time, so that the waters become stagnant. Were the entrance deepened, the stagnant waters would share in the universal and purifying ocean-tide.

There are many social allegiances, and each has its place and its necessity. How this variety may be made consistent with the unity of character is our present problem. It is now obvious that in the differentiation of community the older harmony of the tradition-determined life is destroyed, but it will make the problem so created clearer if we show some of the ways in which during that process the nature and the need of a profounder unity are revealed.

One aspect of the external and uniform character of primitive conduct is the corporate responsibility of group or community, whereby the whole is held accountable for the wrong-doing of any unit, the whole family for the action of any member, the children for the sins of their fathers, and so forth. In the Old Testament the sin of Achan is visited not only upon himself, but also upon his sons and his daughters (*Joshua* vii. 24-6), as the Mosaic law prescribed ; and, similarly, the mediæval church laid its curse not on the offender alone but on all his kin. In the vendetta of barbaric peoples the kin-group avenges the death of the kinsman by slaying

some member of the kin-group to which the slayer belongs.[1]
This sense of corporate responsibility decays as the true
basis of conduct in personality is found. It is only the
primitive mind among ourselves which regards the offence
of a foreigner as somehow the act of the nation to which
he belongs.[2] The reflecting mind can no longer accept
the principle of group-ethics, it demands, as it rests upon,
the self-standingness of every man as an ethical being.
We may recall how the more enlightened ethics of the
Hebrew prophet moved him to protest against the older
code. " The word of the Lord came unto me again,
saying, What mean ye, that ye use this proverb concerning
the land of Israel, saying, The fathers have eaten sour
grapes, and the children's teeth are set on edge ? As I
live, saith the Lord God, ye shall not have occasion any
more to use this proverb in Israel. Behold, all souls are
mine ; as the soul of the father, so also the soul of the son
is mine." [3] The denial of the doctrine of corporate responsibility is, here as elsewhere, the affirmation of the
ethical autonomy of the social being.

This ethical autonomy, we have pointed out, is not
truly opposed to socialisation but only to the reduction
of the person to a uniform social type. This is illustrated by the case of the social genius, the person who,
as it were, cut the steps up which the rest of his society
may learn to climb. No great man conforms to whatever
average standards of thought rule within his society.
His greatness consists in being ahead of these, ahead of
his society in knowledge, in wisdom, in morality, in
religion. In this sense his thoughts are out of conformity

---

[1] Cf. Westermarck, *Moral Ideas*, Vol. I., chap. xx.

[2] Another and very persistent form of the assumption of corporate
responsibility, though scarcely realised by those who act upon it,
is that of sex-responsibility in sex relations, a common source of
misogyny and misandry.

[3] *Ezekiel* xviii. 1-4 ; so also *Jeremiah* xxxi. 29-30.

to those of his society, and that is at once his crucifixion and his greatness. It is why the prophets have been stoned, it is also why the prophets have been willing to endure being stoned. Their society stoned them because they were prophets, but to be a prophet was itself a social function. If it had not been for their deep concern with society, for their socialisation, they never would have been stoned. On the other hand, no man can be great unless his society is *in some measure* fitted for his greatness. A Socrates, Shakespeare, or Kant among South Sea Islanders is inconceivable, and that not merely because the genius is still a member, though exceptional, of his stock and people, but because a genius can no more arise and function in a wholly irresponsive social environment, unsupported by some degree of sympathetic fellowship and understanding, than a living thing can breathe in the void. Genius develops by communication, and communication with oneself is only a metaphor. You cannot even protest your non-conformity except to those who understand your protest. The prophets whom they have raised reflect credit on a people even when they stone the prophets.

Another aspect of the external and uniform character of primitive conduct is the rigorous supersocial sanction attaching to it. This is inevitable where the inner obligation remains undeveloped. Primitive men require supersocial sanctions for social conduct, because the true reason for it, the true necessity of justice, for instance, can appeal only to the autonomous personality. The need for justice, more obvious than the basis of it, created a supersocial sanction. Primitive men are like children who have the intelligence to obey the law but cannot perceive the true reason of the law which they obey. " It is the Law," they say, with the conclusiveness of the animals in the *Jungle Books*.

In the differentiation of community that attitude also passes away. The social meaning of social obligation must be realised before the obligation can itself serve to guide the widened life. The spirit of law-abidingness must rise above the uniformity and externality which characterise all conduct whose purpose is unrevealed. This is another aspect of the emergence of the ethical sentiment. In seeking the reason of the law it transforms the law and discovers an inner sanction for it. The power and the claim of ethical thought is most triumphantly revealed in the transformation of religion. Even though religion continues to provide a sanction for conduct, it is the ethical spirit that is the primary, the transforming power in the creation of that sanction. Religion is brought into harmony with that spirit, for its conception of deity cannot resist the fierce ethical claim of awakened personality.

We may illustrate from the history of the literature of Greece. In the age represented in the Homeric poems few ethical demands are made of the greater gods, and this corresponds to a stage of development in which the external law of social custom rules among men. In Homer there is no true ethical condemnation of the perjurer, the adulterer, the murderer. They are offenders, when they are supposed to offend at all, against the code, the custom of the tribe or city. It is as breakers of the customary law that they are regarded, and it is that law alone which prescribes punishment or retribution, not the outraged heart with its own conviction of the inherent hurtfulness of the offence. But the social status of the heroes of epic places them in a way beyond the reach of customary law, and ethical sentiment has not yet sufficiently advanced to disentangle itself from that law. The conduct of epic heroes is as unquestioned as that of the gods on Olympus, and for the same reason.

They are alike in their degree beyond the operation of
customary law, and the deeper ethical judgment which
goes beyond established law and custom, to transform
them in the end, judging everything in terms of its
inherent rightness or wrongness, has not yet emerged.
On his guilty heroes the poet passes no moral judgment,
but not merely because he is wise enough to perceive
that " poetic justice " may be untrue to life. Odysseus
the murderer, Paris the adulterer, Helen the curse of
men and cities, receive honour and not shame. And
these heroes justify themselves, if they feel the necessity
of justification, in terms of the supersocial sanction, pitting
it against the social need. " Not I but the god in me "
is the excuse of the guilty Helen,[1] just as " Not we but
the gods and heroes " is the boast of the triumphant
Greeks after Salamis,[2] a contrast which reveals the inadequacy of the supersocial sanction. But in the later
poets of Greece the ethical sentiment has awakened, and
they mete out " poetic justice " to the unscathed and
guilty heroes of the earlier epic ; reshaping the old legends
to show that sin from its very nature brings and demands
suffering, that wealth or power will not save him who
" kicks into nothingness the great altar of Justice," that
God will not justify men who " trample on the grace
of holy things." The inevitable conflict that signalises
every process of development is here strikingly illustrated by the story of Stesichorus, the lyric poet of
Himera. In the Homeric story, when the long war is
over, Helen, its guilty cause, is restored to her true
husband Menelaus, lives in honour for many years, and
is fated at the last to pass immortal with Menelaus into

---

[1] *Odyssey*, iv. 261-2 : cf. *Iliad*, iii. 164 *sq.*, and vi. 357.

[2] Herodotus, viii. 109 : cf. Murray, *The Rise of the Greek Epic*,
p. 199. On the whole subject see P. Barth, *Die Frage des sittlichen
Fortschritts der Menschheit* (*Vierteljahrschrift für wissenschaftliche
Philosophie*, vol. xxiii.).

the Elysian fields, becoming a goddess to men. Stesichorus at the end of the seventh century, resenting the lack of ethical justice in the old legend while he accepted the literal truth of the story, in that middle stage of enlightenment inveighed against Helen in the candid speech of moral indignation. The story runs that the impious poet was struck with blindness, whereupon he wrote a " palinode " or recantation, and so received back his sight. Whatever the facts in the life of Stesichorus on which the tale was built, we have here a most interesting glimpse into the transition process in which the ethical judgment fearfully shakes itself free of prescription, of deference to tradition and custom and dogma. In the succession of the Attic tragedians we can observe the ethical judgment still further liberated from that external deference, until in Euripides it is revealed in its own necessity, the fearless and final judge before whose bar every custom and every institution must come, to be justified or condemned according to its ethical worth alone.

The emergence of the ethical sentiment in history is most fully revealed in the conflict of the ethical spirit against the dogmatised ethics of the past. The ethics of the past becomes entrenched in religious forms and is dislodged only after the age-long assault of new ethical claims. For religion can never be separate from ethics, from the social ideal. Religion is the form of an ideal, and in the long run there is but one ideal, an ethical one. If men worship power, that is their ethical ideal ; if they worship beauty, that is their ethical ideal. When a conflict arises between ethics and religion it is in reality a conflict between the ethics of the present and the ethics of the past. This is the great drama of all history, and the history of Christianity might be shown as the greatest act of that drama. Christianity came as the protest of the ethical conscience against the external claim of dogma, the dogma of scribe and Pharisee. It announced for ever the cardinal and inextinguishable ethical principle, the principle of personal responsibility and obligation, the principle that the social individual is the judge and the creator and the redeemer of social claims. It announced that the only value on earth is the value of the " souls " or lives of men, and that systems and creeds are vain and corrupt except as they fulfil these values. It announced that not tribe or nation, not class or station, not sect or school, avails anything, but the men that are born in the race or hold the station or believe the dogma. It announced that the only fulfil- ment and the only reality of empires and principalities and powers are living men. It announced in a word that religion is a life and not a form, and that the true way to serve and love God is to serve and love one's fellows. " Inasmuch as ye did it not to one of the least of these, ye did it not to me." This is the·final principle of all ethics, which refuses to stop at the generality of class and nation, and finds the heart and conscience of particular men. But the church was unequal to the spirit of its message and built greater dogmas in its name. It devised a theological mechanism of salvation out of the very words which breathed the eternal free spirit of ethics. It turned the symbol of the spirit into the shell of the spirit. It found the service of God in the renunciation of the duties and privileges of life. It dis- tinguished offences against God from offences against one's fellows, branding the former phantasmagoric sin as deadly, and counting the latter reality of wrong as venial. It made death more significant than life, and final absolution more potent than the whole conduct of life. It made the acceptance of a creed of more avail than the formation of character. Time and again, often not understanding itself, the ethical spirit has raised its protest, melting the rigid iron of institutionalism in the flame of its indignation. Time and again the institution has rehardened—and it will always continue to reharden until perhaps men learn that the only safety of any institution, and especially of any religious institution, lies in its constant redemption from the letter through its constant subjection to the spirit.

If this ethical claim is dangerous, it is also, we must see, necessary. In the differentiated community the sanctions of the undifferentiated community are simply unavailing. That is proved by their decay. A different unity is necessary for the life of the social being who would be equal to the social opportunities of the co-ordinated community.

All forms of the merely external sanction are subject to the same decay, and therefore it is not possible to solve the problem by leading from one to another. Such a course is sometimes advocated, as in the following passage : " The fact that the weakening of the power of the supernatural sanctions of morality seems to be an inevitable accompaniment of high civilisation, renders the development of the national sentiment a matter of extreme importance ; for in no other way, it would seem, can the great masses of mankind be supplied with motives that will effectively take the place of the motives of personal religion in prompting and sustaining the higher forms of moral effort." [1] But the problem is not adequately put if its solution is conceived in such a form. For it is at least equally characteristic of high civilisation that the *customary* and *national* sanctions of morality progressively diminish—and that for the same reason, because it is the very nature of morality that its sanction must be inner, that you cannot " supply with motives " the developed moral being. His motives are indeed

[1] From an article in the *Sociological Review*, April, 1912.

determined as before by his heredity and environment, but only because these factors determine *him*, his morality being the free expression of his nature so determined. The reason why *merely* supernatural sanctions (wrongly identified in the passage quoted with *all* religious sanctions) fall away is because such a sanction is merely external, like the sanction of tradition, national or other. Their falling away, *if their place be taken by an inner sense of responsibility*, is the witness to the adolescence of social man. Adolescence is a dangerous age. It may be that even the most civilised people has not yet reached the stage where it can trust freely to the guidance of the free ethical sense of its members and can freely criticise its institutions in the light of that morality. But one thing is sure—in so far as in fact the external sanctions fall away and cease to be determinants of men's conduct, it is no use any more herding them back to these, and attempting to supply them with motives. They may attain to a new unity of life—they cannot regain the old.

§ 2. The basis of solution.

All action involves a choice between possible ends of action. If I act at all it is because I choose action before inaction. If I act this way or that, the way I choose is the value I in the moment of action prefer. Even if I act under some overmastering necessity, inner or outer, the menace of death, the imperiousness of passion, the craving for a drug, an alternative is never excluded ; it is still a choice between values. It is not, of course, implied that a man deliberately reckons, or clearly recognises, the alternatives when he acts. Still less is it implied that to choose between values is to choose the greater value. But to act is to choose, to pursue one among alternative ends. Conscious activity is always preferred activity, and all preference is between values.

Every social claim is a demand for the maintenance or the realisation of some value. Every kind of association exists for the pursuit of values, every area of community is held together in that common pursuit. Every interest is in the end a practical interest, determined, that is, by a sense of value.[1] Further, all values are *in practice* comparable. No abstract measuring-rod can be found, but no person can act at all unless he can choose ; the necessities of life and character are necessities of choice. When community differentiates, when social claims are no longer simple but manifold, the necessity of choice is deepened. The widened claim of sociality is an intenser demand on individuality. But the whole social situation implies that values are comparable, that they are forms of a single value. That is the pre-condition of the co-ordination of community, that is also the pre-condition of the unity of life.

No social claim is absolute. It is an estimate of values. No one form of society is adequate to the fulfilment of personality, therefore none has an absolute claim. That belongs to personality alone. There are times when some social claim is so imperative that the individual is called upon to use up his life, to surrender himself wholly to that alone. But that is because though no institution is absolute many are necessary, and when the essential social structure is endangered at any point all within it are called thither peremptorily to its defence. Here as in every other situation a choice among values is offered, and right action, the action which also conserves

---

[1] *Alles Interesse ist zuletzt praktisch* (Kant). Cf. Ratzenhofer, *Die Sociologische Erkenntniss : Abstracte Interessen gibt es nicht ; denn die Abstraction ist gegenüber dem Interessenbegriff ein* contradictio in adjecto ; *der Mensch mit seinem angebornen Interesse ist unfähig, sich interesselos einer Idee hinzugeben, und jedes Interesse wurzelt in letzter Hinsicht in der realen Entwicklung des Individuums, seiner Lebensbedingungen, seines Himmelskörpers, des Universums oder der Urkraft, welche das Leben erhält* (p. 225).

the unity of life, is the choice and pursuit by the social being of the greatest value which he can discover to claim realisation through his conduct. It is of the essence of the distinction between interests and duties that there must always be a choice between interests, but that there can never be a choice between duties ; there can be only one duty where alternative courses of action are open, the pursuit of the highest value the social being is able to conceive within the situation.

A famous case from the ancient world will illustrate this point. Antigone has to choose between two claims, each of which would be a duty were it not an alternative to the other, a religious duty, the fulfilment of the rites of burial due to her brother, and a political duty, obedience to the edict which forbids these rites. The former to Antigone is paramount, the greater value, and in fulfilling it she disobeys the edict of Kreon the king. There is but one duty, therefore, and there is but one tribunal to decide it, the sense of value in the heart of Antigone. Likewise there is but one duty and one tribunal for Kreon, for whom the edict is justified by the treachery of Polyneikes. When Hegel declares : " The meaning of Eternal Justice is shown herein, that both are wrong, because they are one-sided ; but at the same time both are right," [1] this aloof and would-be Olympian utterance defeats itself, offering no solution whatever to the concrete situation. For each of these tragic figures is under a necessity to choose one of two alternatives. Antigone must choose either to obey the edict or, defying it, to fulfil the behests of her religion ; just as Kreon had the choice of permitting or refusing the rites of burial to Polyneikes, and later of exacting or remitting the penalty sanctioning his edict. One of two courses *must* be chosen by each, *one* must therefore be right, not in part but in

[1] *Religionsphilosophie*, II. II. III. c.

whole, for each. Were there ever a situation in which men were given a choice of exclusive alternatives such that the adoption of neither could be absolutely right, such that every choice *must* be wrong, the whole moral universe would be by these alternatives dissolved.

The thought that every possibility of conduct involves wrong as well as right arises from a confused apprehension of the truth that, from the point of view of choice and action, values or goods cannot be wholly harmonised. If I seek one value I must neglect another, nay, I may be able to attain the one only by means that destroy the other. The world is made so. It is a fact over which my present will has no power. It *may* be a condemnation of the world, but it is the justification of the will that follows the greater good. If the world is such that a man cannot dig without cleaving worms, or light a candle without destroying moths, or maintain a State without inflicting loss and suffering on many men, he must still choose one of the alternatives his world provides. The poet may hope

> That not a worm is cloven in vain ;
> That not a moth with vain desire
> Is shrivell'd in a fruitless fire ;

in other words, that the appearance of antagonistic values is illusory. But the antagonism is real and insurmountable for us as ethical agents. The hope of the poet may be vain, but there is a less visionary, if more modest, hope for the sociologist, that of a world where essential values have grown less conflicting and more harmonious.

It is the business of the advocate to show that there are good or evil results of any course of action ; it is the business of the judge to consider whether the total result is more of good than of evil, or more of good and less of evil than any alternative course of action would bring. As social beings we are judges and not advocates. There are arguments against every course of action, against every proposed change of institution for instance —otherwise the change would be already actual ; so there are arguments for every proposed change—otherwise it would never have been proposed. Nothing is justified or condemned because there are reasons for or against it, because it involves some profit or some loss. It is a question of comparative values, the surplus of welfare over hurt, hurt over welfare. Here is the bare formula for the solution of the conflicting social claims of our differentiated social world.

It is easy to exaggerate this conflict, if we consider social claims in the abstract. Within the particular social relations of every personality there is endless choice between interests, but the sense of acute antagonism between their claims is rare. But such situations do arise, rendering it necessary that we should make explicit first the formula of solution and then its application to the particular case.

Every person is a focus of community, and has to reconcile within the unity of his life the claims arising from many social relations. He is never in the strict sense a private member of society, for all activity is relative to social situations. These differ endlessly, not only for different persons, but for the same person, and as they differ so do the calls upon him, his obligations and his rights. His duties as a layman are not his duties as an official, his responsibilities as one in authority differ from his responsibilities as one under authority. But his life has no unity except in so far as he is able to apply a single standard of value to all the diverse situations within which he is called to act. The only universal ethics is that which can be absolutely particularised, and the only being who can ever be truly socialised is he whose ethical individuality is revealed in every social situation.

It follows that in the developed community the main source of law-abidingness is some perception by the great majority of the end or value served thereby. It also follows that in matters of policy affecting the whole of an association or community all important decisions must depend on the will of a majority. Thus only can the claims of personality be reconciled with the necessities of action. It is far from being a perfect way, and we must face presently some of the difficulties which it brings, but there is and there can be no better way. It is also to be remembered that the growth of personality in each which renders the principle necessary involves the growth of the sense of responsibility towards other personalities. It might seem to the superficial observer as if the increase of control, inspection, regulation, under democracy meant a greater abrogation of personality. But it is necessary to weigh liberty against liberty, and then we see that on the whole (whatever criticisms and exceptions we may make) the newer restrictions on liberty are incidental, leaving the essential individuality free, as contrasted with the older restrictions which struck at the very heart of individuality. People cry out that it is the end of personal liberty when they are compelled to attend to their drains or to admit light and air to their factories, or even to educate their children. But what restrictions does the fulfilment of these social duties put upon their spirits ? The unworthiest of all liberties, the furthest from the essential values of life, is the liberty to make or save wealth at the cost of the welfare of one's fellows. Between liberties as between all ends it is a comparison of values. Liberty may be sacred or it may be despicable. Liberty is the final condition of all progress, but the very same name is inscribed on the banners of the blindest and most selfish defenders of unjust privilege old or new.

As community differentiates, the place of force becomes narrowed. Force remains effectual against isolated individuals or small minorities, keeping these law-abiding or at least vindicating against them the law they may have broken. Criminal law necessarily depends on force, the force determined by the will of the great law-abiding majority. But force cannot be effectual against the great and growing non-political associations within community, and it cannot be effectual against the large political groups and oppositions which majority-rule engenders. Here there is no hope for community, and for the State to which it surrenders the right of force, except in the development of the sense of obligation, in the realisation of the greater as against the lesser values alike by other associations and by the State. *The greater the differentiation of community, the greater the need for social education.* It is in the fuller development of personality alone that the dangers can be met which developing personality brings.

The final guide in morals, where there is dispute, must be the conscience of each, the sense which each man owns of right and wrong, of values. Where there is dispute, the claim of a tradition becomes itself a claim of value, and if accepted must be accepted as such, not merely as a tradition or social observance. Doubtless we should be wary of opposing the standards in morals which hold for an age or people, realising that these standards are the growth of long social experience vast and far-reaching beyond our knowledge. Yet these standards live only if they live in us. For we, too, those who assent and those who dissent alike, are the offspring and the inheritors of the past ; we, too, if we are wise enough, may be older in experience than any previous age, since our reason and our conscience are themselves the birth of time. Therefore we can accept tradition only when it is *our* tradition, the tradition that by its nature compels our allegiance. It is no ethical justification of conduct to say that it is " in accord with the spirit of the age," unless the conduct so determined is the best or the only means the age permits of for the fulfilment of ethical ends. To appeal to traditions only because they are traditions is vain, to bid us accept standards that our conscience rejects, merely because they are the standards of others, few or many, or to accept values that contradict the valuations of our intelligence is to solicit us to treachery. That way lies shipwreck. It is not without significance that the greatest of English orators, refusing to admit the right of final judgment that resides in the conscience of each, and bidding men relinquish that for prescription, which is after all but the voice of men's consciences from the past, is at last driven to vindicate the right of prejudice itself, and in that defence is by a nemesis led to speak of moral rights, which in truth express the essential character of human life, as though they were but " pleasing illusions " and draperies to cover the nakedness of life.[1]

Such false views are related to equally false fears. The more the person finds himself the more he finds himself within society, the deeper he enters into the meaning of life the deeper does he strike root in society.[2] There is no opposition between the growth of personality and the security of community, but the reverse. If we

---

[1] Burke, *Reflections on the French Revolution.*

[2] It has been well remarked by Simmel that in antiquity *die Seele ging weder so weit aus sich heraus noch so weit in sich hinein, wie es später durch die Synthese, oder auch Antithese, des christlichen Lebensgefühles mit der moderner Natur- und Geschichtswissenschaft geschehen ist.* (*Soziologie*, p. 758.)

would interpret man and society aright, we must regard as fundamental, not the subordination of the social person, but the maintenance in unity of his sociality and his individuality, not his subjection to society, but his fulfilment within society.

§ 3. Applications of the principle: (1) to a conflict arising from associational claims.

It is clear from what has been said that whenever a conflict arises between social claims, the problem so created falls wholly within the ethical sphere. There cannot under any circumstances be any conflict between an ethical and an economical claim, between an ethical and a political claim, between an ethical claim and the claim of any specific interest whatever. These are all conflicts within ethics, conflicts between values. If the ethical claim is not always and everywhere valid, if any *other* claim can be set against it, the ethical claim itself becomes meaningless. Every association, standing for a specific interest, seeks to advance one form of value, but its claim is relative to the totality of values, never absolute or self-sufficient. No man is a mere " economic man " or a mere " political animal." If he were, ethics would coincide with economics or politics ; since he is not, these latter studies can never justly put forward ideals which conflict with those of ethics, for their ideals can only be aspects of an ethical ideal, subordinate to its unity as realised in the personal and communal life.

Let us illustrate our principle by considering the famous historical opposition which has arisen between the claims of the State and the wider ethical claim, falsely called an opposition between ethics and politics. " It is not, perhaps, the same thing in every case to be a good man and to be a good citizen." (*Ethica Nicomachea*, v. 2. 11.) In this tentative form Aristotle gave expression to a doubt which has often been echoed since his day, alike in philosophic thought and in popular representation. Thinkers and statesmen alike have declared that other than ethical principles *ought* to rule in politics, not recognising the total contradictoriness of such a thesis.[1] To resolve their difficulty, we have clearly to recognise that the political relation is one particular type of social relation. The political claim in not endangered by that recognition, nor its importance and necessity diminished. On the contrary a clear recognition of the claims and services of the State is possible only when its limits also are recognised. Its very definite limits constitute the reverse side of its very definite services, and it cannot fulfil these services unless it observes those limits. The State is *not* " the ethical whole " of the Hegelian doctrine, but a means of realising that " ethical whole." If it seek to be the whole, it is thrusting its externality upon the inner life and thus frustrating its end of protecting and furthering that whole.

There cannot be two opposing *oughts*, one ethical, one political. If life has any meaning, there is always but one *ought*, and the different associational claims are determinants, not absolute expressions, of it.

This conclusion contains the solution of the problem we are considering, but the subject is of such importance, historically at least, that it may be advisable to work out the solution in more detail. There are two forms in which the problem has historically arisen, corresponding to the political distinction between ruler and subject. One, touching the duty of the citizen or subject, may be called the problem of Aristotle, while the other, touching the duty of the ruler or legislator, may be called the

---

[1] Lord Acton, in his introduction to Mr. Burd's edition of Machiavelli's *The Prince*, collected a remarkable number of representative opinions bearing out the above statement.

problem of Machiavelli. The latter may be first disposed of, being more obviously due to a confusion of thought.

Machiavelli sought for the principle by which in an age of corruption a ruler could maintain a united State, and his observation told him it was not by following the recognised principles of ethics but rather by violating these. Hence his famous advice to the prince—" You have to understand this, that a prince, especially a new one, cannot observe all these things for which men are esteemed, being often forced, in order to maintain the State, to act contrary to fidelity, friendship, humanity, and religion." So he boldly declared that right and wrong have nothing to do with government.

The faultiness of this analysis is obvious. The ethics, the right and wrong upon which he turns his back, prescribes law for an abstract being who is a man and yet not a citizen ; his politics dictates to a citizen who is nothing more. Thus his politics by its own false abstractness has given an abstractness to his ethics. Hence a wrong use of abstract terms, and a wrong dilemma. He says, for instance, " Inasmuch as it needs a good man to reorganise the political life of a city, and a bad man to become by violence lord of a republic, it is therefore very rarely found that a good man will desire to acquire rule by bad means, even for a good end,[1] or that a bad one, having acquired rule, will act justly or think of using for good the authority he has won by evil." Strictly speaking, this distinction of good " end " and bad " means " is impossible and meaningless. If goodness or badness is an attribute of will alone, a means cannot in itself, in abstraction, be judged either good or bad. In so far as it is merely means, in so far as the sole reason

---

[1] Cf. the words of Walpole : " No great country was ever saved by good men, because good men will not go the length that may be necessary."

why it is entertained is its causal relation to the end,
so far it cannot be judged as if it stood as end in itself,
but must be regarded in the light of *the* end. So the
question comes to be—Is a certain end such as to justify,
not a *moral* wrong (for if justified it cannot be such :
there is neither here nor elsewhere question of the greater
right set over against the lesser wrong), but a certain
loss of those " goods " which in one way or another
(according to our conception of the moral end) morality
secures ? It is a question not between ethics and politics,
but within ethics, a problem of value, a question to be
answered only in the light of the ethical end, of such a
final standard of value as we are able to set up. Similar
questions arise everywhere in the interweaving relationships involved in the different social activities, and these
are all ethical questions.

For the ruler or statesman the problem seems greater
because the values with which he is concerned are so
great, but it is the universal problem of the comparison
of values. It is impossible to perform a great service
without causing some disservice, to construct a great
good without destroying some lesser good. Sometimes,
especially when community is chaotic and unco-ordinated,
as in the times of Machiavelli, the greater good can be
attained only at heavy cost, but if the good is greater
it is moral weakness to flinch before the cost. There is
no opposition, as Machiavelli thought (and as some of
his commentators still seem to think), between might
and right. Every true cause yokes might to right, every
untrue cause yokes might to wrong. The opposition lies
between right and wrong only, between might and weakness only. Might is an instrument alone, neutral in
itself ; without might there would be no wrong, but,
while wrong exists or is possible, without might there
can be no right.

If we turn next to the side of the subject in the State, another form of the same difficulty presents itself. This form arises ultimately from the fact that political self-government is at best only a partially realised ideal, and that therefore there must be occasions when the law will come as an external command, alien or even antagonistic to the inner principle. The general case is, of course, where the end secured by " loyalty " outweighs in importance the end the law seems to contradict, primarily where disobedience would strike at the security of the State or tend seriously to weaken the habit of law-abidingness so essential to an ordered community. In that case, since the security of the State is indeed the basis of all moral life, since at the least it protects the " life " without which the " good life " is impossible, its claim is paramount. It follows that there is a special obligation to obedience on those who administer, execute, interpret, or enforce the laws, since disobedience on their part strikes a more serious blow to the security of the State and may even involve a kind of treachery, the turning against the supreme or legislative power of the forces which are in the true ordering of the State necessarily subordinate to and dependent on that power. But here again it remains a comparison of values, and it is only out of that conflict of values which is the heart of every moral issue that even this obedience can be established as the *ought*. In a word, it is always " conscience " —or whatever the inner principle of action be called— that is the ultimate court of appeal, even though it err. Because conscience is essentially individual, always, however clarified, a particular *perspective* of the universal, we must always remain at the point of view of the individual, with *his* recognition of a common good.

It is possible to misapprehend this point. It is in no sense an argument for " individualism." The individualism which followed Aristotle did not really solve Aristotle's problem, for while the Aristotelian view seemed to regard man simply as a member of the πόλις, the post-Aristotelian philosophy regarded man simply as an abstract individual, and since the latter being was the greater abstraction of the two, the reaction, as may sometimes happen, represented less the true account. It had not yet become clear that the individuality asserted is a question more of freedom, of spontaneity, in action than of difference in action, that, in fact, the principle of freedom instead of narrowing really widens the area of the common will. The more adequate conception of individuality, the realisation that man is a member of the State and also something more, disposes of the Aristotelian problem by modifying the Aristotelian theory of community. For either the " goodness " of a citizen is not to be regarded solely in the light of State-claims, or else such " goodness " is to be distinguished from true ethical " goodness," and the " good " citizen, like the " good " economist and the " good " churchman, ceases to be identified with the " good " man. But in the latter case, if we talk of " good economist " or " good citizen," we are really using the term " good " in a specialised sense, and no true opposition is logically possible. There is, therefore, no possible conflict between ethics and politics, as if these provided two opposing or even distinct norms of conduct. Even such a question as that of " priority " between the two, elaborately discussed, for example, by Sidgwick,[1] is essentially meaningless.

In conclusion we may indicate, in a word, what real problem underlies the false distinction made between ethics and politics. The inward character of ethical action obviously renders possible an opposition between

[1] *Methods of Ethics*, Book I. chap. ii.

the claim of the State as a whole and the sense of obligation constraining some of its members. We have seen
how obedience even to an alien political end, such obedience being calculated to further the ethical end, may
often remain free or ethical. On the other hand, it is
obvious that cases must arise where the motives inspiring
such obedience cease to bear, where particular conceptions
of the public good refuse to coincide with the State-
conception. This is the real problem—a problem that
does occur, though perhaps rarely—nor, after what has
just been said regarding the nature of ethical action, can
we agree with those thinkers (*e.g.* Plato and Spinoza)
who held that it is in every case the dissentient's duty
to suppress his own conviction in favour of that imposed
by the authority of the State. It is noteworthy that
these philosophers held a purely static view of political
society, whereas perhaps the strongest argument in support of the claim of each to obey his conscience is based
on the developing, progressive character of society. As
a community advances on its way, it must move from
one conception of the end to another. But the recognition of the broader, or the altered, end does not come
as a revelation to a whole community at once. The way
of change is from the smaller to the greater, the recognition moves from a single individual to the whole society.
It operates first at a particular point. It would thus
seem that there are cases where both the antagonistic
views are justified, where the State is justified in suppressing what seems a destructive doctrine, and where
the upholder of it, believing it to mean not destruction
but a better reconstruction, cannot choose but maintain
it. The State must enforce its law, however "con-
scientious" be the objection of the dissentient. The
individual must seek to be loyal to the ethical end, even
when, in rare cases, such loyalty is incompatible with

obedience. Considering the function of the State and its fundamental importance, the cases where disobedience would be the greater loyalty may well be rare, but, considering the difficulty of realising self-government, the cases where obedience finds its ethical justification only in a consideration of the greater as opposed to the lesser good may not be inconsiderable.

§ 4. **Applications of the principle: (2) to a conflict of communal claims.**

We may lastly consider a less determinate but no less real form of social conflict, that between the claims of narrower and wider circles of community. We have seen that in our differentiated world men owe allegiance not to one community only, but to many. When we enter or establish the greater, we do not thereby abolish or abandon the smaller. The primitive tribesman belonged to his tribe alone, the primitive villager to his village alone. *We* are members of a town, of a country, of a kingdom, of an empire, of a civilisation, and must somehow reconcile for ourselves the claims of them all. It is never for us a question of choosing whether we shall belong to one or other, greater or smaller. We must belong to all in some degree, and the only question is " What shall we render to each ? " How shall we live in them all so that we gain the comprehensiveness and liberty of the widest and keep the warmth and strength of the innermost, so that we bring into the greater community a heart animated by the nearer enthusiasms, and retain in the nearer community a mind enlightened by the sanity and justice of the greater ?

That for the member of the co-ordinated community an opposition does arise between nearer and further claims, a very simple illustration will show. Any one who observes the placards issued by newspapers, especi-

ally by evening and provincial papers, will notice that
the framers of them, whose business it is of course to
attract attention, are often divided as to the relative
attractive powers of a small but near event and a distant
but great event.[1] It is because there are two great
springs of the interest we feel in the events of the social
world about us—the nearness of the event and the degree
of intrinsic significance we attach to it. What happens
in our own street or in our own town excites us more
than what happens far away : what happens to a friend
or relative or associate more than what happens to a
stranger. The near event, *ceteris paribus*, is more interesting than the far event. The vaster event, that affecting more people or more permanent interests, is also,
ceteris paribus, the more engrossing. The one measure
of interest, that of nearness, is more emotional, the other,
that of vastness or of intrinsic significance, more intellectual. And the important point is that in our everyday life and thought there is a kind of opposition between
the two claims upon our interest, the nearer and the
wider. We find it hard to comprehend the two. We

---

[1] For instance, I observed during a week or so the corresponding
bills of a particular edition of two evening papers published in the
same town and appealing to the same public. They exhibited the
following contrasts (I call the papers *A* and *B* respectively) :

Oct. 14, 1912. *A*. " Invasion of Servia."
                B. " Heavy Sentence on Local Wife-beater."
Oct. 17, ,,   *A*. " Declaration of Porte. First Naval Battle."
                B. " Prison Experiences of . . . at . . ." (a local convict
                    prison).
Oct. 19, ,,   *A*. " Typhoid in . . ."
                B. " War by Microbe."
                    (*A* referred to a local outbreak, *B* to a supposed
                    outrage in the Balkans.)
Oct. 22, ,,   *A*. " 1600 Greeks killed."
                B. " Murder of English Inspector."

In no case did either bill refer to the event or rumour to which the
other gave prominence.

On a newsbill, issued by a Scotch newspaper, I once observed the
following contrast : At the top, in heavy type, " Strong Language
by Local Bailie," below, in small type, " Great Earthquake in China " !

tend to lose either the near enthusiasm or the wide sympathy.

As there arises a conflict of interests, so there seems to arise a conflict of claims. Many a man is deeply interested in national politics who cares nothing for the affairs of his city ; others are so preoccupied with local interests as to lose sight of their relation to national interests. Thus various spiritual errors beset our social service, parochialism, false " patriotism," empty cosmopolitanism. Many a man professes, and really feels, a deep interest in the welfare of his country who yet gives very little thought to the welfare of his employees, though his power to increase their welfare may be his best lever to improve that of his country. It is only a true recognition of the relation of the narrower to the wider circle which can save us from the perverted service of either, a recognition of the interdependence and ultimate oneness of all social values.

As that recognition grows, the conflict between the claims of the nearer and the wider circle becomes transformed into a certain harmony. The co-ordination of community is the necessary external condition, the recognition of the common meaning of social values is the inner condition, of that transformation. Immanent in us, waiting the appropriate social stimulus, is the spirit of attachment to many degrees of community, from village or town right out to the world of humanity itself. " A peculiarity of the group-sentiments," it has been said, " which renders them powerful to move men in many circumstances is that a man may acquire a hierarchy of such sentiments ; sentiments of attachment to each of the successively wider or more inclusive groups which themselves form a hierarchy. Thus a soldier may share in the group-sentiment of his company, of his regiment, of his army corps, or of his particular branch of the

service, and, at the same time, in that of the army as a
whole. And in a properly organised character the several
sentiments of such a hierarchy are in no sense antagonistic to one another, but rather the sentiment for
each lower group lends whatever strength it has to add
to the strength of the sentiment for the more inclusive
group. For, just as the individual identifies himself and
is identified by others with his group, so each group is
identified by himself and others with the more inclusive
group ; so that the good of the larger becomes for him
at the same time the good of the smaller group, and
vice-versa." [1]

This reconciliation, we must carefully note, is an inner
one, the expression of the unity of life attained by personality in society. There can be no external rule to
reconcile the conflict of claims. No mere rule of pre-
cedence will suffice. This is a truth often forgotten,
especially in the instruction of the young as to their
duties in the now so wide world of community. I may
quote as an example of such instruction the following
advice of Lord Rosebery to some Midlothian Boy Scouts :
" Therefore, boys, remember you are first members of
the Empire, next Scotsmen, and thirdly, Midlothian lads." [2]
But such a mode of reconciliation is too formal and
external to be effectual. What sort of inspiration will
a man find if he bases his social activity primarily on the
fact that he is something which he shares with Australian, Canadian, Indian, and Boer, but not with Frenchman,
American, or Dutchman ? In the near and necessary
life of every day how will that formal priority serve
to guide his relations with his fellow-men, with friend,
kinsman, and townsman ? Our service of the large community must be mainly through our service to the small

[1] Dr. MacDougall, in *The Sociological Review*, April, 1912.
[2] From a speech delivered July 20th, 1912.

community, and we can do so much more, most of us infinitely more, for the small than for the large. In fact, if we *must* have an external order, the order should be reversed, for the richer in content should come first, and to be a Midlothian lad is to be also a Scotsman and a member of the Empire. It is a mistake to regard community in an external way. In space, in externality, the larger circle includes the lesser, but in the world of community it is the near relation which includes the wider. But again, no external priority of any kind will serve as guide to the unity of life. For, finally, every man is more than any of his memberships, and it is only in the unity of his own self that he can find the focus of the thousand social circles wider and narrower. The qualities realised in the small and in the great community are in fact complementary, and so their claims become complementary when men, establishing the co-ordination of community, seek therein the unity of the individual life, bringing each social claim after its kind to that responsive centre. Only when a man has found in himself that unity can he fulfil these many social obligations of our ever more complex world. When a man has found that unity, he cannot help fulfilling them all, for to fulfil them is to be true to himself, and he need no longer measure by external rule the extent of his duty to town and country and empire.

The whole history of society bears out this truth that only at the last and in his full development does the social being find the social focus in himself. To the primitive man the group is all. He finds himself in the group, but he never finds *himself*. He is not a personality, but one of the bearers of a type-personality. He is summed up in the group, the clan or tribe. So it is with the boy, the analogue of primitive man. He need not be bidden to remember that he is first a member of a school or family and then an individual. To his undeveloped mind the group is a circle with no centre, for he can find a centre only when he finds himself. The boy has a passion for uniformity, and regards all divergence from the group-custom—the school-custom or whatever it is—with something of that abhorrence which filled the mind of the primitive tribesman in beholding the violation of his sacred tribal law.[1] More and more, as the boy grows and as the community grows, the centre of initiative and responsibility becomes the individual. So the individual becomes the focus of his own personality, to the enrichment of personality, thus to the enrichment of community.

So the smallest circle is revealed at last as the centre of the greatest. In realising the most intimate society, finally in realising ourselves, we are most realising humanity. It is in the attainment of personality, the progressive union of sociality and individuality, that community is fulfilled, and the law of the small and the law of the large community reconciled. This is no doctrine of egoism but the reverse, for the only enduring self is a focus of social values, and the greater the self, the more social values does it comprehend. Such a reconciling individuality, instead of loosening the bonds of community, makes them strong, for they become conscious inner bonds, imposed by no external power or unreasoning instinct, but revealed as the very fibres of personality, bonds no longer, but essential threads of life.

[1] This is well illustrated by the life of the public school, where the boy has the opportunity of forming a little community of his own. The spirit of Eton, for example, with its rigid customary laws prescribing minute details of clothing and minute forms of observance (even to the side of the street on which a boy must walk), with its taboos and its horror of non-conformity, reminds one strongly of the spirit of the primitive village or tribe. The schoolboy carries something of that spirit into the university, but it dwindles in the widened life.

CHAPTER VI

SECOND LAW OF COMMUNAL DEVELOPMENT: THE CORRELATION OF SOCIALISATION AND COMMUNAL ECONOMY

§1. General statement.

If we compare any two communities which, as measured by the criteria we have already discovered, stand on different levels of culture, we find that the activities pursued by these differ not so much in kind as in the mode of their pursuit and in the relative prominence assigned to each within the life of the whole. The social forms under which interests are pursued, as well as the importance assigned to various types of interest, change as we pass from lower to higher. These changes conform to a certain general principle which we must now set forth.

If we use the term " economy " in the widest sense, to signify the conservation of values not only material but spiritual, the conservation of life itself, the conservation of the means of life, and the conservation of personality or the intrinsic values of life, we may call the principle which these changes reveal *the principle of communal economy*. There is throughout the development of community a constant transformation of social relationships which can be understood only as fulfilling this principle. Many ends of human activity remain unchanging, and must ever so remain, but the way of the attainment of *all* ends is transformed.

Outside society there is no economy and no question of economy. Economy is relative to purpose and intelligence, and can be established only in so far as purpose and intelligence are revealed. As purposive beings we seek ends, but as intelligent beings we seek them in the least wasteful manner—that is the meaning of intelligence. The lower the intelligence the smaller the economy, and the absence of intelligence is necessarily the absence of economy. Nearly all naturalists in these latter days have been struck by the seeming wastefulness of " nature," how " she " produces myriads of seeds in every generation of life for every one that attains fruition, so that the total potentiality of life becomes infinitely greater than the amount conserved and made actual. A single plant or tree of almost any species produces so many fertile seeds that, did they all come to fruition, they would in a few generations cover the whole earth. In a few years of like unimpeded fruition the sea would become solid with fish, and the land would have only standing-room for its multitudes of animals. But this most profuse expenditure cannot be named waste. Waste is needless expenditure, expenditure without return or without the greatest possible return. Nature's expenditure is not superfluous, for only by the multiplication of chances is life conserved in a world in which intelligence has not eliminated chance.[1] The sum of expenditure is necessarily directed not to the development but to the multiplication of life. Whether we say that this very multiplication is itself the work of intelligence, certainly over the multiplied lives chance and not intelligence rules, and only in the multiplication of chances is chance defeated.

There are still some among us who do not perceive that the difference between the expenditure of lower

[1] Cf. Lester Ward, *Psychic Factors of Civilisation*, chap. xxxiii.

nature and the economy of man is due to the absence of intelligence in the one and its presence in the other. They even bid us turn and follow the methods of lower nature. This is mere atavism. When you have a calculating machine, it is waste of time to go through the ordinary processes of addition and subtraction; without the machine it is not waste. Where you have mind it is waste to employ the ordinary methods of nature; without mind, in nature itself, it is not waste. Those who bid us " follow nature " are bidding us throw aside our calculating machines.[1]

In the degree in which society comes into being, a method other than that of the multiplication of chances is introduced. For society is the first creation of intelligence. As soon as society reveals itself, the excess of reproduction over survival diminishes, and it continues to diminish in the degree of the development of society. In the animal world the higher animals, at once the most intelligent and the most social,[2] are remotest from the amazing fertility of herring and cod. Within human communities the same general principle holds; birth-rate and survival-rate approximate more and more as we pass from the most savage to the most civilised. Here is the primary economy revealed in society, that economy of the stuff of life which is the saving of energy for life's development.

Could we regard this primary economy as a sufficient criterion of development, there would fall to be recorded a vast communal advance within recent history. It is recorded that in London in the year 1730 there were

---

[1] We may note in passing that the " waste " of nature serves man's ends in many ways, making his food-supply easy, giving him a remarkable control over nature and power of experiment. The " waste " of nature is thus a means to the economy of man, but the waste within human life is a means to no end whatever.

[2] To be social is not necessarily to be gregarious.

17,118 births, and that in the same year 10,368 children
under two years of age died, an infant mortality-rate
representing nearly two-thirds of the total birth-rate.[1]
Before the end of the nineteenth century the ratio had
fallen from two-thirds to one-fifth. In the twentieth
century the economy of life has advanced at a yet faster
rate, not in any automatic way, but through the purposive co-operation of a more enlightened people. The
following extract from the latest published (1912) Annual
Report of the Registrar-General of Births, Deaths, and
Marriages in England and Wales [2] reveals strikingly this
truth. " Of the 486,939 deaths registered during the year
in England and Wales, 82,779, or 17·0 per cent., were
those of infants under one year of age, corresponding
to a mortality-rate of 95 per 1000 births. This rate was
30 per 1000 births, or 24 per cent. below the average in
the preceding ten years, and 23 per 1000 births, or 19
per cent. below that of 1906-10. It was the lowest rate
on record, being 10 per 1000 births below the lowest rate
previously recorded, that for the year 1910, while during
the nineteenth century the proportion of deaths had never
been lower than 130 per 1000 births. These facts illustrate the rapidity with which infant mortality has fallen
in recent years in this as well as in most other European
countries." These figures have a vast significance if we
have the imagination to interpret them into terms of
human health and human happiness. Nor is there any
reason to suppose the limit of progress has been reached.
It has been stated by a competent doctor [3] that 60,000
lives of infants could in this country every year be saved,
and there is still a vast loss of ante-natal as well as post-
natal life due to mere parental unenlightenment.

[1] These figures are quoted from De Greef, *Le Transformisme Social,*
p. 405.

[2] Cd. 7028.   [3] Dr. Elizabeth Sloan Chesser.

We may note in passing that this primary form of social economy affords a progressive resolution of that opposition between perpetuation and individuation on which Herbert Spencer laid such stress. The opposition only arises as the individual life realises its own worth, and the conditions which create it break it down again. The lower creatures devote to reproduction all the energies not expended in the sustenance of their own lives. The plant lavishes its strength first on the flower-stalk, then on the ripening of the seed. The life of the animal is largely determined by the special necessities which the reproduction of its species involves. But we cannot say that in these cases there is any opposition between reproduction and individuation, for that has meaning only where these are offered as alternative ends. It is only where life wakes to clear self-consciousness that such an opposition can arise, and concomitant with that clear self-consciousness is a social economy which breaks down such opposition. Where the excess of reproduction over survival is reduced to a minimum, reproduction and individuation cease to be alternatives for social beings in general. Special circumstances may indeed create an accidental opposition, but these special circumstances nearly always mean an imperfect social economy of another kind, poverty and inequitable distribution of the means of life, and are not due to any proper opposition between the claims of individuality and the necessities of reproduction. For, as the sheer waste of life is diminished, the reproduction of life fulfils the individuality of the parent-lives, the compensations of parenthood vastly outweigh the burdens which it imposes, and the sex-society becomes from every point of view a form of life's fulfilment.

In so far as a lower birth-rate is due to a lower death-rate it is sheer gain. It means, on the one side, the better upbringing of the children, an increase in the quality and the standard of life ; on the other, the deliverance of the parents from unavailing care and toil. As the parents are able to devote themselves to the betterment, as distinct from the mere sustenance, of offspring, they find in that devotion a means to their own greater happiness. The mother, in especial, through the limitation of the mere necessities of reproduction made possible by the greater protection of young life, is saved from becoming the mere drudge-servant of the race, and serves the future the more as she ceases to serve it at the cost of the present. If there is not complete harmony, there are yet infinite possibilities of harmony between the needs of each generation and the needs of the race.

It should be noted that we are here concerned simply with the relation of birth-rate to survival-rate. The raising of the survival-rate has without doubt a correlation with the lowering of the birth-rate, and it is in that aspect only that we have here considered the birth-rate. But many other questions arise in connection with this development, and some of these will demand our consideration presently.

The primary economy just described is but one form of order within the vast system of social economy. The meaning of society lies in the purposive relations of social beings. Society is therefore meaningless, or more strictly non-existent, except in so far as men are conjoined in efforts for the preservation of values, except in so far as its members, by the union of will and intelligence, raise themselves above the non-economical ways of lower nature. Economy in this wide sense is a necessary aspect of all society. There *is* society only in so far as

All, as in some piece of art,
Is toil co-operant to an end.

This economy develops wherever society develops. It is the stimulus of that progressive transformation of social activities which we are next to describe.

§ 2. The economic significance of the formation of secondary common interests.

In our analysis of community we discussed the various ways in which will may be related to will and interest to interest. We saw that there were two great classes of interests, designated discrete and common, and that one kind of discrete interests, designated like interests, had in especial to be distinguished from common interests. The results of that earlier analysis, and the meanings attached to the various terms in our analysis, must be kept in mind in what now follows.[1] We are to consider a progressive transformation of the modes by which men pursue *like* interests, *i.e.* interests in the attainment of the same or similar objects, material or other, regarded not as a common or comprehensive good but pursued as the separate or discrete good of the several *units* who pursue them.   In the earlier analysis we regarded, for simplicity's sake, the single person as the unit in question We may now add that for the relations between associations or groups the same terminology holds.   Thus when each of a number of associations or communities pursues as a separate or discrete unit an interest like or identical *in type* to that which every other pursues, we may call the interests they severally pursue *like* interests.   Within the unit there is then a common interest, but as between the units we have like interests only.   We shall find that the formula of transformation can be expressed as follows :
The development of community involves the gradual transformation of conflicting and parallel like interests into con-

[1] See pp. 99-105.

cordant like interests through the establishment of secondary common interests. And we shall find that this formula is one particular expression of the general law of communal economy.

If we consider the ways in which men or communities can pursue their several like interests, they will be found to fall under the following heads :

A. *The method of direct antagonism.* Under this fall all relationships in which the activity of one individual or group is directed to cripple or destroy the activity of another individual or group. The perfect type of this method is war, involving the reciprocal destruction of a portion of the active manhood of communities. In all direct antagonism effort is destructive of effort, not constructive of something beyond the struggle. We are in the region of purely conflicting interests, or rather of interests regarded as such, and no common interest is recognised.

B. *The method of isolation.* This is the absence of all relationship between individuals or groups in the pursuit of their like interests. We are in the region of parallel interests, and here also common interest is wholly absent.

C. *The method of competition.* Under this heading come all relationships in which it is primarily ends and not means or activities which are opposed. Here the success of one individual or group in part or in whole thwarts the success of other individuals or groups. It is distinguished from the method of direct antagonism because it involves an ordered system within which the conflict falls. There is community beyond the opposition of interests. Beyond it there stretch the wider common interests of town and country, of class and party and the inclusive State, of church or other cultural association. There is opposition in respect of one particular interest, not of all interests. In direct antagonism the opposition is absolute, in competition it is partial. Hence the essential difference of the two methods. When men run a race, they do not trip up one another. When merchants compete, they do not endeavour directly to prevent one another from offering and selling their goods, they do not destroy one another's goods, still less one another's lives. Because the opposition falls within community, it is subordinate to common interest. Here we may perhaps make a further distinction. If in respect of the particular interest they pursue by way of competition men recognise no community, but only in respect of further interests, then competition is pure or unmodified. If even in this sphere they realise some degree of common interest, then competition is modified. It is so modified when, for instance, competitive merchants yet make common cause in seeking to advance the status of their occupation, when they make certain agreements in respect of selling prices and so forth, when they unite to secure more favourable terms from manufacturers. Practically all competition is to-day thus modified. Especially in the professions is the edge of competition blunted by the clear recognition of important common interests within the actual sphere of competition. In pure competition the interest in question is wholly conflicting, in modified competition it is partly conflicting and partly concordant. In the latter case a secondary common interest is already established, but being, perhaps necessarily, imperfect, it does not involve the co-operative pursuit of the interest, it only limits competition.

D. *The method of co-operation.* Under this heading come all relationships in which the activity and success of one directly furthers the activity and success of others. In so far as co-operation exists, the like interests of men or groups of men have become concordant. Thus it differs from the method of direct antagonism, according to which like interests are treated as purely conflicting, and from the method of competition, under which some like interest remains at least partially conflicting. Wherever the method of co-operation is established, a secondary common interest (if no more) has been created which renders some like interest concordant. So men pursue directly the general or common interest, the success, say, of a trading company, and find therein the fulfilment of their particular like interests.

Within this sphere we may distinguish two types of co-operation, which may be called (a) partial and (b) complete. When men barter or exchange goods, when one buys and another sells, when one renders some service in return for the service rendered by another, there is a certain degree of co-operation involved, for the activity and success of the one contributes to the activity and success of the other But only in part, for there remains an opposition of ends. There is a gain on the whole transaction or it would not take place, there is therefore co-operation and common interest ; but the cheaper the buying the less (within limits) the gain of the selling, and the more valuable the service the more (within limits) its cost, thus there remains a conflict of interests. The interests of buying and selling, of demand and supply, the interests involved in all exchange of services, are complementary, but only up to a certain point. They, therefore, create secondary common interests, but not such as to make like interests wholly concordant. For this reason this form of co-operation must be distinguished from complete co-operation.

We may now set out summarily the ways in which like interests can be pursued, as follows :

A. *The method of direct antagonism.* (Interests conflicting, no common interest.)

B. *The method of isolation.* (Interests parallel, no common interest.)

C. *The method of competition.* (a) *Pure competition.* (Specific interest conflicting, wider interests common.)

(b) *Modified competition.* (Specific interest partly conflicting, partly concordant ; wider interests common.)

D. *The method of co-operation.* (a) *Partial co-operation.* (Specific interest complementary, hence partial common interest.)

(b) *Complete co-operation.* (Specific interest common.)

It will be observed that the modes of the pursuit of like interests set forth above are arranged in a certain order, according to the absence or presence of common interest, and in the latter event according to the degree in which common interest is present. Both in direct antagonism and in isolation there is no common interest established, but in the former case the relationship of activities is the direct opposite of that relationship which corresponds to common interest. It destroys the potentiality of common interest, whereas isolation merely fails to realise it. Hence direct antagonism stands at one end, and complete co-operation at the other.

We have now to show, what indeed requires little demonstration, that the order so expressed is also the order of increasing economy, and finally that the development of community means a gradual substitution of the more economical for the less economical form of relationship. The more a common interest is established, the more is society established, and every increase in society is an increase in economy.

It is obvious, at any rate if we look at the whole situation and do not narrow our gaze to either side alone, that the method of direct antagonism, the method which destroys potential common interests, is of all methods of attaining ends the most wasteful. It is the nullifying of activity by activity, not only such that the success of one side must be won through the failure of the other, but also such that there is necessarily a nett loss within the whole field of interests. It is a method of attaining one value through the destruction of other values. This is the economic condemnation of war, and it applies in particular to warfare between peoples at similar cultural levels. For in these circumstances an alternative method is always possible, and it is in these circumstances also that war is most truly war, the equal clash of forces and not the mere overwhelming of the inferior by the superior. The method of direct antagonism, unlike every other method of pursuing interests, is destructive only. Competition, though it involves opposition, is a stimulus to creative activity, for it is the pursuit of ends beyond the struggle. Success in competition, though it means the comparative failure of others, means also doing better than others in some constructive way, manufacturing better, selling better, understanding better what the public wants. Even if it mean only advertising better, it is still the means of satisfying interests, something created or constructed, that men advertise. The activity of each competitor is free, the direct pursuit of ends, not the nullifying of their pursuit by others. There is thus on the whole nett gain, as opposed to the nett loss of war. Further, in estimating the total result of direct antagonism, we must include the waste involved in the preparation for it, a waste that becomes greater in proportion to the civilisation attained by communities. It is the same kind of energy, of skill, and of sacrifice which produces the agencies alike of destruction and of construction, and so far as both men and means are devoted to the one they are lost to the other. It is the same social beings who practise the destructive art of war and the constructive arts of peace, and so far as they are devoted to the former they are lost to the latter. In all preparation for antagonistic activity there is therefore a twofold loss, and this form of waste, though not to be compared with the waste of war, itself constitutes at the present time an enormous and wholly unprecedented drain on the resources of our civilisation.   It is due to a failure or absence of society, the absence of established intercommunity between States.

Closely connected historically with the method of direct antagonism, and in many cases both the cause and the effect of that method, is the method of isolation, the isolation of groups or communities. This comes next in the order of economy.   Mere isolation neither destroys nor realises the potentialities of common interest.   It means the waste of values through the failure to establish common interests.   There is no loss of present values, but there is a vast loss of potential values.   All the advantages of co-operation are lost, and the extent of that waste is measured only when we count the gains of co-operation.   To illustrate, over large parts of India, until quite recently, the small villages among which the greater part of the population is scattered remained almost completely isolated from one another, although separated often only by a mile or two.   The economic isolation of each district was thus extreme.   When there was an abundant harvest, the district did not export, when there was a failure, it could not import ; in the one case wasteful plenty, in the other needless penury. The establishment of communication has checked both forms of waste, given a new stability to social life, created new forms of industry, new specialisation, and consequently new resources.[1]   Isolation always means waste, for community always means economy.

The economic advantage of competition over direct antagonism and over isolation has already been indicated, and is in fact so obvious as to require no exposition.

[1] Cf. Lt.-Col. E. Roberts, in *The Sociological Review*, Vol. II.

But one point is worthy of special notice. The method of antagonism is appropriate only when the interests pursued by different individuals or groups are conflicting in their entirety. Now interests are conflicting in their entirety when they are directed towards an exclusive object such as is incapable of increase or development through co-operation. There is only one material object which fulfils that condition, *i.e.* land, for all other objects may be to some degree increased (or, in the last resort, replaced by substitutes) through the co-operation of men. Further, the one object which human ingenuity cannot increase is itself the source of the multitude of objects which human co-operation does progressively increase. Again, non-material exclusive objects, such as distinctions and offices, fall within a social order which makes their pursuit by the method of direct antagonism meaningless. Hence the only form of opposition which is in general justified by the objective nature of interests is the competitive form, under which opposition is partial only and relative to an inclusive community. Because material objects are exclusive, the element of competition must always remain, but because they are expansive, the method of co-operation must increase until the limit of co-operative benefit is reached. Now every increase of intelligence, as will appear in the next section, places that limit further back, and makes the method of co-operation more and more an alternative to the direct forms of competition.

Where the two methods are in fact alternative, the method of co-operation is necessarily the more economical. The social process since the first establishment of industrialism is one long proof of that statement. Since under co-operation ends are not directly opposed, a great waste of effort is avoided. There is no longer the exhaustion of strength on that indirect countering of effort by effort which corresponds to the direct collision of activity in war. There is less of that social friction which, like mechanical friction, impedes the progress of the whole and wears its parts. Competition undoubtedly tends to develop certain anti-social qualities, particularly deception and ill-will, while co-operation tends to develop the contrary social qualities. Finally, and this is the decisive consideration, free competition involves the exploitation of all who are inferior *as competitors*, although the well-being of these may have vital importance for the whole community. In this class must be included not only women and children—whose exploitation in industrial competition, now mitigated in most countries though far from absent in any, has inflicted grave harm on the common welfare—but also all workers of every condition who, owing to the stress of competition, are compelled to excessive periods of work or to excessive application, or who are subject to the wearing anxiety of irregular employment, or who receive a return for their labour inadequate to the demands of healthy existence. Such conditions induce that chronic depression and fatigue which really means a poisoning of the whole organism, and which, as it develops, reduces not only industrial efficiency but every wider value of life.

To sum up, direct antagonism is appropriate only where interests are entirely conflicting, and wherever society exists, interests cease to be entirely conflicting ; competition is appropriate where interests remain partly conflicting though partly concordant, and all development of society, involving the development of intelligence and of constructive power, makes interests more concordant and less conflicting ; co-operation is appropriate in so far as like interests are or can be made concordant. It is to be remembered that we are considering here *like* interests only. The primary common interests, not being exclusive, can be effectively pursued only by means of co-operation. Strictly speaking, one scientist cannot compete with another in the pursuit of scientific research, but only in respect of incidental distinctions, and one patriot cannot compete with another in the service of his country, but only in respect of incidental distinctions ; in so far as men are scientists or patriots or seekers after religion or any other inclusive end, they cannot compete.

The whole of the above argument may be granted and still an objection be raised against the conclusion. For, it may be and often is said, there are values to be considered other than those directly sought for through antagonism and competition, further values which these methods themselves bring into being. It is true that war and competition are wasteful in respect of the immediate interests concerned, but are they not the means, " Nature's " means, to unsought gains, to values undreamed of by combatants and competitors ? Is not war the spring of national unity, the great stimulus to effective solidarity ? Is not competition similarly an incentive to the activity of individuals and groups, a spur to inventiveness and industry, so that the whole gains through the competing activities of its members ? If these further values are served by war and competition, the order of economy established by the narrower argument may not be the true order after all, for there is loss as well as gain in the substitution of the method of co-operation.

This objection is seen to be a false one, if we understand *why*, with the growth of culture, the methods of direct antagonism, competition, and co-operation become in reality alternative, and why the order of preference, when they become alternative, corresponds to the order of economy. The change is one aspect of that supersession of blind by conscious forces which marks the development of mind. Every living thing that is to maintain or improve its place in the order of life must have such a stimulus, extrinsic or intrinsic, as will spur it to constant endeavour. Where the intrinsic stimulus is weak or absent, the extrinsic stimulus must be strong, but where the intrinsic stimulus is strong, it proves infinitely more effective than the extrinsic.

All life is warfare, it is said, and all history but the record of warfare, but we must see, if we have eyes to trace the broader movements, that in the course of it new forms of conflict arise as substitutes for the old. Through conflict all things grow strong, but there are many forms of conflict. Intelligence brings ever less wasteful forms. The spasmodic conflict of war, that begins in hatred and fever and clamour, and ends in revulsion and the counting up of loss, becomes super-fluous as a stimulus when men enter into the endless and fruitful struggle involved in the mastery of environment and the conquest of essential evils. Apart from other considerations, the latter provides a better stimulus than the former. For war, from its destructive nature, can spur a people only to occasional endeavour. Where war is the chief stimulus to solidarity, its necessary intervals are full of danger. It is the warrior who, away from war, becomes luxurious and degenerate, it is the war-sustained people which, when it ceases to fight, falls into decadence, simply because the more persistent stimuli involved in constructive effort cannot so effec-tively appeal to these.

The end is life, not the struggle for life. It is life, life's maintenance, increase, fulfilment, that we will ; we must not make any of the means to it an end, thereby rejecting other and perhaps better means. If war the divider itself heal division, shall we call it good in dividing or in uniting ? If in uniting, must not war be evil in that it also divides ?   What absolute claim can so broken an instrument make on that intelligence which, as it grows, finds ever new means and forms of unity ?   What is true of the relations of individuals is true of the relations of their communities : in both alike, as the next chapter will more fully show, the more the struggle is a struggle for life, a direct struggle of living thing *against* living thing, the less is life itself fulfilled ; the more each is set against each, the less does the inclusive whole attain ; the greater the energy expended in extrinsic conflict, the more does society become an exchange of losses instead of the exchange of gains.

Competition, it is said, works a further unintended good.   " Countless times it fulfils that service which besides itself love alone fulfils, for it discerns the inmost wishes of another before they have become conscious even to himself."   (Simmel, *Soziologie*, p. 286.)   It is claimed that in all competition the rest of the community is a *tertius gaudens* blessed in the service which the competitors render, not because they seek to serve the community, but because they are competing for the rewards which service brings.   But this further value, so far as it is real, cannot count for so much as to reverse the order of economy already set out.   For, in the first place, the gain of the public is diminished in that it must pay somehow the cost of competition, the cost of the multiplication of activities, agencies, machinery, and so forth, which it involves.   It is diminished also in that the measure of success in competition need not coincide with the quality of the service rendered, but may depend much more on the effective employment of the competitive methods themselves.   Again, no properly organised co-operation does away with the incentives to effort which competition possesses, for such co-operation is capable of enhancing the rewards of service.   It is an outworn fallacy that co-operation must mean the slackening of activity and the equalising of rewards. Finally, in so far as competition benefits the third party at the expense of the competitors, they are competing to their own hurt. But this *sic vos non vobis* does not appeal to any intelligent beings, and competitors in the degree of their intelligence seek to diminish it, organising themselves to renounce the wasteful elements in competition ; in other words, to limit or even abandon competition. Hence agreements in respect of selling prices and rebates, hence rings, amalgamations, cartels, and trusts of every kind, so that the end of competition is monopoly. True, it may be said, but this monopoly is one of the evils of co-operation. But, we must answer, if it bring loss to those outside the co-operation, it is because it brings gain to those within it. And further, it is only by corresponding co-operation on the other side, say by a co-operation of consumers over against the co-operation of producers, or by a wider co-operation still, say by the concerted action of the State, that these evils can be met. Many questions are here involved, which obviously cannot be discussed within our limits, but enough may have been said to show that the order of social economy already established is not reversed when we take account of the further values involved.

Economy, the utilisation of means for the conservation and increase of values according to their kind, is a necessary consequence (as well as a cause) of socialisation. It must follow, therefore, if we remember the relation of socialisation to personality, that where men are most autonomous, most prosperous, and most intelligent, there the less economic ways of pursuing like interests are most relinquished in favour of the more economic ; in a word, that where men are most advanced, they are least isolated in small groups, they compete more readily than they fight, and they co-operate more than they compete. Every page of history will illustrate this law. To trace the growth of community from the dim origins of "Cyclopean" family-community, through primitive clan and tribe and horde, through isolated or semi-isolated communistic village, through warring city-community and badly integrated empire, through feudal confusion on to the close-knit social life of modern Western States, is to follow the process, indirect, indeterminate, broken, yet victorious, by which human life has been reclaimed from the waste as the principle of co-operation has more and more become active within it. Isolation is broken down wherever culture develops. As intelligence grows, the impediments in the way of good life found in geographical differences and spatial barriers become less and less, and the services rendered by these differences become greater. As intelligence grows, it discovers the means and the utilities of intercommunication of every kind. Money-currency succeeds kind-currency, and on the new basis a vast international banking system comes into being. Men learn to exchange not only material goods, but also those cultural gains the exchange of which involves no loss of that which is given in return for what is taken. The most advanced peoples carry the principle the farthest. In England, France, and Germany there is a degree of social co-operation unknown to Spain or Turkey. The most advanced periods are periods of the greatest social co-operation. Lastly, the most advanced classes of a community always co-operate the most—lawyers, doctors, and parsons do not advertise, and do not " cut " prices against one another. It is said that the modern world is pre-eminently an age of competition, but, as an eminent economist has pointed out, this statement has certain false implications, the real characteristic of the modern industrial world being, not competition, but the self-reliance, independence of judgment, and deliberate forethought which characterise its members.[1] It is true that the first age of industrialism introduced new forms of competition, but we have to remember that on the other side it enlarged the competitive unit, substituting in many instances the factory for the home, and thus increased the range of co-operation as well. Further, the increase of competition which it involved is now generally admitted to have been an evil rather than a good, and the classes who specially suffered by it, the working classes, are now, in their turn, as they become more educated socially, defeating these evils by their own co-operation. Thus the test of experience, here for its vastness merely indicated, is conclusive. The law of success is the law of co-operation. Man to succeed must subjugate nature, the whole world of laws that hold outside his purposes, not by opposing or breaking these laws, which he is powerless to do, but by bringing them into his service. And the greatest means employed by mind in that transformation is co-operative service.

We have in this section been considering how the discrete interests of men, the interests determining every man in the maintenance of his own life and the satisfaction of his own needs, the *distributive* interests in earning bread, finding shelter and comforts, pursuing personal advantage generally, are affected as to the mode of their pursuit by the progress of community. It is these like interests, unharmonised, that in our still primitive world of civilisation create endless chasms within the unity of the common life, and it is the progressive harmonisation of these like interests that most clearly

[1] Marshall, *Principles of Economics* (6th ed.), p. 5 ff.

reveals the immense potencies of community. The mode
of harmonisation we have now seen ; it is the creation
of secondary common interests wherein men unite to
pursue their like interests, so rendering them concordant.
It is a mode not only of harmonisation but of economy,
and is thus a particular case of the general principle that
the development of society is the development of social
economy.

We may now turn to consider the way in which the
pursuit of interests already established as common,
whether secondary or primary, is transformed in accordance with the same general law.

§ 3. The economic significance of the development of secondary common interests.

Economy or efficiency in the pursuit of interests is
relative not alone to the extent or area of socialisation but
also to its character and degree. Thus the development
of community is a process not only of the formation of
common interests but also of their transformation. As
men grow in intelligence they increasingly pursue common
interests, but they pursue these in changing ways. Here,
again, the correlation of economy and society is revealed.
For the transformation of common interests instituted
by the growing intelligence of men means at the same
time a higher degree of socialisation and a higher degree
of economy.

What are the factors, we must first enquire, which
determine the degree of success of any association ? We
have seen that the increase in extent of an association,
the increase in the number of those who share a common
interest, is an increase in economy *in so far as* it means
the co-operation of those who were previously antagonistic or competitive. We cannot, however, infer that
every increase in numbers is an *absolute* advantage, that

the larger the association the greater its absolute economy and efficiency. This is true only under certain limitations which cannot here be discussed, but we may say at least that every increase of the other factors determining success makes it possible also for a greater number to associate to the absolute advantage of them all. This will be evident if we reflect on the character of these other factors. They fall into three classes, which may be distinguished as psychical, institutional, and material. By psychical factors I mean (1) the strength, persistence, and unity of the common will relative to the interest, (2) the degree of intelligence which directs the common activity so inspired, and (3) the authority and prestige with which, for whatever reason, the association is invested. Intelligence and authority form the subjective means which both shape the institutional conditions of success, and develop and utilise the material conditions. Intelligence above all is the primary means which adapts to the needs of the intelligent being both the institutional order and the external world, the inner and outer environments in and through which it works and lives.

The institutional factors of success we must presently discuss more in detail. It is obvious that certain forms of social co-ordination and organisation are more advantageous than others, and it is the differentia of the more advantageous forms which we are seeking.

The material factors of success consist of all material resources regarded as and employed as agents of production, as means. These are summed up by economists under the terms " land " and " capital." For our special purpose it may be well to add " machinery " as a further category, or, at least, to insist on its peculiar character as a form of capital. Intelligence develops all material resources, but it does more than develop, it constructs machinery. Thus intelligence not only utilises the " gifts of nature," not only develops the environmental conditions favourable to success, it *creates* two forms of order for its purposes, an inner and an outer mechanism, the institution and the material machine.

It is important to note that all these factors are in some way interdependent. Intelligence, the primary and creative factor, is itself dependent for its growth and manifestation on appropriate environmental conditions. It is the same intelligence which both creates the inner or institutional environment and transforms the outer or physical environment. Again, it is through institutional means that intelligence is enabled to transform so completely this outer world. Finally, the discovery and utilisation of mechanical means involve a transformation of the social order.

Our special object is to show that all institutional changes towards increased economy, towards the greater conservation and completer attainment of values, are changes involving a deepened and developed socialisation. If we can show this to be the case it will be evident, in view of the interdependence of all the factors of economy, that any increase whatever in social economy, or, in other words, every increase in the success wherewith men pursue their common interests, means a further development of community itself.

The chief institutional factors which determine success are obvious. It is obvious that the greater the ease of communication between those united by a common interest, the more effective will their pursuit of it be. The machinery of communication belongs itself to the material means, but the effective concentration which it makes possible is an institutional factor. If, for instance, there are ten thousand lovers of music scattered through a country and forming an association, they will constitute a less successful association than if they were united within a single great city.   Their organisation will be different, less " economical," less effective.   It is again obvious that the general co-ordination of the community within which an association falls is a factor in the success of the latter.   If, for instance, an association of scientists pursues its interest in a country where there is hostility displayed against science, say by a powerful church, it will be less successful than where the general advance of culture provides for it a congenial community.   Once more, it is obvious to every one to-day that the division and the sub-division of labour is, at any rate up to a certain point, a factor in economy.   When the pursuit of a common interest is so organised that each worker or group of workers performs unlike and specialised operations, the organisation so constituted is a factor in economy.

The division of labour forms a test case for our purpose. It is clear that the other institutional factors to which we have referred are dependent on the progress of social-isation, but it has often been asserted that the division of labour means the division of society as well.   If it were true it would be the complete refutation of our general principle.   For division of labour is the most striking characteristic of all economic development.   It has been continuously advancing since the very beginning of civilisation, and has received a vast impetus with the coming of a mechanical and industrial age.   It is also a process which is confined to no sphere of human activity, but prevails within them all, being as necessary to the successful pursuit of cultural interests as it is within the strictly economic sphere.

It is objected that this vast and seemingly endless process destroys the earlier unity of communal life, that the specialisation of interests narrows the common ground on which the members of a community can meet.   It is also objected that the division of labour, perfected as it is through mechanical developments, renders the work of men also more mechanical, narrower, and more monotonous. If these objections are sustained, then the development of social economy is not necessarily in every case a process of socialisation, the development of society itself.

The former objection has been so completely met by M. Durkheim in his study of the social consequences of the division of labour,[1] that it is perhaps sufficient merely to refer to that remarkable work. In a word, M. Durkheim shows that the division of labour creates a new kind of social solidarity, which he distinguishes as " organic " in opposition to the " mechanical " solidarity characteristic of more primitive life. The one is based on likeness alone, the other is built on reciprocities involving unlikenesses. The one is relative to the absence of individuality, the other exists only through the development of individuality. It is, indeed, obvious that the more considerable the division of labour the more interdependent men become, each being dependent in new and more complex ways on the whole of which he is a member, and on the variant activities of many groups and associations within that whole. It is not, we must insist, on differences alone that the division of labour depends. Unless unity underlies differences, there is no division of labour, for division of labour and co-operation are two names for a single fact (or two aspects of a single fact), and if men co-operate it is in view of common interests, to which their differences must be both subsidiary and subservient. Men never, consciously at least, co-operate, like the parts of a machine, to effect some result whose attainment serves themselves in nothing, as means to an end in no wise their own. If they fulfil an end beyond

[1] *Division du Travail Social.*

themselves, they fulfil it in fulfilling themselves. This
is why the relation of men, in their pursuit of variant
activities is incomparable with the relation between the
parts of a machine. Dr. Bosanquet has suggested, with
perhaps conscious humour, that, " If minds were visible,
as bodies are . . . they would not look like similar
repeated units, but rather each would appear as a member
of a mechanism pointing beyond itself and unintelligible
apart from others—one like a wheel, another like a piston,
and a third, perhaps like steam." [1] On the contrary, if
minds were visible, they would be just as like and just
as unlike as the bodies are by which they manifest themselves. It is unnecessary at this stage to repudiate the
suggestion that community is mere mechanism. Men
do not, even in respect of their specific functions in the
sphere of labour, form a mechanism properly so called,
but become, in Kant's language, " reciprocally ends and
means," means to the ends of *other* men, means thereto
because other men in the same process become means
to them, means only because they are ends to *themselves*,
and fulfil their own ends by serving also the ends of
others. It is only because the likenesses of men are
deeper than their differences that division of labour is
possible between intelligent beings, and itself intelligible.
The basis of social unity is always likeness.

The only inherently evil division of labour is, in fact,
such as would reduce men to the place of parts within
a machine, one a wheel, one a piston, and so forth, so
that the very incompleteness of each became the condition
of his service, so that work and worker were alike fragmentary. The efficiency of workmen secured by their
reduction to such a condition would not be economy,
but that most tragic form of waste, the form practised
by the miser, the saving of the means of life at the cost

[1] *The Value and Destiny of the Individual*, p. 50.

of the ends of life. If, as some allege, the new " scientific management " proposed by some recent writers [1] would create such a condition, it would be in the wider sense most uneconomic. But the actual division of labour has not this consequence. To make this clear we must consider the second objection, the charge that division of labour brings narrowness and monotony into the work by which we live.

It must first be noted that in the sphere of cultural interests specialisation is often largely due to, and is always promoted by, the intensity of interest felt by the worker. In all the higher forms of labour it is the specialist who is the ardent devotee, it is he who finds completest satisfaction in his labour. It is true the satisfaction may sometimes appear a narrow one, but this is often only the view of the outsider who cannot perceive the complexity and depth of interest enclosed within seemingly narrow bounds. If the satisfaction is indeed narrow, it can only be, in a world which encloses infinite space within a nutshell, because the mind itself is narrow to which it makes its appeal.

The charge has greater relevance in respect of machine-determined industrial labour, but even here it can be raised, as a general accusation against the principle of the division of labour, only by those who refuse to survey the whole situation. We have at the outset to remember that if the work of men becomes specialised and in that sense narrowed, it is because their world is becoming more varied and more complex. What is lost in one way may thus be more than restored in another. If

---

[1] Taylor, *Principles of Scientific Management* ; Münsterberg, *Psychology and Industrial Efficiency.* I do not think the general principles advocated by these writers need lead to such a result, although sometimes the exposition of them certainly does too much suggest the " man-machine " idea. The inevitability, the peril, and the advantage of " scientific management " are well pointed out in Josephine Goldmark's fine study, *Fatigue and Efficiency* (New York, 1912).

man loses variety in his work he gains it in his world ;
and since specialisation is a process of economy, so that
less expenditure of time and energy are necessary to
produce any determinate result, it may leave the worker
a greater leisure, and more physical and spiritual energy,
to enjoy the world his work contributes to make.   If
it does not, then there is a failure of economy somewhere
else.

We have here assumed that the effect of industrial
specialisation is, in fact, to make work generally narrower
and more monotonous than before, but this assumption
must itself be disputed.   For it is just the mechanical
necessities of life which can be taken over by the machine.
It is routine, monotonous repetition, of which alone the
machine is capable.   In so far as the machine takes over
these tasks, persons are liberated from them.   Machines
as mere means can take the place of persons as mere
means, and allow the persons to become ends as well.
It may be answered that the technical worker is tied
down by the nature of the machine to an exceedingly
monotonous service of it, and this is true in many cases.
But the more monotonous and mechanical the task
becomes the greater the possibility that a further development of machinery will transfer that task itself to the
machine.   Further, the persons who perform the most
mechanical services are those who would otherwise have
been driven, in vastly greater numbers relative to the
size of the community, to perform the labour which the
machine performs instead.   Before any portion whatever
of a community can be free for higher or cultural pursuits,
it must command a vast amount of mere drudge-service.
The process of civilisation has meant the gradual redemption from such service of an ever-greater portion
of the community.   The existence of a preponderating
slave-class was a necessary condition of all ancient

civilisations, for the slave was the "animate tool" who released his master from like servitude. Before the age of machinery, even where slavery in the strict sense disappeared, the great majority in every community, however free in name, remained in a state of real serfdom. Without the machine men remain the slaves of their necessities, even when no longer the slaves of one another. By aid of the machine the amount of *mere* drudgery and the comparative number dedicated to it have already been vastly diminished. We can never escape the whole of this unloved burden of work which brings no joy to the worker, but if social wisdom and mechanical ingenuity increase together, we may well look forward to the progressive deliverance of an ever-greater majority. When we condemn the necessity imposed by the machine, let us remember the necessities from which it delivers us. Let us remember, for instance, that the engineer often loves the engine which drives his ship through the sea, but no ancient galley-rower ever loved the oar.

In considering the effect of specialisation on personality, we must further distinguish between specialised work and specialised ability. Specialised work may make demands on the general ability of the worker, not merely on a special facility of a limited kind. "Manual skill," according to Professor Marshall, "that is so specialised that it is quite incapable of being transferred from one occupation to another is becoming steadily a less and less important factor in production. . . . We may say that what makes one occupation higher than another, what makes the workers of one town or country more efficient than those of another, is chiefly a superiority in general sagacity and energy which is not specialised to any one trade." [1] "Further, just as industrial skill and ability are getting every day to depend more and

[1] *Principles of Economics* (6th ed.), p. 207.

more on the broad faculties of judgment, promptness, resource, carefulness and steadfastness of purpose—faculties which are not specialised to any one trade, but which are more or less useful in all—so it is with regard to business ability. In fact, business ability consists more of these non-specialised faculties than do industrial skill and ability in the lower grades : and the higher the grade of business ability the more various are its applications." [1]

Finally, we should note that the development of machine-determined specialisation involves in general a gradual reduction in the value of the mere physical energy of men and a corresponding gradual enhancement in the value of human intelligence. The development of machinery puts at the disposal of men an amount of physical force vastly greater than that which their own bodies can generate. To-day, for example, in the United States, it is computed that every workman controls on an average an amount of physical energy equivalent to the physical force of twenty workmen unaided by animal or machine power. It follows that physical force, relative to human intelligence, is becoming cheaper, and thus we are approximating nearer to the ideal that man, as compared with inanimate objects and impersonal forces, should be as dear as possible, that man should count for less and less as himself a mere machine, a mere producer of energy, and for more and more as a personality, a value to whose service the impersonal forces are bound. [2]

These considerations are sufficient to show that the division of labour is in itself both a form of social economy and a factor of socialisation, that it serves at once the development of personality and the solidarity of com-

[1] *Ibid.*, p. 313.

[2] Cf. André de Maday, *Le Progrès* (*Revue Internationale de Sociologie*, Juin, 1913).

munity. We can now affirm that every transformation of the pursuit of common interests due to the principle of economy means an increase in sociality. We have seen that society and economy are correlative, we now see in particular that where economy is greatest there society is most.

We might regard the argument as now complete, but to do so would be to leave a false impression as to the perfection of the social economy at present attained by the most developed communities. It must be borne in mind throughout that we are concerned with comparative estimates, that the communities we call most developed are so only in comparison with others at still lower stages, and that any goal of development, so far from being attained, is yet invisible. Every increase in social economy reveals unattained possibilities of social economy, just as every advance of community reveals the way to further advance. Viewed from the standpoint of present attainment the immense incompleteness of our social economy is only too apparent.

The means which serve life and personality have been enormously increased. The gains of each generation, what it has instituted, what it has wrought and discovered, are in large measure handed on, so that the total resources of community are growing constantly greater. The control of man over nature, due to scientific discovery, is already sufficient, if applied intelligently, to provide all men with all the equipment needed for the enjoyment and realisation of life. But for all the legacy of the past and the power of the present, multitudes are being dwarfed through mere material privations, embittered by the sordid necessities which cramp their desires, and reduced to despair in the unequal fight for the mere animal requirements which foxes and birds can satisfy more easily than they. Waste and superfluity in one direction, destitution in another, convict society of economic incapacity to apply the power it possesses, to direct its forces in due proportion to production and distribution, to utilise proportionately to the needs of life and personality the means to life and personality.

It must be remembered that every increase in human resources, in the control of environment, opens up alternative ways of application, alternative possibilities of satisfaction.   Thus every development of industrial power makes possible either (a) the increase of luxury or refinement, or (b) the diminution of poverty, or (c) the development of cultural interests.   (The third is made possible because increased industrial efficiency releases more members of the community from the necessity of industrial toil, and also provides completer material equipment for the pursuit of certain kinds of cultural interest.)   The alternatives are not completely disjunctive, for all three forms of satisfaction advance together as a rule, but a certain opposition does arise.   The opposition is sharpest and most direct between the first two alternatives, and undoubtedly raises a fundamental problem in social economy.   If material wealth is concentrated in the hands of a small minority, the demand for luxurious forms of satisfaction tends to turn productive activity excessively in that direction, and superfluity and destitution appear in evil and dangerous fellowship.   The problem may be as insoluble as many seem to think, it is none the less a problem, and its existence is none the less an exceedingly grave defect of social economy.

Yet it is not unreasonable to suppose that this problem, too, is progressively soluble.   It is not within the scope of this work to consider possibilities of development nowhere yet realised, but one or two inferences from our study may be drawn.   If intelligence and economy, and again society and economy, are correlated as we have seen reason to believe, then any further development of intelligence among men, or any further development of sociality among men, will necessarily bring them a stage further towards its solution.

There are facts connected with the recent development of community which encourage this hope. Of these perhaps the most significant are the facts which prove the falsity of the forecast of Marx that wealth would become the possession and power of an ever-richer and ever-smaller minority. On the contrary, all the evidence goes to show that the number not only of the wealthy but also of the moderately well-to-do increases both absolutely and relatively to the whole population. What is most significant, a general tendency, fostered by but not wholly dependent on legislation, is revealed whereby the land itself is ceasing to be the absolute property of a few great land-owners, and is passing into the hands of a vast number of small proprietors. In some parts, as in France, Holland and Bavaria, this process is almost complete; in others, as in Russia, Galicia, and Ireland, it has rapidly advanced in recent years ; elsewhere, as in England, there is a slower movement in the same direction. The import of this change can scarcely be exaggerated, and its universality is evidence that here is a phenomenon not due to accidental or transient causes, but marking a stage of communal development.[1]

It is most noteworthy that the failure in economy we are considering involves also a failure in sociality. So long as great numbers are, through no fault of theirs, destitute and expropriated, they cannot attain any adequate socialisation. They cannot root themselves in community, for com-

[1] For the facts and figures relative to this movement, see Makarewicz, *Sociale Entwicklung der Neuzeit*, in the *Archiv für Rechts- und Wirtschaftsphilosophie*, April and July, 1914.

munity means for them merely a system of driving outer forces to which they are subject, and which they cannot in the least control. On the other hand, the industrial conditions which produce this expropriation have also made wealth, in the form of capital, more completely alienable from the personal significance of the possessor than any form of possession the world had previously known. Undoubtedly the right of conveyance, especially conveyance by bequest, is the crux of the position ; for when a man transfers wealth he transfers not merely an external thing which may benefit its new possessor, he transfers also power over other men,[1] it may be a power of life and death. This transference is a vital concern of society, and may well be limited by considerations of social welfare. Control over property is control over men. If then the few defend a socially unlimited control on the ground that property is necessary for personality, shall not the many reply, " Are we too not persons " ?   If on the ground that they have created this property, shall not the many reply, " Have you then also created us " ?   If on the ground that to limit property is to limit power, shall they not say, " It is also to limit our powerlessness " ?

There can certainly be no real development of community which does not mean an increased economy.

§ 4. The economic significance of the development of primary common interests.

Outer necessities are the first springs of action. Pain, hunger, thirst, the pangs of appetite, these are the almost automatic determinants of animal activity in the highest as in the lowest. But in the lowest the activities so determined sum up the whole of life, in the highest they

[1] Cf. Professor Hobhouse, *The Evolution of Property*, in *Property : Its Duties and Rights*.

fall within a life which consciously pursues further ends, more intrinsic ends. As in the growth of a child the outer necessities come first and the intrinsic interests gradually supervene, so in the growth of community. This is in accord with the principle that social development means the growth of co-operation at the expense of antagonism and competition. For where interests are intrinsic they are essentially common interests, so that antagonism necessarily impairs and co-operation necessarily furthers them. Further, the different modes of activity are at the same time different stimuli of activity. Now the stimulus of direct antagonism cannot enter in the pursuit of intrinsic interests, while the stimulus of competition is merely an extraneous aid which becomes increasingly less valuable for all who have come to find in any pursuit not an external necessity of life, but life's realisation. Thus, for instance, in the education of youth competition is at first a very useful stimulus to activity, in so far as the end sought is nothing to the seeker,[1] being merely imposed by an outer authority which recognises its value for him ; it is less valuable in the higher stages, where the enfranchised student, the student in his own right, pursues knowledge because he himself desires it, seeking not merely its incidental reward ; and it is perhaps valueless in the very highest stage, wherein the pursuit of knowledge has become the essential fulfilment of the seeker. So far as stimulus is found in social relationships at all, the only form which can appeal at this stage is the stimulus of co-operation, the stimulus found in the aid and appreciation of fellow-workers pursuing a common end, above all in the thought that each is seeking a value that is a value for all men. This

---

[1] Note in passing that competition is a necessary stimulus in all games, simply because the end immediately sought in them is nothing to the seeker.

social stimulus provides indeed one of the highest and most enduring of human satisfactions. In co-operative activity we best realise the integrity, the unity, and the worth of that commonweal towards which our eyes are turned.

All interests which are pursued for their own sakes, and not as mere means to some further interests, not as mere necessities of life, may be called intrinsic interests. Through these interests personality is directly fulfilled, in the pursuit itself and not merely by aid of its results. It is obvious therefore that with all substitution of intrinsic for extrinsic interests there goes a development of communal economy. Both community and economy increase, for instance, whenever the conditions of work are so altered that men are enabled to take joy of their work, to express and find their nature in and through it. It is significant that the demand for the joy of work should only have arisen in very recent times, even though some of those who voice it have cast longing eyes on past ages wherein, as they suppose, that joy was present in fuller measure. Now nothing contributes more to this fulfilment than the sense of responsibility, and nothing creates the sense of responsibility so much as co-operation. The more men are devoted to the common interest, the more they realise themselves within it. This, too, is economy, for the pursuit has value no less than the end attained. It is clear that it is in the pursuit of primary common interests that the greatest social economy is realised.

Blind forces, as seemingly mechanical in operation as those which rule external nature, guided all the activities of the primitive world ; but as the child passes from outer to inner guidance, so does mankind. Men eat the fruit of the tree of the knowledge of good and evil. Conscious forces supersede, in whatever measure, blind forces. Intelligence, seeking to save the values which are revealed to it, discovers that in everything the way of economy is the way of community.

CHAPTER VII

THIRD LAW OF COMMUNAL DEVELOPMENT: THE CORRELATION OF SOCIALISATION AND THE CONTROL OF ENVIRONMENT

§ 1. Community and environment.

The growth of community, involving the transformation, in the manner already described, of the relations between the members of it, involves also a transformation of their common relation to an external world. This transformation is also a continuous process, admitting of endless degrees, and each degree is directly concomitant with, and causally related to, a degree of development within community. The changes within the relations of men which we have seen to mean a development of their sociality, these are changes correlated to changes in their common relation to their environment. Men cannot alter their relations to one another without at the same time altering their relations to the whole universe ; and, on the other hand, in seeking to control to their purposes the world lying outside them, they inevitably widen and deepen their social relations. The growth of knowledge is the progressive revelation of this most significant of all truths, that the inner and outer worlds, the world of mind and the world of " nature," are in the end one world. " The mind is organic to the universe," and cannot function either in isolation from, or in opposition to, the rest of it. One aspect of this unity concerns us especially as students of the development of community, the law of concomitance connecting the growth of sociality among men with a definite process of transformation of the modes of their relationship to the environing world.

We have already seen in general how the development of community has involved the transformation of the physical environment. If, for instance, common life in Aristotle's time meant only the life of a few thousand people within a single town, while to-day common life may extend over continents, this difference, so momentous for the spiritual development of man, has been made possible by the extension of man's control over physical forces. It might likewise be shown that every great social development is accompanied by an alteration of the physical conditions of life. Here we are thinking of the direct action of mind upon the physical world, but in this way we will never reach the heart of the problem or understand the full principle of correlation. For the nearest environment of mind is the organic body, which in one sense lies intermediate between the psychical and the outer physical worlds. The body must in a sense contain the harmony of both spheres, be the resultant of both sets of forces. The growth of society means not only a progressive control over outer physical forces, it means in especial the modification of the relation between the organism and *its* environment. Psychical and physical forces meet, though how we may not understand, in the organism, and the development of psychical forces revealed in the growth of purposive relations, in the development of community, transforms the mode in which the organism is dependent on physical forces. How this happens may also be beyond our understanding, but the fact is clear and the process may easily be traced and its significance revealed.

But before doing so we must explain, in view of certain prevalent confusions, the universal relation of life to environment, we must explain, in other words, the very meaning of environment. We have already pointed out how material law is a basis or condition of vital law. This truth we have now to make explicit.

§ 2. The two ultimate factors of all development.

The connection of life and environment is as inseparable as that of subject and object. For environment does not mean simply that which is external to life, but that external correlative of life apart from which life would remain an unconceived and inconceivable potentiality ; just as object means not simply that which is external to subject, but that external correlative of subject apart from which its being and activity as subject would be meaningless and for ever unrealised. Life apart from environment *of some kind* is as impossible as motion apart from some material thing. Environment pierces to the very heart of life. If we probe to the beginnings of life, it is there no less intimately dependent on environment than in its completest manifestations. We never find and never can conceive life pure, unenvironed.

So intimate is the relationship that every difference whatever of life from life involves a difference of environment from environment. Not only is life incarnated in endlessly diverse organisms which themselves reflect every change of the life-activity within them, but every kind of organism has a different kind of outer environment, a different place in the world, *and every change whatever in the state of any organism involves some change of the environment in which it lives.* This statement will appear exaggerated only if we fail to understand what a complex and specific thing an environment is. We all inhabit a single world, but the world is somehow different for every species, nay for every living thing within it.   Thousands of species of organic creatures live side by side, yet each has an environment not wholly that of any other.   The earth is infinitely diversified, a house of very many mansions for the reception of living beings, and each somehow finds a different mansion.   Each kind of organic creature selects and uses in different degrees the different elements and situations of the common world of them all, and thus *makes* an environment for itself.   For environment is not simply the external world, but the external world as it is related to life.   This will be shown more explicitly in the following section.

The study of the correlation between specific types of physical environment and specific forms of social life is one of the most interesting and one of the most successful pursuits of present-day sociology.   We might instance in particular the work of Demolins and his collaborators in *La Science Sociale*.   Such work, though liable to a certain misinterpretation which will presently be pointed out, reveals in a very impressive way the constant relativity of life and environment.

Environment is the means, the opportunity, and the home of life.   In the organism life and environment meet in a manner more intimate than we can understand, while the organism in turn mediates between life and the outer physical environment.   Life is that which feels and knows and wills, that for which values exist and which itself exists as value.   Each life is environed at once by an organic body, by an outer physical medium of the organism, by other lives likewise incarnated, and by the social order which together they create.   It is thus obvious that environment is an exceedingly complex and many-sided factor.

If then every change of life is relative to a change of environment, it is clear that there are two ultimate factors determining all development, (1) what we must call, though it be merely naming the unknown, the inner potency, that energy or spirit of life which must never be identified with the environment it finds or chooses, with the physical nature whose laws it both commands and obeys, and (2) a world so various, so complex, and so plastic, as to provide a continuous succession of environments corresponding to and making possible every impulse of life towards fulfilment. We have seen how the social environment changes with the development of life ; we have next to see how, correspondent to that change, the relation of the organic environment of living beings to the outer world of nature is by their own activity transformed. To this end it is very necessary to insist on the twofold determination of all development, on the equal necessity of native capacity or endowment on the one hand and of favourable environmental conditions of every kind on the other. This seems a truism, but it will appear that many theories of development fail to recognise its truth.

It is impossible to say that either of these factors is more *important* than the other, since both are absolutely necessary. But the inner capacity is logically prior, that of which environment is but a necessary condition, as the channel is of the stream. Environment gives or withholds opportunity, determines direction, but it is the life-capacity which seizes opportunity, which follows this or that direction. The way in which life responds to environment, changing to its every change, is not to be regarded as a witness to the characterlessness of life, but rather as evidence of its infinite capacity for seizing every opportunity which environment provides. Thus a change of outer environment does not mean merely a *proportionate* change in the organism, as if development were the simple resultant of two like forces. The change is the opportunity for a further revelation of life, wholly incalculable in advance. We find not simply " varia-tion," but, as de Vries has so completely shown, " muta-tion." To illustrate, the common primrose (*primula officinalis*) has a variety which loves damper and cooler soil (*primula elatior*), but we do not have all degrees of approach to the latter variety according to the degree of humidity of the soil. Instead we find a plant of a distinctive character in one kind of environment, a variety of a distinctive character in another. Differences of outer environment are measurable and continuous, varieties of organism are immeasurable and discontinuous. It is as if the incalculable Proteus-principle of life, eternally lying in wait behind material phenomena, wrought of every physical change an organic means for its own revelation.

So within the sphere of human society we can on the whole say what conditions of physical environment are most favourable for the appearance of new energies ; we know, for instance, that certain climatic conditions are good and others bad : but the quality, the ideals, so evoked and made actual through the favourableness of environment, these no man can predict. Life is no quantitative thing whose increase is the mere adding of like to existent like.

The constant relativity of the two factors of develop-ment places, we must admit, a serious obstacle in the way of the determination of their respective rôles in any given situation. We cannot refer absolutely the differ-ences between members of the same species, stock, or family to one or the other alone. Environment is in-finitely complex, never quite the same for any two living creatures ; it is ever present, never to be entirely known or estimated ; it is modified by the beings whom it modifies, in an endless and never wholly calculable reciprocity. But at least the same reciprocity is decisive against any theories which deny the significance of either factor, which attribute development wholly either to conditions of environment or to the inner potency of life. It may be well to examine briefly certain of these theories, since they stand in the way of the law of correlation we have finally to set forth.

One form of error is the explanation of all differences of development as simply due to differences in environment. This appears generally as a reaction against the opposite and more popular mistake. Thus Mr. J. M. Robertson,[1] while finely protesting against the facile theory which attributes to distinct racial capacities all differences of social and political development, seems to deny any differences whatever of native endowment and capacity between peoples. He protests, for instance, when Lord Morley [2] speaks of " peoples so devoid of the sovereign faculty of political coherency as were the Greeks and the Jews." But conditions, even on the most favourable hypothesis, will not explain everything. Switzerland is more mountainous than Greece, and the Swiss are divided in tongue and race and religion in a way unknown to Greece ; but in striking contrast to the Greeks the Swiss have created the longest-lived of federal unions. If we say that it was the menace of surrounding hostile States which inspired the federation, can we deny that Greece was exposed to an equal peril ? If, therefore, the Greeks failed to federate successfully, must they not have lacked a faculty of political coherency which the Swiss possessed ?

It is certain that every difference of environment corresponds to some difference of life. Just as in every different situation of the material world—in air, earth,

[1] *The Evolution of States*, Pt. I. chap. iv., and *passim*.

[2] *Compromise* (ed. of 1888), p. 108.

and sea, in every latitude and every soil, in alien growth
on plant and tree and animal, and out of the corruption
of death itself—there is bred a different form of life for
every difference of setting, as though behind all that
variety there moved a universal force everyhow and everywhere seeking what incarnation it can find ; so in especial
human life breaks out into the myriad differences of
humanity, the highest creative form of that universal
life, driving towards expression through the ever more
plastic-growing media of the environments which it
builds. It may therefore be that, looked on *sub specie
aeternitatis*, all life would appear as the manifestation in
greater or less degree of some one spirit of life. But
even so we cannot conclude that the differences of environment in any given historic situation wholly account
for differences of character. The type, the stock, is
already formed through endless past processes of interaction between life and environment. As life appears
in each new generation it cannot be regarded as some
mere undirected force, wholly shaped by the conditions
there represented. Doubtless the recreation of the type
in every birth and generation saves life from the fate
of imprisonment in its created forms. The plastic
capacity of development in every new generation stands
in contrast to the hardening of the once plastic form of
every older generation. But it is always the plasticity
of a given form, always the modification of a given
character. The Hottentot, the Egyptian, the Teuton,
placed at birth in the same general environment both
material and social, would certainly respond differently
in virtue of pre-determined capacities. It is the characteristic of a superior people that they can respond in
more complex ways to the calls of environment. It has
often been observed that the members of primitive peoples
attain their maturity very early in life, their character

becoming fixed and stereotyped in each much more quickly than that of more highly developed peoples. This means a difference in the power of response to the calls of environment. It is evident, therefore, that, *starting from any historical situation*, we cannot explain simply in terms of environmental conditions all the differences between people and people.

We do not explain a thing if we " explain it away," if we resolve it into its own " conditions." The wind may no more blow where it listeth, for we know something of the conditions which determine its direction and its power, yet the wind is no more its conditions than before. As once the wind, so still the spirit of human achievement seems most unaccountably to come and go, but even were our ignorance completely removed that spirit would not a whit be resolved in its revealed conditions, for it is itself underived, itself also an integral force.

Probe we never so far into causes, there remains a point where our search must end. We have been using the metaphor of plasticity, but at the last this metaphor, like all metaphor, proves defective. For the responsive power of life is not mere plasticity, not the mere potentiality of the clay to take on whatever shape the hand of the potter may devise, still less the characterless fluidity of water that will flow by whatever channel we dig. The reaction of life to environment is a true response, not a mere following or flowing ; the response of a *nature*, not the mere accommodation of some formless stuff (named psychical) to the impress of a die. Life is itself the prior force in its own unfolding. Life is itself the shaper, not environment. Character is the expression and form of life, not of environment. Environment is the occasion, the stimulus, and not the source of character. If material forces have their own specific natures, are psychical forces mere resiliences ?   It is surely foolish to write as if every external and material force had its own proper and definite nature, while spirit alone existed featureless and blank, the name of an unknown impressionability, until these outer forces gave it character.

The form of error we have been considering is, from the practical standpoint, less dangerous than the other false extreme. The opposite error, which belittles the significance of environment, discourages that struggle for its control which we shall see to be a determinant of development. If the native force of the human spirit is anyhow dependent on conditions of environment for its manifestation, direction and fulfilment, it is of paramount importance that we gain what mastery is possible over them. Our knowledge of the immense determinative power of that greater body of our spirits which we call environment is the revelation of the incalculable importance of social co-operation. To know these environmental forces is to know that we are more than they, for it is to know our power over them, the prior power of spirit over body which alters body for the sake of spirit. The keys of life itself are in our hands. Each owes his very birth to the will of the most intimate and primal of societies, and the environment into which each enters has been essentially determined by the willing of a myriad generations. If our impotence in the face of natural forces is vast, so is our power. In our hands is the sling with the little stone which may bring down the giant circumstance. Circumstance dulls the sense of the earth-bound labourer as it sharpens the pitiful precocity of the city waif, it turns the primal instincts of the street-woman to wretched viciousness, it leads the native endowment of the child of undisciplined luxury into the service of inept vanity—just as it evokes skill and courage, patience and strength, in the leader, the thinker, the worker. It is in great measure the activity of men in community which has created the differences of circumstance to which these differences of character correspond, and if men realised more fully their dependence on community-created conditions of environment they would will more earnestly and unitedly the transformation of unfavourable conditions.

Some forms of the opposite error, that which denies or minimises the significance of environment, must next be considered. We have already noticed in passing [1] the grosser fallacy of attributing to a peculiar race-endowment all the achievements in culture and civilisation which a particular community or any member of it may have achieved. There is indeed a still grosser form which attributes to the pure race-endowment of some one people not only all their own achievements in culture, but all or almost all that humanity itself has achieved, so belittling both culture and humanity for the greater glory of a figment. But this fallacy, dear to Herr Stewart Chamberlain and the *Politisch-Anthropologische Revue*, leads its champions into such blunders that it needs no other refutation.

There is a prevalent biological theory which maintains that the direct modifying influence of environment upon the organic character of the individuals of any generation or succession of generations has no effect whatever upon the race, upon the native endowment of the individuals of further generations. This seems to involve a denial that the correlation of life and environment holds at the very source of life. If this were so, it would be the destruction of the principle we have set forth. We must therefore examine the implications of the theory in question, that we may see how far, and on what grounds, it denies our principle. Here it is necessary to offer

[1] See pp. 264-5.

2 A

an apology. For the proper function of the sociologist is
to make the accepted conclusions of biology the data of
his own sociological conclusions. But in this case, especially in view of the conflicting social imperatives deduced
by biologists and others according as they accept or
reject the theory in question, the sociologist is to-day
compelled, at whatever risk, to study the facts and draw
his own conclusions.

The theory in question is of course associated chiefly
with the name of Weismann, though for the social inferences drawn from it not Weismann but his putative
disciples must be held responsible. (Many of these inferences do not, in fact, follow from the doctrine as stated
by their authority.) It may be well to consider, as
briefly as possible, what the actual doctrine of Weismann
is in this regard. Since that doctrine varies somewhat in
the successive statements of its author, we must here limit
our consideration to a single one of these. The short
systematic statement in *The Germ-Plasm*,[1] containing
as it does the essentials of the theory, will serve our
purpose.

What follows, it must be premised, is not in the least
a criticism of the general theory of heredity enunciated
by Weismann. We are not at all concerned with the
question whether this or that character is transmissible.
We have merely to vindicate the principle that life and
environment are always and in every respect correlative
and interdependent, and we shall see that this is in nearly
every respect admitted by Weismann, and that in the
one respect in which it seems not admitted the logic of
the case leads to the contrary conclusion.

(1) *The meaning and significance of "acquired characters."* In his chapter on " The Supposed Transmission

[1] *The Germ-Plasm : a Theory of Heredity* (Cont. Science Series,
1893).

of Acquired Characters," Weismann gives the following definition : " By *acquired* characters I mean those which are not preformed in the germ, but which arise only through special influences affecting the body or individual parts of it. They are due to the reaction of these parts to any external influences apart from the necessary conditions for development." [1] The preliminary question arises, How can any one ever say what " characters " are or are not " preformed in the germ " ? If, as we have seen reason to believe, every phenomenon of development is manifested in and through an environment, we can never distinguish among characters exhibited by a living thing some that were preformed and some that were not preformed in the germ. The only distinction we can make is between characters revealed as correlative to normal environments and those called out by abnormal environments. But if we realise the infinite complexity of environment we see that there can be no hard-and-fast division between " inborn " and " acquired " characters, since, of course, all characters are both. To make a hard distinction between " inborn " or " blastogenic " and " acquired " or " somatogenic " characters is to repeat the old fallacy which underlay the psychological dispute that raged in the seventeenth century round the doctrine of " innate ideas."

Must we then understand that those characters which develop in normal environments are transmissible, and those which develop in abnormal environments nontransmissible ? Or is the theory the more logical one that the line of evolution passes direct from germ-plasm to germ-plasm in the successive generations, the body being in each case but an epiphenomenon in the process ? But the nature of the germ-plasm is known only by the bodies which it builds, and how shall we distinguish at

[1] *The Germ-Plasm*, p. 392.

all *within those bodies* characters which are and characters which are not heritable ?

Let us look next at the types of " character " which Weismann distinguishes as " acquired." They are *injuries, functional variations*, and such variations as " depend upon the so-called ' *influences of environment* ' " —in particular climatic variations. Now injuries cannot be called " acquired characters " at all, in terms of Weismann's definition. If, for instance, a mouse has its tail cut off, the loss is in no sense " a reaction *of that part* " to external influences ? In the first place, the part is no longer there to react ! If there is reaction, it is that of the body, not of the tail ! It is true that Lamarckians sometimes pursued their doctrine to the absurdity of supposing that the accidental loss of its tail by a parent cat, to take an actual instance quoted by Weismann,[1] was responsible for taillessness in the offspring, and in the correction of all such crude theories of descent Weismann has done signal service. But it shows a curious lack of logic to imagine that, by cutting off the tails of nineteen generations of mice and discovering that the tails of the twentieth are as long as those of the first, you are contributing any evidence whatever for the solution of the real question at issue. For the real question is this, *Does the special development or decay of any character in a parent, occurring as a response to external influences of a particular kind, tend to increase or diminish in any degree the response of his offspring in respect of that character, when placed in the environment in which the character specifically developed in the parent ?* " In any degree," because there is, of course, the double parentage to be considered, as well as the influence, through each of them, of two whole ancestries.

[1] *The Germ-Plasm*, p. 397.

It is evident that, since every character appears in relation to an environment, the term "acquired character" has to be limited to characters due to special and, from the point of view of the biologist, accidental and transient conditions of environment. Now the more accidental those conditions are, the less, on any conceivable theory of inheritance, must their influence be upon the race. The amputation of a limb does not seriously affect the head, why should it be supposed to affect the germ-cells ? On the other hand, there are injuries which do affect the whole balance of the organism, *i.e.* nervous injuries, *and it is just in regard to these that there is evidence of their modifying influence on the germ.* The crucial experiments of Brown-Séquard on guinea-pigs have never been adequately met by the Weismannists.[1] But in any case, as we shall see presently, in respect of such forms of injury, Weismann and his followers really admit—and this is all we are contending for—the influence on the germ-cells of their bodily environment.

The case of functional variations, variations due to the use or disuse of parts, can merely be touched upon. Here, too, Weismann has disposed of the too simple doctrines of the Lamarckians, but here, too, the direct negative offers difficulties. It is admitted that organs no longer of use to the race gradually degenerate. This may be due either to transmission or to selection—or to both. Those who deny transmission can always fall back on selection. There is always an alternative hypothesis, and in this particular case no possibility of *proof* either way.

Finally, as to such variations as are due to changes of climate, of nutrition, and so forth, *appearances* certainly favour the doctrine that the bodily environment

---

[1] See the criticisms of Brown-Séquard's conclusions in Thomson's *Heredity*, chap. vii., § 11.

affects the germ. The effect of heat or cold in the determination of differently-coloured varieties within a single species (*polyommatus phlaeas*) of butterfly provides an illustration. We know from experiments that the differences in colour are *in some way* actually dependent on differences of temperature, and since these differences permanently distinguish the varieties found respectively in northern and southern regions, the theory that they are due to the cumulative effect of environmental influences working on successive generations is at least a possible explanation. But an alternative theory is also possible. Weismann holds that the true explanation is found in the direct influence of temperature at once on the " determinants "—hypothetical particles of germ-plasm—in the wings of each individual and on the germ-cells of each.[1] But if the external influences can affect even the secluded germ-cells, how can we wholly deny the influence of the nearer environment, the body itself, upon these ? This brings us to the whole question of the relation of the soma to the germ-cells.

(2) *The relation of the body to the germ-cells.* All the evidence goes to show that the germ-cells cannot be regarded as completely independent of the influence of the body as a whole. This is largely admitted by Weismann. Take the following passage, for instance : " The removal of the sexual ' glands ' from young mammals and birds prevents the development of secondary male sexual characters. Castrated cocks, for example, retain the appearance of hens, and do not develop the beautiful tail or the large comb and spurs of the male bird, nor do they crow ; and conversely, when hens become sterile from age, or if their ovaries become degenerated, they take on the external sexual character of cocks. I possess a duck which no longer lays eggs, and has assumed the

[1] *The Germ-Plasm*, p. 401.

coloration of the drake. Men who have been castrated in their youth retain a high voice like that of the other sex, and the beard does not become developed." [1] Even if we suppose with Weismann that the *alternative* secondary sexual characters were latent in the soma, it is still a change in the germ-apparatus which determines their appearance. If, then, the germ-cells influence the soma, why not the soma the germ-cells ? The soma is the nearer environment of the germ-cells, and it would require better evidence than a series of hypotheses to prove that here alone, and in one direction alone, environment counts for nothing.

But this, too, is in part admitted. " The body bears *and nourishes* the germ-cells." [2] Weismann acknowledges the importance of nutrition, and suggests that differences of nutrition may determine variations. [3] It is well known that in the case of bees the female larvae when poorly fed develop into sterile workers, when well fed into fertile queens, and that a similar relation of nutrition and fertility holds in the case of ants and termites. Weismann points out that this environmental influence is properly a stimulus to which the organism responds in a predetermined manner. [4] Now this principle may lead us very far. If oscillations of nutrition have so significant an effect upon the germ-cells and the germ-plasm, what other effects may they not have ? And what of other oscillations, those nerve-oscillations which, as Weismann admits, affect nutrition, those *psychical* " oscillations " whose effects on the organism as a whole are manifest to every one ? Where then can we stop ? It is, for instance, admitted by all impartial students of the subject that poisons such as alcohol so act on the body as to affect the germ-cells, harming not

---

[1] *The Germ-Plasm*, pp. 358-9.   [2] *Ibid.*, p. 5. Italics mine.
[3] *Ibid.*, p. 417.   [4] *Romanes Lecture*, 1894.

only the individual but his offspring also.[1] But if the toxins of the body affect the germ-cells, why not the " anti-toxins " ? If we believe that stocks or peoples may acquire specific immunities from disease, these immunities must be " acquired characters," if any are ; and they may be due to specific " anti-toxins." Every condition of the body may involve specific toxins or " anti-toxins," just as we know the condition of fatigue to involve the former. And again where can we stop ? " Microbe or toxin," that is the reply of the Weismannists to the conclusions drawn from such experiments as Brown-Séquard's. Call it what you will, it is all the admission we require to establish the reciprocity of environment and life.

Once more, germ-plasm must occur, as Weismann admits, in the general tissues of the organism as well as in the special reproductive organs. Otherwise there would be no possibility of reproduction, as in the case of plants, from cuttings, grafts, buds, and even leaves, and no possibility of regeneration, as, for instance, in the case of newts and lizards, of parts accidentally lost.[2] So we see that the soma, in certain organisms at least, forms an even nearer environment to the germ-plasm than we might at first have supposed. May this not indicate that the organism is itself a more integral unity than the doctrine we are considering will allow ?

[1] It is not admitted by the Professor of Eugenics at London University, but the evidence against him is quite conclusive. The investigations of Dr. Laitinen of Helsingfors in regard to infant mortality are alone a sufficient refutation. Laitinen's experiments on animals (as also those of Hodge and Bluhm) prove the fallacy of the favourite argument of the " natural selectionists " that the alcoholism is merely a symptom and not at all a cause of degeneration. For a short summary of the effects of alcohol-poisoning see Schallmayer, *Vererbung und Auslese* (2nd ed.), c. viii., § 1.

[2] Weismann remarks, " The tail of a lizard, again, which is very liable to injury, becomes regenerated, because . . . it is of great importance to the individual." (*The Germ-Plasm*, p.122.) Contrast this with the case of the mutilated mice.

The evidence for the environmental influence of body upon germ-cells, whether we affirm or deny that this means the "transmission of acquired characters," could be extended indefinitely, but the foregoing considerations may suffice.[1] They justify us, I believe, in our contention that life and environment are *always* correlative. It was necessary to meet the difficulty involved in the much-vexed problem we have just been considering, because if we found a single exception to that principle of correlation, the principle itself would have been undermined. But every development of life implies and necessitates the modification of its whole environment. We have seen how such development means a transformation of the social environment, the forms and institutions of community ; it means no less a transformation within the physical environment, so that, as it changes, life becomes dependent upon it in different ways than before. Each step in the growth of community is correlative with a change in the conditions of the organic life of social beings. The law of this process we must now endeavour to set forth.

§ 3. The transformation within community of the principle of adaptation to physical environment.

The law of life, we must conclude, is relative to the kind of life, and changes with its changes. Thus can we differentiate natural from vital law. For material law has an absoluteness denied to vital law. Where there is no life there is no response, no growth of a power revealing itself *in difference* in every stage of growth. The stone is moved and lies. The dead tree is a log. The living cell alone resists. Within it is that power of response that acts back in being acted upon, in ways incalculable until they are actually made manifest. The

[1] Some further evidences appear in § 5. See also Appendix C.

growth of life is revealed not as quantitative increase alone, but as qualitative difference.

If a principle of life is discovered to be active in the lower organic world, and more and more suspended in human society as it grows, it is the curious obsession of certain biologists that it *ought* to be made operative among men also, although the more obvious inference might seem to be that, unless some other explanation is forthcoming, the relative absence of the principle in the human sphere is due to its humanity, in a word to its advance. The obsession of the biologists in question is increased because they often regard these principles as absolute in the lower organic spheres, thus confusing material with vital laws. In reality, as we shall see, they are only partially realised within them—a fact of great significance. They are *never* like the laws of the material world, descriptions of invariable sequences or concomitances. They are not laws at all as the physicist understands the term " law." *The true laws of life are laws of concomitant variation*, laws of concomitance between the growth of life and the transformation of its inner and outer conditions.

The " laws " which the biologist deduces from the study of lower organic life are summed up under the expressions, " adaptation to environment," " struggle for life," and " natural selection." Although these expressions are often used as equivalent names for a single law, it makes for clearness if we take each of them separately, and show that it expresses only a relative, partial, and partially supersessionable principle, the degree and form of its operation being relative to the degree of communal development.

Nothing illustrates better the confusion of material and vital law than the frequent mis-statement of the principle of " adaptation to environment." Regarded purely

in its physical aspect, every organism is always adapted
to its environment, since there is no break in the order
of physical causality. But this law must be clearly distinguished from the law of life of which it is merely the
basis. Mere adaptation to environment may mean for
the living being either progress or retrogression, either
the increase or the decrease of the amount and quality
of life. All the organic beings on the earth, low and
high, strong and weakly, healthy and diseased are alike,
as physical beings, perfectly adapted to their physical
environments. The tree with the young foliage of spring
is no more and no less adapted to its environment than
the tree shedding the withered leaves of autumn. The
mulga shrub, hard, dry, and stunted, is no less and no
more adapted to its environment than the luxuriant vegetation of the Amazonian selvas. The pinched children
of the poverty-stricken are no less and no more adapted
to their environment than the healthful children of the
well-to-do. Is it not because the former are so adapted
that they are pinched ? Every being is always adapted
to its environment if it lives at all, and when it dies its
death is the final triumph of adaptation. The phenomena
of retrogression furnish as good illustrations of continuous
adaptation as do the phenomena of progress. The rotting
leaf is adapting itself to its environment by rotting, the
neglected rose by reverting to the wild. The beaver,
harried by man, forsakes his wonderful dams and sinks
to a less constructive, less social mode of life,[1] and that
degeneration is also adaptation. This truth was pointed
out just fifty years ago by Huxley,[2] but owing to the
prevalent confusion of material and vital law it is still
far from being universally recognised. There is here no
imperative for the living creature. It is needless to bid

[1] Fouillée, *Les Elements Sociologiques de la Morale*, p. 216.
[2] *Criticisms on the Origin of Species*, 1864.

us be adapted in this sense to our environment, for we always are so adapted, and even as we change it we become adapted to its changes.

It is when we state this universal law of causality in the form of an imperative law of life that confusion arises. We say that to succeed or to survive every organism *must* conform to the conditions of *its* environment. If this *must* is an imperative, we are construing adaptation in quite another sense. We mean that under certain conditions of its physical environment an organism, in the process of adaptation, decays or perishes, and that to thrive or survive it must find or create other conditions. And this is an imperative not of conformity but seemingly of non-conformity. But, if physical adaptation is universal, how can an imperative of such a nature be possible ? To answer this we must pass from the sphere of material to the sphere of vital law. We must take account of that formative life-activity which characterises every living thing. Then it appears that we are concerned with a relative principle, relative to the kind of life.

Every living creature in some degree determines its own environment, and the more developed the life the greater the control of environment. This increasing control is secured chiefly through the increase of social co-operation.

We have seen that the physical world provides endless possibilities of new or different environments. Environments are not separate spaces pre-allotted to the different kinds of life. The environment of each species —and in a lower degree of each individual—depends in some way on the active nature of each. The allotment of each environment to each species is not accidental, the organism is not passive in acceptance of its environment and active only in conforming to it. All life is endowed with mobility—even the most vegetative, for its seeds wing themselves or are transported over the earth, its roots may pierce from the dry to the moist soil, from sand or rock to clay, and its leaves turn from the shade to the sun. These least mobile of organic forms are thus actually choosing between environments, not merely conforming to one pre-determined situation. If this holds for vegetative life, it holds in ever higher degree for animal and human life. In general the plant has a minimum power of choosing between different *given* environments, while the more mobile and creative animal has both a greater variety of choice within existing environments, and, still more important, an increasing power, relative to its intelligence, of *modifying* these environments. This latter power, on which all human progress ultimately depends, introduces an essential relativity into the principle of adaptation, for in the degree in which man (or any other organic being) possesses it he becomes master no less than servant of circumstance, so that his purposes are armed with conscious might against the blinder mights of outer nature.

Such a power in no way contradicts the universal principle of physical adaptation, or, to use a less misleading term, causality. It is because men cannot be other than " adapted " to their actual physical environment that they endeavour to transform it, so that it shall be a different actual environment which makes this ungainsayable demand. Adaptation to a more favourable environment means progress, adaptation to a less favourable environment means retrogression, the necessary harmony of adaptation being in itself no value, but the condition of values, and the condition of evil no less than of good. It is here the vital law appears in contradistinction to the material law. Man changes his environment so that his necessary adaptation to it shall further and not hinder his pursuit of ends or values.

The less intelligent the species, the more must it accept the existent conditions of its environment; the more intelligent, the more can it refuse to accept these conditions in the knowledge of its power to alter them. So civilised man most of all builds up his new world within the old, his world of community. In this highest level of achievement each builds least for himself alone, and most as fulfilling some part in a concerted whole of endeavour. Thus only, by the increase of society, does he gain progressive control over environment. Community, we have seen, implies co-operative activity towards common ends. This co-operative activity is in the main directed towards the control of physical conditions, so that human life is raised from that mere subjection to them, that " state of nature " which is so full of misery, insecurity, internecine struggle, and squalor of every kind, to that mastery of them, that social state wherein the struggle for insufficient means is gradually transformed into the co-operative and thus productive pursuit of more abundant means.

Finally, it is probable that the higher the life the lower its *organic* plasticity. This, at any rate, is the conclusion to which many facts of comparative zoology lead. To illustrate, the more highly developed the organism the less easily can it regenerate lost parts.[1] Now this principle means that the higher the organism the less can it directly change in response to changes of environment so as to maintain its life throughout these changes. It was the opinion of Lamarck that while environment had direct power in changing plant-organisms it had no such power over the more active animal-organism. It may, however, be a question of degree. In which case

[1] There are exceptions. The power of regeneration seems to be slighter in fish than in more highly organised amphibians, such as *Triton*.

the relevant law of life would be that *the higher the life the less is it directly modified by the changes within its physical environment and the more does it modify that environment and its changes into conformity to its own purposes.* Intelligence in its degree fences a space of life against the immediate and minor surges of the environmental flux, so that life may reveal itself within that space the more.

Since we have seen that the degree of intelligence measures the degree of society, the correlation between socialisation and the control of environment is now definitely established. In the remaining sections we shall consider some more particular aspects of that correlation.

§4. The transformation within community of the principle of the struggle for life.

The two expressions " struggle for life " and " natural selection " are often used as practically synonymous. But there are two kinds of struggle which need to be clearly distinguished, the struggle of living thing *against* living thing on the one hand, and, on the other, the endeavour of living things to maintain their lives and purposes against the unfavourable conditions of their environment. Here we shall consider only the former of these, leaving the latter for consideration under the wider rubric of " natural selection."

We have already seen that in the process of communal development the modes of the activity of social beings are transformed. We have seen that the principle of the " struggle for life," understood as the direct struggle of living thing *against* living thing, is modified or even abrogated in that process. In civilised society, the struggle is not for life but for a kind of life, and the goal of the struggle is attainable not in direct conflict with others but by their direct and indirect aid. The full

significance of this fact becomes clear when we understand the correlation of environment and life, in particular the necessity by which life as it grows greater
controls and modifies in greater measure the conditions
of its environment. To that end the activity of social
beings must become increasingly a co-operative activity,
and in that direction must their co-operative activity
be increasingly turned. We can now, therefore, complete
the argument of the preceding chapter by showing that,
under the conditions of environment corresponding to,
and dependent on, the increase of life, the necessity and
the value, no less than the extent, of the individualistic
struggle are continuously reduced.

The contrary argument may be summed up as follows :
(1) the law of individual struggle rules lower organic
life ; (2) it is a beneficent law for such life, securing the
elimination of the weak and the diseased, and the survival
of the strong and healthy ; (3) it is, therefore, a good
thing that this law *should* remain in operation within
human society. Again we have the statement of a supposed universal law of lower life, again also the transition
from a descriptive to an imperative law, from what is
or is supposed to be in the lower organic world to what
ought to be in the higher. And again we shall see the
transition to be false. Nay more, in this case we shall
see that the descriptive law is itself unsound.

The principle of the individualistic " struggle for life "
is not absolute at any level of life. Strange though it
may seem, under the conditions of environment which
determine survival for the lowest forms of life, the principle is non-existent. Where there is no determinate
purpose there can be no struggle of this kind. When
purpose first clearly emerges, the direct struggle for life
does appear, but as purpose grows with the growth of
mind, the struggle for life becomes, as we have already

seen, modified through social co-operation. What then becomes of the descriptive law ?

In the lowest regions of life there is no proper *struggle* of living thing against living thing. If of the multitude of seeds and fruits of nearly every tree, only one or two survive to carry the species on through time, it is not because the race is to the swift or the battle to the strong. " Time and chance happeneth to them all." It is truer of Nature's sowing than of man's that some seeds fall by the way-side and are devoured, others upon stony places and are scorched, others among thorns and are choked. Likewise of the countless eggs of the low forms of animal life, marine and terrestrial, there is here no struggle to survive nor fitness in survival. The drift of the tides, the mercy of the winds, the accident of escape from the devouring mouths, these are the conditions of survival, no merit of the surviving units of the host. As well say that in a modern battle, when the collective fire of many guns and rifles sweeps the extended lines, it is the individual brave or keen-eyed or clear-brained who are spared by shell and bullet. When next we mount the scale of life and observe the dawning of clear purpose, the principle of individual struggle appears as a very partial and limited condition of survival. The intelligence which makes it possible is always breaking it down again. All higher animals are to a certain extent, some to an amazing extent, social animals, and have broken the struggle for existence by co-operation. Further, it is not between members of the same species but between members of different species that the process of elimination is most ruthless, and this is " rather accommodation than struggle." It depends scarcely at all on individual differences. It is not the difference of speed between deer and deer that decides which the lion shall make his prey. It is not the difference between sparrow

2 B

and sparrow that decides which shall fall a victim of the hawk. A moment's reflection will show that here is no law of individual struggle, but a process shaping the conditions of the survival of species. One way in which a species is fitted for survival in the face of its enemies is rapid multiplication, but this means no increase of strength or skill to the individuals of it, rather the reverse. The law of racial survival has here no implication of individual development. In fact, it might seem that the ordinary statement of the law of struggle—implying as it does that the better-equipped units survive—can apply only to a struggle between *likes*, where strength is pitted against strength, fleetness against fleetness, cunning against cunning. In such a struggle, *when the arena is cleared for it*, the stronger and the fleeter and the more cunning do for the most part triumph. But such a struggle, although often taken for granted even by distinguished scientists, seems in fact somewhat rare in nature. It is most clearly exemplified in the strife between members of the same species, a kind of strife best known in human society. In truth one is sometimes tempted to think that the law of organic struggle, in the individualistic interpretation usually given to it, applies scarcely at all to nature outside certain kinds and stages of human society. It is significant that Darwin himself acknowledged that he was led to his doctrine of selection through struggle by the reading of Malthus. But Malthus was concerned with the competitive and purely human struggle of likes of the same species, not of unlikes of different species. It would be curious if here too, as so often elsewhere, our interpretation of nature turned out to be anthropomorphic at the last.

But we have already seen how in the development of human society the struggle suffers transformation. The control of environment is possible only through a social

unity which contradicts the principle of the "struggle
for life." The history of civilisation shows that one form
of conflict is substituted for another, for the barbaric
conflict of like against like the constructive conflict of
likes towards the mastery of nature, the discovery of her
laws, and the utilisation of her resources.

This truth, obscured or seemingly contradicted while
the first triumphant discovery of the principles of organic
evolution still dominated scientific thought, is only now
beginning to be realised. It was Huxley, in his justly
famous Romanes lecture on *Evolution and Ethics*, who first
clearly championed the method of socialisation where it
differs from the "individualism" of lower life. But Huxley
expressed the contrast between " cosmic " and social law
in too extreme a form. He still spoke as if men in their
social activities simply reverse some earlier process, the
ways of ape and tiger.[1] " Let us understand," he said,
" once for all that the ethical process of society depends,
not on imitating the cosmic process, still less in running
away from it, but in combating it." The road turns
back upon itself. But in truth the ethical process is
more an upward spiral ascent, involving at no point a
sudden change of direction. If we interpret the law of
struggle in the only sense in which it can be called a
law at all—as a condition of the survival of *species*—
the sheer antagonism Huxley found between the cosmic
and the social process is broken. The social process
means the increasing socialisation of the human species
or portions of the human species, through the increasing
application of inventive mind, with its principles of
economy, order, and the direct adaptation of means to
ends, for the furtherance of the unity of individual and

[1] One wonders if those who pretend to believe in the supremacy
of the " ape and tiger " ways ever reflect on what has befallen those
animals themselves, how the tiger is confined within an ever-narrowing
belt of jungle, and the ape makes sport for children !

social good. The rudiments of that process exist already in lower organic nature, and so far as it exists the process works the same advantageous effects for the socialised species as it does for man. But it is only very partially exhibited because free inventive mind is almost wholly absent in the underworld. Animal societies lacking this guidance lack the success it brings, but this does not mean that animal life owes its development to an opposite principle, to anti-social antagonism among its members and to the passive acceptance of whatever good or evil the environment may contain. With greater truth we might say that it owes its lack of development to the comparative absence of this principle of socialisation. Wherever this principle is introduced *ab extra* into the lower organic world, it ensures the rapid development of the species concerned, as every breeder and horticulturist will bear witness. The breeder and the horticulturist are employed all the time in modifying natural conditions, no doubt for their own purposes. But if only the animals and plants themselves possessed inventive minds, they would modify for their own ends, as men for theirs, these natural conditions.

There is not, therefore, any antagonism of principle between the law of success in lower organic life and in human life. It is not so much that there is present in nature a mighty organic law, running counter to the law of society, as that there is absent the mighty social law. In human social life a transforming element has appeared and become operative. Mind reveals a new road to success, a new means of attaining ends hitherto attained, if at all, in slower and more imperfect ways. I do not know if mind tends to substitute altruistic action for egoistic. There is altruism and egoism at every different level of intelligence. But I am sure that mind increasingly discovers, in ways before undreamed of, the de-

pendence of the interest of each upon the interest of all.
It reveals that the fundamental needs of each are best
realised in the community of all, and that, as Plato saw
clearly long ago, " in respect alike of pleasure and repute
and utility the approver of social justice speaks the truth,
and the disapprover is all unsound and knows not what
he does in disapproving." [1] It reveals that the measure
of the socialising of man is the measure of the development of man.

As the struggle changes, so does the meaning of victory
change, and therewith the quality which ensures it.   The
whole work of that reason which builds community is
the endeavour to ensure that what is revealed to it as
best shall be at the same time strongest.   It seeks so to
control the conditions of life that they shall less and less
advantage the socially worse and more and more advantage the socially better.   All progress everywhere can be
resolved into this, the control of the conditions of values
for the securing of values.   However imperfect the attainment, there is the goal which every community, which
every true association must pursue.   Further, though no
one can say that this power, even were it to become fully
reasonable, will ever become supreme, though no one
knows what limits a " step-motherly nature " without
or a failure and arrestation of the social spirit within may
set to this control, we must acknowledge that never in
history has it been so great as it is to-day.   " The distinguishing characteristics of our time are that civilisation
for the first time has the upper hand, that the physical
conditions of life have come and are rapidly coming more
and more within human control, and that at least the
foundations have been laid of a social order which would
render possible a permanent and unbroken development." [2]

[1] *Republic,* 589 c.   I translate τὸ δίκαιον by " social justice."
[2] Hobhouse, *Social Evolution and Political Theory,* p. 163.

§5. The transformation within community of the principle of natural selection.

The effect on the race of the individual " struggle for life " was supposed to be the maintenance and increase of its vigour, since only the strongest and " fittest " survived to reproduce their kind. To the same end the whole of existence also conspired. The organism grows in a world full of ordeals for it, fraught with the conditions of pain, misery, and disease. The old-world view regarded these as simply evil, due to a spirit of evil seeking its will over man, though destined to final overthrow. A newer-world view dramatically reversed the doctrine, conceding indeed, as it must concede, that these were evils for the individuals who succumbed to them, but adding that they were the essential conditions of the progress of the race. Not only was there a soul of good in seeming evil, the latter was the very condition and origin of good.

Unfortunately this vindication of " the cosmos " was the condemnation of the activity of man. For that activity is directed just to mitigate those evils which, if the vindication holds, are blessings in disguise. Man seeks—and cannot help seeking—to conquer his poverty, to heal his diseases, to raise himself from subjection to those forces which, on this doctrine, are the very means of his salvation. To-day, for instance, man seeks to overcome the " sinister trinity " of diseases, tuberculosis, syphilis, and cancer, which threaten his whole civilisation, and he is told, in respect of the first of these, that " if to-morrow the tubercle bacillus were non-existent it would be nothing short of a national calamity." [1] So, in spite

[1] So the doctrine is interpreted in a speech delivered by the President of the Australasian Medical Congress at Sydney, September, 1911 (quoted in the *Economic Journal* for September, 1912). But why *national* ?

of the vindication of nature, the ways of nature and man still seem at strife, or rather, a more implacable strife takes the place of the old. For man must, by his very constitution, seek relief from misery and disease, he must in the degree of his intelligence, pursue those researches into the conditions of life whence he comes back armed with greater power over them. He is so constituted that he must seek to destroy the conditions of his welfare ! His gods have disguised themselves so terribly that he must always continue to attack them as demons instead !

The application of the principle of the relativity of life and environment relieves us, I believe, from so ironical a situation. It enables us to comprehend under one law what truth underlies both the newer and the older doctrine. The older doctrine looked forward, the newer doctrine looks back. But life and environment are always changing together, and as environment differs for different kinds and stages of life, so does its selective force. There is no one constant operation of nature which we can call " natural selection." Every environment is selective according to its kind, but the kind of selection and the operation of selective forces vary with the kind and the activity of life.

Let us again, as a convenient starting-point for the application of this principle of relativity, set out the extreme doctrine of those who seem to admit it least. They hold (1) that the principle of " natural selection " is the main determinant of all the evolution of life, (2) that the attempts of man to eliminate or modify " natural selection " defeat themselves or, if they succeed at all, do evil instead of good. They therefore tell us (3) that we *ought* not to interfere with the operation of that principle. Once more we have the transition from the descriptive to the imperative law, and once more we shall find the transition to be invalid.

(It is significant, we may note in passing, that a similar imperative is discovered whenever men begin strenuously to control the *social* environment.   The same *laissez-faire* was proclaimed when the first serious attempts were made to protect men and women and children from the operation of uncontrolled industrialism, and is again proclaimed at every transition from competition to co-operation as between individuals, associations, or communities.   The same spectre cries " Back " at every turn of the road, and it is to be laid everywhere in the same way.)

The principle of " natural selection," so far from being absolute and alone determinative of evolution, is (1) at no stage of life an all-sufficient explanation, and (2) less and less adequate, as community grows, to account for each successive development of life within community. The principle of " natural selection " looks upon life simply as acted upon by natural forces, but the more life grows the more it acts back on these.   The development of life is the development of selective forces of another order than those we call " natural."   *The kind of selection is relative to the kind of life.*

(1) It is impossible within our limits to set out the evidence which has led the great majority of modern scientists to regard " natural selection " as by itself an inadequate explanation of organic evolution.   It is indeed unnecessary for us to do so, if we can show the gradual diminution of its rôle within the world of community. It may, therefore, suffice to repeat that all life is active and itself makes in part the conditions under which alone selection can take place.   If life displays an infinity of forms, if in its highest manifestation it reveals an infinity of individualities, the very existence of these is sufficient proof that environment provides no single and inexorable test of fitness to survive within it.

(2) All socialisation involves the increased operation of socially-determined selective forces and the consequent decrease of the selective activity of the forces of outer nature. We may point out some of the ways in which this principle is revealed.

(a) The growth of socialisation, involving as it does increased economy of and control over material resources, takes the edge off the " struggle for life." It does not diminish struggle but it transforms it, so that it becomes a struggle for something other than mere life, for the goods of life however understood. Now, where the struggle is not for life, failure in the struggle does not necessarily mean the forfeiture of life. The defeated in the struggle neither die nor cease to reproduce their kind—on the contrary they often breed the more for their adversity, so completely is the principle of selection transformed by the very existence of society.

(b) The less prolific a species is, the less possible is its salvation by " natural selection." The method of " natural selection " presupposes a considerable preponderance of birth-rate over survival-rate, the surplus being eliminated as less " fit," less " adapted." Now we have seen that with the growth of society the surplus of birth-rate over survival-rate diminishes constantly, and therefore the method of a selective death-rate becomes less and less effective.

When Huxley, only twenty years ago, was discussing the possibilities of human control over environment, he saw one grave difficulty besetting that accomplishment. " The Eden would have its serpent, and a very subtle beast too. Man shares with the rest of the living world the mighty instinct of reproduction and its consequence, the tendency to multiply with great rapidity. The better the measures of the adminstrator achieved their object, the more completely the destructive agencies of the state of nature were defeated, the less would that multiplication be checked." [1] Consequently, as multiplication advanced, " the fierce struggle for existence must recommence and destroy that peace, which is the fundamental condition of the maintenance of the state of art against the state of nature." But it is now manifest that as civilisation advances multiplication does not also advance. In the lower world multiplication does not mean increase, because the high death-rate counterbalances the high birth-rate. In the world of civilisation a different equilibrium seems in process of being attained, one not imposed but willed. The transition from one to the other, like all transitions, is perilous, but the process cannot be denied. Nor should we regard it as necessarily evil. It is needful to protest against the blind and clamorous arithmeticians who can count heads but cannot read the signs of the time, who measure the progress or decay of a people by the increase or decrease of its surplus of births over deaths, never reflecting that there waits somewhere a limit beyond which increase may be disastrous, and that there are for peoples, and for all mankind, periods and stages of numerical equilibrium determined, according to the development of life, either by ruthless outer forces or by the spirit of equilibrium within society. Again we see that the greater the development, the more inadequate the method of " natural selection " proves.

How inadequate that method proves within society is seen if we consider some conditions which stimulate the growth of population. " Misery promotes population," ran the early-Victorian formula,[2] and the wretched population so produced breed new misery for themselves and a further posterity—a vicious circle of misery. " In degenerate families," according to Dr. Tredgold, " where

---

[1] *Prolegomena* to *Evolution and Ethics* (1894).

[2] Cf. Thornton, *On Overpopulation* (1846).

children are passed over to the special schools, there is an average of 7·3 children, excluding still-born, as compared with 4 for families whose children attend public elementary schools." [1] These facts illustrate in the first place the general law that the less advanced breed the most, but there is a further point to be noted. These degenerate families live in a social world which not they but their superiors have built, and actually endanger its welfare by sharing its advantages. For outside the world of social law these certainly would never have lived on to reproduce their kind. Here, then, is a socially-created danger, and the dangers it creates society itself must overcome.

We have nullified the methods of " nature," which lead down from barbarism to savagery and the dark worlds of lower life, and we can never restore these methods unless we ourselves take again that downward road. Besides, these methods, like all unintelligent methods, were spendthrift, imperfectly efficient, repressive of good not less than of evil. But the services rendered by that imperfect and ruthless ministry are still necessary. Since the " natural " selective agency diminishes, the more perfect and direct selective agency of human purpose must increase. *The " natural " method is a selective death-rate, now of less avail because it selects too late ; the finer method is a selective birth-rate, the only adequate method in a world in which the excess of reproduction over survival constantly diminishes.*

(c) The selective efficiency of *disease* becomes less with the growth of society. In wild nature, disease claims its victims more rapidly, and leaves them no opportunity to reproduce their kind. It is quite other under human conditions. Those who fall victims to the very worst diseases, those who do not recover, yet linger on to

[1] Quoted from Mr. and Mrs. Whetham, *The Family and the Nation*, p. 71.

reproduce a weakened offspring. In fact, the curious reversal of " natural selection " which we have already noticed seems to hold here also, for these are often more productive than the healthy. If they mated with themselves alone, the disease might, by its earlier incidence in the successive generations, act selectively, in other words, eliminate its victims ; but intermarriage does not follow these lines, and no such result is actually attained. There is only one way left, it becomes necessary not simply to combat disease where it already exists, but still more to prevent it. To that end social man is now beginning, none too soon, to apply the resources of society. The trial of the organism by disease is not as individualistic an affair as our forefathers' conception of the day of judgment. In society the stronger and the weaker are so bound up together that in certain respects the weakness of the weaker weakens the strength of the stronger. The perception of this fact changes our whole outlook. Take the simplest of all cases, that where the wage-earner of a family is struck down by some disease. If no cure be found, his dependents, the healthy members of the family, become destitute, suffer privation, are weakened, and perhaps in turn contract the disease, to the endangering of a wider community. If, on the other hand, medical skill, under that social control which should always accompany social interdependence, find a cure, it means not only the restoration of the affected member, but also the probable preservation of the health and vigour of the rest. Again, social conditions greatly increase the dangers of infection from disease, so that it has opportunities never given to it in nature. Now it is the young who are most endangered by infection,[1]

[1] " Young animals are capable of being infected by a smaller quantity of microbes than adults." (Archdall Reid, *The Principles of Heredity*, p. 129.) " Young English soldiers perish more readily of cholera and dysentery than adults." (*Ibid.*, p. 173.)

and therefore it is vitally important for the race that society should protect its children from the dangers it creates for them. If the lives of individuals were isolated, disease might perhaps be regarded as a purely beneficent agency, but how can we hold to that doctrine if we realise the interdependence of men ? In truth disease becomes a poorer selective agency as society advances, and we must find better agencies to replace it.

It is said, on the contrary, that the preventive agencies of man are useless or worse, and that " Nature is solving the problem for us." [1] Nothing could be more erroneous. " Nature " solves no problem which society creates. We have seen that in society disease does not eliminate itself by eliminating its victims—it is alas ! too obvious that to wait for " Nature's " aid is to wait on the bank till the stream runs past. It is, happily, also becoming clear that the purposive activity of man can, here as elsewhere, progressively control his environment. Whether or not the bold prophecy of Sir E. Ray Lankester be true, that " by the unstinted application of known methods of investigation and consequent controlling action, all epidemic disease could be abolished within a period so short as fifty years," [2] it is certain that in a much shorter period, since men have begun to realise the need of control, most encouraging results have been attained.[3] The posi-

[1] Cf. Karl Pearson, *Tuberculosis, Heredity, and Environment,* p. 45.

[2] *Romanes Lecture,* 1905.

[3] Professor Karl Pearson, in his pamphlet on *Tuberculosis, Heredity, and Environment,* provides graphs showing that the *rate of fall* in the death-rate from tuberculosis in this country has decreased since the fight against tuberculosis has become most active. Whence he argues that the fight in question is useless or pernicious. If we take his own figures and omit others which tell a very different story, the conclusion remains curiously illogical. If a man digs a pit, let us say, and finds that the deeper he goes the less is the *rate* of progress, it would follow, on the same reasoning, that his activity was hindering the work ! Has Professor Pearson never heard of the law of diminishing return ? Really, it is curious that so eminent a statistician, who can give you in exact percentages the correlation of sympathy, truthfulness, dutiful·

tive character of these results, the elimination of small-pox for instance, stands in striking contrast to the dubious results achieved when " Nature " is allowed to solve the problem for us.

The *laissez-faire* argument rests entirely on precarious hypotheses. It is not established either (1) that those who are immune from attack escape by reason of their essential life-fitness, or (2) that those who are attacked and recover are stronger and not weaker for the battle they have fought, or (3) that those who are attacked and eventually succumb leave the race the stronger for the elimination of the weaklings. The last of these hypotheses is disposed of by the considerations we have already set forth. The other too may be briefly discussed. (1) The theory of immunity, except for certain very special cases, is yet unverified. It is in any case certain that the immunity " naturally " acquired by a people, say against consumption or malaria, is always of a most partial character, contrasting sharply with the immunity which man has secured for himself against certain diseases. Again, recent researches tend to show that, where immunity does exist, it is of a specialised

ness, and so forth, as between husband and wife, should fall into the obvious errors that disfigure the pamphlet in question.

It may be well to give some positive evidence. In France, two public-spirited men, Professors Calmette and Courmont, instituted a consistent " fight against tuberculosis " in Lille and Lyons respectively. " That the results were excellent was shown by Calmette's figures. Before 1901 the public health office in Lille recorded yearly from 1000 to 1160 deaths caused by tuberculosis. In 1907, after six years' work of the dispensary, the record was 860 deaths among 205,625 inhabitants, and in 1911, 704 deaths among 217,807 inhabitants. Similar results had been observed in Lyons. From 1900 to 1904 the average death-rate from tuberculosis had been 35·4 per 10,000 inhabitants ; in 1911 it had gone down to 26·1 per 10,000." (From the account given by Dr. E. Rist at the Conference on Tuberculosis held in London in 1913.)

It may be added that in Germany, where the fight against tuberculosis has been very systematically conducted, the *rate of fall* in the death-rate from tuberculosis has *increased* in recent years. In Prussia since 1892 the death-rate from tuberculosis has declined about 50 per cent.

character, in other words, it is not that the body as a whole is rendered stronger and therefore more resistant, but that special protective substances are evolved to counteract the poisoning agencies. Immunity, so far, would mean not general fitness, but fitness in respect of immunity. We do indeed find a champion of " Nature " telling us that measles confers distinct benefit on people by making them immune—to measles ! [1] One may note in this connection that perhaps the most recent theory to account for the *relative* immunity of Europeans from tuberculosis—that of Professor Metchnikoff—regards it as due to the existence of mild strains of the disease with which the young unwittingly inoculate themselves. " It is a matter of chance," so Sir E. Ray Lankester expounds the theory, " whether on the one hand, the child thus becomes infected with a comparatively mild or benign ' strain ' of the bacillus producing only scrofula or hip-joint disease, or possibly no noticeable malady, but resulting in protective immunity, or, on the other hand, has the misfortune to infect itself with a deadly ' strain ' producing pulmonary phthisis and consequent death." Whether this be so or not, it is quite clear that in respect of that other disease which most of all endangers the life of future generations and which is alarmingly prevalent in the civilised world to-day, neither is immunity being acquired nor is infection a consequence (but only a cause) of physical disability.

(2) The victory may or may not be to the strong, it remains unproved that the victors emerge stronger and not weaker for the battle. The virulent bacillus is a kind of poison, or poison-producer. Is it, then, a good thing for the organism to be tried by poison ? We shall see presently how difficult it is to answer in the affirmative.

A further point may be made. There is indisputable

[1] Cf. Archdall Reid, *Heredity*, pp. 112-3.

evidence that, however well selected men may be in respect of previous health-character, they fall victims to the diseases favoured by unhealthy conditions. For instance, soldiers, a selected body in respect of general health, suffer far more from tuberculosis than the general population, because of barrack-conditions. It is also quite clear from statistics [1] that the life lived in prisons, nunneries, etc., increases susceptibility to tuberculosis. We must therefore ask of those who hold that this kind of " struggle " is good for the race, How much of it is good ? The amount which our prison-conditions induce, the amount which our city-conditions induce, or how much ?

(d) An analogous argument holds in respect of all conditions of life which have evil effects on the present generation—these are, at any rate wherever society is firmly established, evil also for the race, for the future generations. The case of alcoholic poisoning, already referred to, is here apposite. We cannot admit here the easy doctrine of immunity which the natural-selectionists uphold. " It is an absolute rule to which there is no exception," says one of them, " that, given an abundant supply of alcohol, every race is temperate strictly in proportion to its past experience of the poison." [2] This is an entirely misleading statement, as the case of France alone is sufficient to prove. And again, which is more temperate in respect of opium, England with its little experience of it or China with its great experience ? If it be said that the supply is less abundant in England, that, so far as it is true at all, is due to *social* conditions.

Or take the case of those who work in poisonous materials such as lead. The effect of their trial by poison is undoubtedly to lower the general average of

[1] Cf. Hirsch, *Geographical and Historical Pathology*, III., p. 222 ff.

[2] Reid, *The Principles of Heredity*, p. 199.

health as well as to increase the mortality-rate and to decrease the birth-rate.[1] The effect of industrial poisons on women-workers is especially serious. According to Dr. Hirt,[2] the mortality among infants born of women employed at a certain form of glass-making is 55 per cent., and for the children of women who work in lead it is 40 per cent. The selective birth-rate is not improved by the selection, but worsened, worsened in proportion to the activity of the selective agent. Prince Kropotkin has observed that " those who survive a famine, or a severe epidemic of cholera, or small-pox, or diphtheria, such as we see them in uncivilised countries, are neither the strongest, nor the healthiest, nor the most intelligent. No progress could be based on those survivals—the less so as all survivors usually come out of the ordeal with an impaired health, like . . . the garrison of a fortress which has been compelled to live for a few months on half rations, and comes out of its experience with a broken health, and subsequently shows a quite abnormal mortality." [3] The more our knowledge extends the more evidence have we that the general standard of ill-health is highest in the classes where the death-rate is highest, and therefore a high death-rate cannot be regarded complacently as working for the welfare of the race.[4] For

---

[1] Cf. Legge and Goadby, *Lead Poisoning and Lead Absorption* (1912). The diminution of the birth-rate is a specific result of the poison.

[2] *Die gewerbliche Thätigkeit der Frauen.*

[3] *Mutual Aid* (2nd ed.), p. 73.

[4] The introduction of a National Insurance Act has been the means of providing more exact evidence of this fact. Here is an illustration. " One panel doctor with a large East End practice has had through his surgery within the year 81 per cent. of all the people on his list. Another in South London has had 88 per cent. He declares emphatically, and doctors in other towns and in other parts of London bear the same testimony, that what these people are suffering from is essentially want of nourishment, want of warm clothing, want of decent housing, and want of rest—in short, extreme poverty." (From the report on the working of the Insurance Act issued by *The New Statesman*, 1914.)

it is due to evil conditions which continuously do injury
to the successive generations.

In all these cases the selective agency is in some measure
the cause or even the essence of the degeneracy which it
also in some measure eliminates. This truth is either
ignored or denied by those who rely on these agencies of
selection. But the evidence is clear. Consider the
crucial instance, the selective action revealed in infant-
mortality. " It cannot be too distinctly recognised,"
says Sir George Newman, " that a high infant-mortality
rate almost necessarily denotes a prevalence of those
causes and conditions which in the long run determine a
degeneration of race." [1] The two exhaustive reports [2]
prepared by Dr. Newsholme, the Medical Officer of the
Local Government, confirm this statement, showing in
particular that, all over the country, the infant-mortality-
rate and the death-rate at subsequent ages go together.

It follows, as a general principle, that social conditions
which are bad for " the individual," *i.e.* for the members
of the present generation, are bad also for the race.   It
is those who are most immersed in the whirl of the struggle
against misery and poverty whose health—to say nothing
of other qualifications of life—is most endangered and
enfeebled.   It is those who strive most for life whose
own lives suffer the most.   It follows also, on the positive
side, that the development of society is, and must always
be, bound up with the development of the principle of
rational or purposive selection, as distinct from the
principle of " natural selection."

Merely to state this fact is to raise a cloud of prejudices.
Those who believe in the undiminished operation of

[1] *Infant Mortality*, Preface. This work, and Dr. Newsholme's
reports, should be studied by everyone who is interested in this fundamental question.

[2] *Local Government Board*, 1910, Cd. 5263, and 1913, Cd. 6909.

"natural selection" among men are sometimes least ready to admit the operation of rational selection. Others discover under the expressions " selective birth-rate " and " rational selection " the methods of the cattle-breeder, with perhaps a despotic State as master of the stud. But such ideas are grotesque distortions of the principle we have stated. The operation of State-control is necessarily most limited, and can only prevent the reproduction of those who reveal so deep-rooted and fatal a defect that it taints the source of life, and gravely endangers, in the interdependence of men, the integrity of the lives of those around them, as well as of the possible offspring of themselves. The conditions which fall under this condemnation are chiefly syphilis and certain forms of insanity ; and all who know the social effects of these realise the absolute necessity of positive measures in respect of them.[1] An extension of that knowledge would open the eyes of the whole world to the necessity of control. It is significant that in recent times that knowledge has in fact been growing.[2] There will doubtless

[1] It is sometimes said that, since many men of genius have revealed symptoms of insanity and come of stocks tainted with insanity, these measures would diminish the uprising of genius. This objection has been answered by Mr. Havelock Ellis, who well protests against the reckless methods of those alienists who regard as insanity all divergence from the mean. Adopting, as a means of determining genius, an objective and impersonal scheme of selection on the basis of the *Dictionary of National Biography*, he finds that :—" In not one per cent. can definite insanity be traced among the parents of British men and women of genius. No doubt this result is below the truth ; the insanity of the parents must sometimes have escaped the biographer's notice. But even if we double the percentage to escape this source of error the proportion still remains insignificant." He concludes :—" There is no need to minimise the fact that a certain small proportion of men of genius have displayed highly morbid characters, nor to deny that in a large proportion of cases a slightly morbid strain may, with care, be detected in the ancestry of genius. But the influence of eugenic considerations can properly be brought to bear only in the case of grossly degenerate stocks. Here, so far as our knowledge extends, the parentage of genius nearly always escapes. The destruction of genius, and its creation, alike elude the eugenist." (*Contemporary Review*, Oct., 1913.)

[2] One might instance, as in most significant contrast to the earlier attitude towards this subject, M. Brieux' play, *Les Avariés*.

some day result a directer activity, social and not merely political, to overcome the evils thus revealed.

For the operation of social selection is an infinitely wider and more continuous process than the direct activity of any State. All social activity, being purposive, is selective, and thus social selection increases in intensity as society grows. It operates most directly in the form of sexual selection. Now this becomes more direct and intimate with the growth of personality, and it depends in great measure upon the standards and ideals developed within a community. Thus the ideals of each generation determine—not the ideals alone, but—the very life and character of all that succeed.

The selective forces operative within society are exceedingly complex and diversified, and the attempt even to enumerate them would carry us far. But this much is obvious, that these are not outer forces merely active upon men, but forces revealing and springing from their actual natures. They are purpose-determined forces, and are themselves rational in so far as human purposes are rational. The development of community means, therefore, the increase of rational selection.

We may here point out some forms of social selection still operative among men which are the reverse of rational, and which therefore are incompatible with any complete development of community. (1) In so far as those otherwise less fit are preferred in marriage because of their *economic* advantages, and those otherwise more fit are prevented from marriage because of their economic disability, there is operative an evil process of social selection. (2) Likewise, in so far as social conditions of any kind favour the celibacy of the vigorous in mind or body, there is operative an evil process of social selection. This was the crime of which Galton so eloquently accused the

Roman Church.[1] It is probable also that the segregation of military conscripts into barracks for two or three years, not only enforcing a temporary celibacy, but delaying the period at which they can attain an economic position such as would justify marriage, as well as creating habits opposed to married life, works in the same direction.[2] (3) The institution of war is an evil selective agency, for it always destroys a portion of the youth and strength of warring nations. It was pointed out by Darwin himself that the more " civilised " war becomes the more it proves a maleficent selective agent, passing over the weaklings and choosing for its victims the healthy and vigorous. If war, as some still blindly assert, were beneficent in its selective work, Central Europe, after the terrible ordeal of the Thirty Years' War, would have emerged stronger in will and fibre. In fact it emerged crushed, broken, and wretched, in parts so stricken that they required centuries to regain their previous vigour. The evil selective influence of war has been recently pointed out in a convincing way by the American biologist, Professor Jordan.[3] How disastrous its effect was on the civilisations of Greece and Rome, the remarkable work of the historian, Otto Seeck, reveals.[4]

These are but some definitely evil forms of social selection. But social selection is ubiquitous within society, though constantly changing its form as society changes. It works good in so far as human purposes are both good and enlightened, evil in so far as human purposes are evil or, more commonly, determined by ignorance of the means to good.

[1] *Hereditary Genius,* in the chapter entitled " Influences that Affect the Natural Ability of Nations."

[2] See Forel, *The Sexual Question,* pp. 335 ff.

[3] In various works, of which *The Human Harvest* is the most notable.

[4] *Geschichte des Unterganges der antiken Welt,* Vol. I., Bk. II., c. 3 (3rd ed., 1910).

§ 6. Conclusion.

It appears that after all one of the chief *results* of selection has been the evolution of intelligence. It would be unfortunate if " natural selection," which is said to have evolved the brain, should then forbid us the use of it ! Already the mind of man, though it casts only a small circle of light, infinitely small in contrast to the darkness which rings it round, has found, if it has the strength to follow, the way of its own welfare. In truth, if mankind were only willing to accept the aid of that one most obvious and indisputable law, that like tends to beget like, they could ensure for ever—or till that inconceivable time when physical conditions can no longer be controlled to the service of life—health of body and of mind to the successive generations of their race. Men have never tried to cure many of the social evils which they call incurable. They are incurable only if they cannot *will* to cure them.

The enemy is not civilisation and not culture. We have not been thrust out of Nature's Eden because we have " become as gods, knowing good and evil." It is not civilisation that we must blame for our evils, but what remains uncivilised in our civilisation, not culture, but what remains uncultivated within our culture. It is the evil social conditions, perhaps above all the evil economic conditions, which we have—not positively willed or made, but failed to destroy, the evil social conditions which have been the unwilled accompaniments of our willing, the unpurposed effects of our purposes, and whose abolition demands not less but more willing, not poorer but fuller purpose, not a surrender to nature but a completer dominion over her.

Men reply, " You improve at your peril. Look at the cultivated animal or plant, it is no longer able to

face natural conditions, it is an alien in its world." But
there is a difference. The animal or plant has been
bred in a particular direction by a creative purpose outside its own. When that is removed, it is no longer
sustained by any inner force. But social man has bred
himself. His development is the revelation of creative
purpose within humanity, it is the manifestation of his
own nature. And you cannot remove that creative purpose without removing humanity. Furthermore, the contrary argument presumes that "nature" is only a few
centuries or millenia behind us, whereas it is unknown
aeons back. Or rather, this state of nature never did
exist for man. Because life and environment are correlative, the "state of nature" never was the environment of man ; where it existed, man did not yet
exist.

It seems a legitimate inference that man is right in
going forward unflinchingly to the further development
of mutual service and protection, is right in his persistent
battle against disease and pestilence and every organic
evil. Doubtless there is peril in going forward, but there
is peril also in standing still, and in standing still there
is no reward, no further conquest, but only the final
certainty of all standing still—defeat. Our instincts have
led us into the great adventure, our reason must carry
us on. There is no return.

And the adventure is at any rate worth while. We
are not tethered animals living the unthinking, instinctive,
self-adjusted, merely animal life. Untethered, we may
lose our way—the animal cannot, having none to lose—
but the risk is insignificant beside the prospect of gaining
the ever farther horizons, lands of the promise of ever
higher fulfilments.

To-day we can never solve to-morrow's problems, we
cannot even know how to-morrow's problems will appear.

Therefore it is wise for the social philosopher to take no thought for the morrow, in the sense of seeking the solution of difficulties which are still to come. For the morrow will have its own better and better-placed thinkers to answer its own questions.

CHAPTER VIII

SYNTHESIS

WE have now seen the unity that underlies all the forms of communal development. It is the unity which life, if we seek deeply enough, always reveals. As in each life, so in the continuity of life through successive generations, all the characters of development reveal a single principle. All growth of personality in the members of community involves a correspondent change in their relations to one another, in the social structure, in the customs, institutions, and associations of community. The development of persons and the development of interpersonal relations thus form a single field of study, though we may centre our interest on one or other aspect. In this work our interest has been centred on the interpersonal or social aspect, but we must start from the unity of both aspects in order to understand it. This was revealed in our first law, which gave the clue to the whole development. Socialisation and individualisation develop *pari passu*. The unity of these two factors is revealed in every life as well as in the whole they constitute, for that unity is personality. This must be the basis of any account of communal development. *The actual development of personality attained in and through community by its members is the measure of the importance these attach to personality both in themselves and in their fellow-men.* By aid of this clue we can bring all the other aspects of communal development, the growth of communal economy, the growth of environmental control, under a single law.

To show the unity of communal development is to show also the *line* of communal development, the direction of a road that stretches, who knows, to a yet undreamed-of distance. Community has advanced along that road, not in any steady progress, but in spite of halts, wanderings, and retreats. As it has advanced, the meaning of its march has become, though still dim, yet clearer. Blind impulses are superseded by conscious forces, whereupon it appears that much that was blind in its operation—blind to us whom it impelled—was yet not meaningless, but continuous with what now reveals itself as our own conscious purpose. If that purpose grows still clearer, the movement of community will become more straightforward, towards an age for which the records of this present time will be a memory of " old unhappy far-off things."

APPENDICES

APPENDIX A.

A CRITICISM OF THE NEO-HEGELIAN IDENTIFICATION OF "SOCIETY" AND "STATE"

(Extract from an article contributed to " The Philosophical Review" of January 1911)

IT is a noteworthy fact that most of the serious attempts, during the last century and a half, to reach a comprehensive political principle, have owed their inspiration to Hellenic ideas. This is as true for Rousseau, " citizen of Geneva," whose abstract love of " nature " transmuted itself into a very concrete affection for a city-state, as for certain writers of our own day, and especially Professor Bosanquet, with his ideal of " Christian Hellenism," [1] itself inspired by the Hellenic thought of Hegel. This Hellenism has indeed taught us so much that it may seem ungrateful to accuse it of misleading us. Yet the conditions of our modern life are in some respects very different from those of Hellenic society. In particular, within the small circles of the Greek world certain distinctions lay concealed which in the wider reach of the modern community are or should be manifest. An application to modern life of a purely Hellenic theory is on that account dangerous, and seems to the writer to have in fact misled many of those theorists who, from Rousseau onwards, have adopted it—who have found in Hellenism the key to the modern State.

Within the small circle of the Greek city, the distinction of State and community lay concealed. It might be interesting to trace the rise of this distinction in the political consciousness of later ages,[2] but here it must suffice to say

---

[1] *Essays and Addresses*, p. 48.

[2] Ritchie (*Principles of State-Interference*, p. 157) quotes an early instance, viz., St. Thomas Aquinas (*De regimine principum*) translates the πολιτικὸν ζῷον of Aristotle by *animal sociale et politicum*.

that the distinction is an essential one, and that its validity is shown by the incoherence of the logic which obscures or denies it. In particular, the theory of the general will is, in the hands of most of its interpreters, a virtual denial of this necessary distinction, and I propose before going further to examine briefly the forms of this doctrine held respectively by Rousseau, Hegel, and Professor Bosanquet, and to show that in every case they are vitiated by a too narrow Hellenism.

1. The General Will, said Rousseau, is the true sovereign and ultimate authority in a State, and, in its obvious sense, this is the accepted doctrine of all democratic States, whose machinery is so constructed that, in one way or another, the ultimate decision lies with the mass of voters, the " people." Politically, then, the " general will " is and must remain sovereign. So far Rousseau is justified. But Rousseau, not content with the necessary political sovereignty of the people, went on to show *not* that such a sovereignty was a moral thing, but that it was *identical* with a moral sovereignty. The general will, Rousseau explained, cannot err. The rightful sovereign *must* act rightfully. Now, that the sovereign " can do no wrong " is a logical and obvious legal position. Legality cannot transcend law ; morality can, and it is just the necessary moral righteousness, not the legal rightness, of the sovereign that Rousseau was concerned to uphold. For him the political organisation was in no way made distinct from the complex and indeterminate social structure, and therefore the bonds of State were just the bonds that keep a society together, the moral sanctions of society. Thence arose the refinements of theory by which Rousseau vainly tries to maintain the identification. First, the general will is distinguished from the " will of all "—not, in truth, a distinction between two kinds of *political* willing—and then it is asserted that the former always wills the good, though it may be unenlightened. The legal formula asserts the legal rightness of the sovereign's action and leaves its moral rightness open, but the dictum of Rousseau asserts its moral rightness and thus makes the political sovereign an anomalous " person " liable, it may be, to intellectual error but in every other respect infallible—a " person " absolutely good but somewhat short-sighted. It is the danger of modern Hellenism

to confound the actual with the ideal, and in this strange
conception of inerrant will united to fallible judgment we
have a good instance of that confusion.   Here already we
find Rousseau losing hold of the political principle, seeking a
political sovereign which no State can ever recognise because
no State can ever find it.

Rousseau identified the common will with the good will,
but without going into the difficult places of psychology we
may say that, although it may be to the general interest or
good that the general will should be fulfilled, the general
will is not therefore the will for the general good.   And the
practical difficulty is no less than the psychological.   A will
which cannot be determined by any positive standard can
never be a legislative authority or source of positive law.
Will is liable to persuasion, and the persuading will is therefore sovereign over the persuaded.   So the will of the people
may be the will of a single individual, does sometimes mean
the will of two or three.   To analyse the complex of influences
moral and social determining a given act of will, a specific
act of legislation, is difficult in the extreme ; to isolate among
these determinants an original or sovereign will is impossible.
For all practical purposes we must find a definite sovereign,
a political sovereign ; we must ask not whether it is Pericles
persuading the demos or Aspasia persuading Pericles, but
what will it is that wills the decree, that actually commands
or consents.

The whole attempt to identify the principle of democracy
—as any other political principle—with that of morality is
fore-doomed to failure, and ends in setting on the political
throne a crowned abstraction.   For a will that is not realised,
that is no man's will, is meaningless.   What profit is it that
this " general will " does not err—if it does nothing at all ?
Even if on any occasion the " general will " as understood
by Rousseau came into being, it would simply be an interesting social fact, a coincidence ; for political purposes it would
be identical with a *majority*-will.   In every case, therefore,
the majority-will—which extended far enough becomes the
" will of all "—must be the political principle, and to determine political obligation in terms of any other is worse than
useless.

It is his consistent attempt to identify the political with the social order that leads Rousseau into the vagaries of his political logic. Why cannot the people be represented or act through deputy ? Logically there seems to be no reason why the general will should not will legislation by its representative. But Rousseau is thinking of the whole complex of ideals and interests and aims animating a society—and that cannot be represented. Why, again, does the *Contrat Social*[1] afford us that strangest of all spectacles, the apostle of freedom prescribing " dogmas of civil religion," declaring that " if anyone, after publicly acknowledging those dogmas, acts like an unbeliever of them, he should be punished with death " ? Again the answer is that Rousseau has utterly failed to distinguish the sanctions of all social order from the proper bonds of the political organisation.

2. Hegel[2] finds fault with Rousseau because, while rightly adhering to the principle of will, he " conceived of it only in the determinate form of the individual will and regarded the universal will not as the absolutely reasonable will (*an und für sich Vernünftige des Willens*) but only as the common will that proceeds out of the individual will as conscious." This is to accuse the author of a political treatise because he has not written a work on metaphysics when the writer has in fact merely mixed up the two. After all, is there not a common will, and is not this common will the basis of any State or organisation ? Behind the definite institution, the work of conscious will, the philosopher may look for a rationality or universality which that conscious will yet has not for itself. It is at least permissible to search. But no fact is explained away by the greater rationality of another fact, and for the State, for any *organisation*, the fact of will is just the fact of " common will, proceeding out of the individual will as conscious." The will on which State-institutions are based must be a conscious will, the will of the citizens, or they would never come to be. State-institutions are not built like the hexagons of a beehive, by an instinct of unconscious co-operation. And though, in the construction of any institution, we may build wiser than we know, the plan of

[1] *Contrat Social*, Bk. IV., c. 8.

[2] *Grundlinien der Philosophie des Rechts*, § 258.

the building and the co-operation of the builders must be consciously resolved upon.

To Hegel as to Rousseau there was ever present the tendency to interpret the State in terms of Hellenism, and that in spite of his being credited with discovering the distinction of State and society. In reality his account of that distinction is neither clear nor satisfactory. The society which he distinguishes from the State—what he calls *bürgerliche Gesellschaft*—seems to hang strangely between actuality and ideality. It is a community resting on the " particularity " of desires, on economic need, and yet in discussing this economic community, which is " different " from the State, Hegel treats of law and police, essentially State-institutions. On the other hand, the economic system is not the only social grouping, though a primary one, which can be distinguished from the State organisation; we might equally distinguish, *e.g.*, the institutions through which arts and sciences develop, the educational system, ecclesiastical institutions, charitable institutions, and so on, terms which cover a kaleidoscopic variety of constantly re-forming elements.[1] But the State cannot be regarded as absorbing within itself the free and living interplay of all these social forces ; for one thing they are many of them not bounded by the limits of any State ; and therefore it is absurd to say, *tout court*, that the State is " developed spirit," " the world the spirit has made for itself," and so forth.

3. The foregoing argument bears directly on the misconception of the " general will," and I propose next to consider the more or less Hegelian account of that doctrine set forth in Professor Bosanquet's book *The Philosophical Theory of the State*. In no modern work are the inconsistencies and contradictions of applied Hellenism more apparent.

Professor Bosanquet's general position is as follows : Liberty is the condition of our " being ourselves " or willing ourselves, and this liberty is identified with the life of the State. " It is such a ' real ' or rational will that thinkers after Rousseau

---

[1] Hegel's incidental treatment of these parts of the social system is bewildering. What is to be made of such a statement as the following : " Inasmuch as consciousness (*Wissen*) has its seat in the State, science (*Wissenschaft*) too has it there, and not in the church " ? (§ 270.)

have identified with the State. In this theory they are follow-ing the principles of Plato and Aristotle, no less than the indications which Rousseau furnished by his theory of the general will in connection with the work of the legislator. The State, when thus regarded, is to the general life of the individual much as we saw the family to be with regard to certain of his impulses. The idea is that in it, or by its help, we find at once discipline and expansion, the transfiguration of partial impulses, and something to do and to care for, such as the nature of a human self demands." He adds two considerations " to make this conception less paradoxical to the English mind." " (a) The State, as thus conceived, is not merely the political fabric. The term State accents indeed the political aspect of the whole, and is opposed to the notion of an anarchical society. But it includes the entire hierarchy of institutions by which life is determined, from the family to the trade, and from the trade to the Church and the Uni-versity. It includes all of them, not as the mere collection of the growths of the country, but as the structure which gives life and meaning to the political whole, while receiving from it mutual adjustment, and therefore expansion and a more liberal air. The State, it might be said, is thus con-ceived as the operative criticism of all institutions—the modi-fication and adjustment by which they are capable of playing a rational part in the object of human will. . . . (b) The State, as the operative criticism of all institutions, is neces-sarily force ; and in the last resort, it is the only recognised and justified force." [1]

The first and greatest confusion into which Professor Bosanquet falls is that he uses the term State in two quite different senses. We find him, on the one hand, defining the State as a " working conception of life " (p. 151), or even, after Plato, as " the individual writ large " (p. 154)— and it is clear that here he means by State the unity of all the social forces at work in a community of human beings ; on the other hand, when he comes to talk of State-action, it is at once obvious that he is now using " State " in its proper signification of " *political* society," with its definite form, its definite and limited type of action. Hence we are

---

[1] *The Philosophical Theory of the State* (1st ed.), pp. 149-152.

told that the means of the State are not *in pari materia* with
the end (p. 187), and are left with the anomalous conclusion
that the " real will," the " rational will," " the will that
wills itself," can never will any positive action whatever, much
less " itself," can only " hinder hindrances " (p. 191). Hindrances to what ?

The same confusion underlies Professor Bosanquet's distinction of " real " and " actual " will, by means of which
he attempts to solve the problem of political obligation. The
distinction intended is itself a true and suggestive one, though
wrongly expressed. It rests on the primary distinction of
" good " and " seeming good." People will what, if they
knew the case fully and truly, they would no longer will.
They will the seeming good because it seems the good. It
is an obvious fact enough, but I may set down as an illustration an instance mentioned by Balzac in the novel *Cousin
Pons*. " The mortality in French hospitals," he declares,
" caused by women who take food privately to their husbands
has been so great that physicians have now resolved to enforce
a rigid personal search of the patients on the days when
their relatives come to see them."   Now Professor Bosanquet's
distinction of " real " and " actual " rather obscures the
psychological relations here involved, and suggests a false
antithesis of " real " and " actual " will. The opposition is
not between two wills, a " real " and an " actual," but within
the single act of willing, between the actual consequence of the
object willed, *i.e.*, the giving of food, and the end it was meant
to serve, the restoration to health of the husbands. There is
but one object willed, the giving of food. We cannot say even
that the health of the husbands was " willed," still less the
death of those husbands. A motive or end is not an act of will,
" real " or otherwise. Would Professor Bosanquet say that
these women " really " willed the recovery of their husbands,
but " actually " willed the giving of food ? [1]

It has to be remembered that Professor Bosanquet introduces this distinction of " real " and " actual " will in order

---

[1] It looks as if Professor Bosanquet's distinction rested on such an
opposition as this : They " really " will the recovery of their husbands,
they " actually " *cause* their death—not an opposition in terms of will
at all.

to answer the question of political obligation. " We have thus far been attempting to make clear what is meant by the identification of the State with the real will of the Individual in which he wills his own nature as a rational being ; in which identification we find the only true account of political obligation " (p. 154). But this, in fact, does not touch the real problem. It is only too obvious that an " actual " State is not the " real " State of Professor Bosanquet, and the question of political obligation is : " On what grounds and how far is a citizen bound to obey the actual laws of the State ? " What might be the principle of political obligation in an ideal State—where the question would never arise— is very different from what must be the principle under actual political conditions. The will of an actual State, in respect of any definite act of legislation, is and must be based on a majority-will. It is not because he finds his " real " will embodied in legislation from which he actually dissents that the citizen is obedient to the law. A thorough-going identity of will is in the nature of the case impossible, and we must look instead for some persistent identity of interest, giving unity to the fundamental will on which the State, like any other association, must rest, and ensuring consent— but only consent—to the secondary acts of will through which the State fulfils its end. We ask too much if we expect an identity of will. In an actual State no individual can have this ideal, this harmony of his will and the State-will, realised all the time. Granting the first unity—the primary will for political life resting on the primary good of political life— we must thereafter be content to rest political obligation on common *good*, and at most only indirectly, through that notion, on common will.

Professor Bosanquet, in fact, refuses to recognise the neces- sities of the situation. To avoid Rousseau's difficulty that where a portion of the people must accept the will of another portion there is no freedom, Professor Bosanquet would declare that the general will is the rational will and thus true freedom—a double confusion for, first, the *political* principle must be the majority-will, and second, supposing *per impossibile* that the majority-will were purely rational, yet to identify freedom with enforced subjection to reason

or good, and to call such subjection self-government, is indeed
a "paradox." Doubtless a man may be forced to be free—
Rousseau's own dangerous paradox contains a certain truth
—but to identify such enforcement with "self-government"
is to strain language and meaning to the breaking point. It
involves an impossible identification of good and will.

On both sides Professor Bosanquet's account fails to answer
the concrete question of political obligation. The conception
of an abstract self willing an abstract good will never be an
explanation of why and when the actual citizen should loyally
identify himself with the positive commands of a very concrete government, enforcing measures whose ultimate conformity to his own "true" nature he may not unreasonably
refuse to take for granted.

The basal fallacy of all such views lies, as I have pointed
out, in the identification of State and community, in the
refusal to draw a clear distinction here. "We have hitherto,"
says Professor Bosanquet, "spoken of the State and Society
as almost convertible terms. And in fact it is part of our
argument that the influences of Society differ only in degree
from the powers of the State, and that the explanation of
both is ultimately the same" (p. 184). This position vitiates
the whole of Professor Bosanquet's account of the State.

Note.—I ought to add that Dr. Bosanquet, in the course
of some private correspondence which has passed between
us, has expressed the view that the distinction between
society and the State is one of importance, and points out
that he has made more of it in the Introduction to the second
edition of *The Philosophical Theory of the State*, though maintaining the essential truth of his general theory of the State.

APPENDIX B.

INTERNATIONAL COMMUNITY IN RELATION TO THE INSTITUTION OF WAR

(An extract, with some additions, from an article contributed to " The International Journal of Ethics," Jan. 1912)

TO-DAY it is States and not communities that go to war, for there is no community which is separate and independent to-day. A war to-day between civilised peoples is essentially " civil war," because the peoples are all to-day *inter*civilised. That war should have meaning at all it is essential that the State should be co-extensive with community, that a people should be as independent of any other people as a State is of any other State.

If we once realised how the civilised world is being transformed from separated, isolated, independent communities into a single continuous community, international questions would at once appear in a new light. We should see, *e.g.*, that the cessation of war does not depend on federations or treaties arbitrarily entered upon by independent self-sufficient States, not on the mere fiat of high contracting parties, not simply on the convenience of governments or the intrigues of diplomacy or the relations of monarchs, but on the silent widening social will that ultimately all governments must obey. The mass of society, the great working mass of every people, have an interest in peace and not in war. Their interests are one in every State ; they form a single common interest. Common interest when recognised begets common will.

The members of western States are already and are becoming more and more members also of this greater community. This greater community is becoming conscious of its common interest, and in turn will establish, through the co-operation

of States, the means for its security. It has already begun
to do so by " international law," and by the recently established international courts. Many people regard " international law " as law in name only, and international courts
as courts in name only. What, they ask, is law that has no
force behind it, or a court that can neither summon offenders
nor execute its decrees ? Is not law without power a shadow
or phantom, and the tribunal entrusted with administering
it but the vain pulpit of impotent idealists, pitting moral
suasion against armed force ? Such an objection is seen to
be ill-founded if we realise that the ultimate factor in government is not force but will. What is lacking to " international
law " in the first place is not common force, but common will.
Given the will, the force necessarily follows. It is because
common will is still so inchoate that " international law " is
so imperfect and insecure. But even in its present form it is
not futile. You are perfectly at liberty to deny to it the right
to the term " law," but you must admit a certain degree of
efficacy nevertheless. States do not sign Berlin treaties or
agree to Hague or Geneva Conventions without meaning something by it. And there are many rules of international law
that no civilised State would dream of violating. Would any
civilised State to-day commence hostilities against another
civilised State without declaration of war, or suffer its nationals
to shoot down in warfare the ascertained bearers of a flag of
truce ? The " law of nations," which even Napoleon declared
to be universally observed by civilised States, has been
hitherto concerned more with regulating war than peace, but
if it can regulate war, the denial of community, are there not
a thousand reasons why it should be still more authoritative
to regulate peace ?

Force, indeed, of some kind the law must have. But
whence, in the first instance, does the law acquire its force ?
From governments or judges or armies or policemen ? Simply
from the social will to uphold the law, the will to obey it.
Without that will not a government or court of law could
exist for an hour. It is that will that evokes the force that
waits behind the law, to enforce the law on any reluctant
minority. Government is simply a medium of the will of
society.

The assumption that law is only possible within a State is an unnecessary one. There was a time in the history of civilisation when there were laws and no States, effective social laws. No legislature had ever enacted them, no chief had ordained them, but they ruled the tribes, were recognised and obeyed, upheld only by public opinion and the power of social approbation and disapprobation. So far as we can discern the dim beginnings of civilised life, first in the history of peoples came the law, never enacted or proclaimed, next the court, the jurisdiction, the " doom," revealing but not making law, and last of all the legislature took law into its charge. As in Old Testament history, after the Judges came the Kings. *International law is following exactly the same course.* The law itself has been growing into being from remote antiquity, the famed " law of nations," the " law which all men everywhere obey," dimly realised in the troubled political consciousness of the Greeks, interpreted by the Romans for the peoples within the Empire, and after the pitiless wars of the Middle Ages first formulated by Grotius as a rule for independent States.

Here is the first stage, the slow revealing of the law. The second stage has now arrived. Two permanent international courts have now been called into being, the Hague permanent Court of Arbitration, founded 1899, and the Hague International Court of Appeal for naval prizes, recently established. This is the beginning of the jurisdiction that comes after the law. Lastly will come the international legislature, to take into its keeping, maintain, modify, and enlarge the international law. Why should not such a legislature be as authoritative as, say, a Federal Legislature ? It is the fulfilment of the present process of the nations. It would leave the integrity of nations unimpaired, or rather ensure it, for it is war that has always threatened the independence of peoples. It is a means neither to imperialism nor to cosmopolitanism, two false extremes. It would maintain the autonomy of States, as law maintains the liberty of individuals. And it would protect community. For while State is totally independent of State, and nation, sometimes, clearly defined and separate from nation, community is one, and links the nearest to the most remote and may make the most remote indispensable to the nearest. "I say, there is not a red Indian hunting by Lake Winnipeg can quarrel with his squaw, but the whole world must smart for it ; will not the price of beaver rise ? " If not sympathy or understanding, then at least commerce forms its nexus.

Even were they bound by this strong band alone, it would be enough to make war disastrous both to the warring nations and to the neutral peoples with whom they form one community. This economic interdependence has recently been very strikingly illustrated by Mr. Norman Angell in his book *The Great Illusion.* I do not think, however, that the new economic conditions alone are our greatest security against war. War has always been expensive, and has rarely paid itself to the conquerors, but this has not prevented wars. The surer safeguard is the growing intercommunity of the nations, of which the economic interdependence is rather a sequel than a cause. It is isolation that sets the people to war. "They isolate themselves, expecting war," wrote Bastiat, "but isolation is itself the commencement of war." When nations are isolated, the strength of one is the weakness of the other, the pride of one is the disgrace of the other. When nations are intersocialised, the weakness of one is the weakness of the other, but the wealth, culture, and progress of the one contribute to the wealth, culture, and progress of the other. For it is an elementary fact that within a community every gain of the part is a gain of the whole directly in proportion to the solidarity of the community.

It is not like interest or like culture which constitutes community, but like interests become common through recognition and establishment. There have been periods during which there has prevailed over a wide area a single type of culture, without any adequate realisation of the community thereby made possible. Thus the extensive culture of the Middle Ages came through political and ecclesiastical hierarchies, so that the leaders alone entered into wide social relations. In religion alone did likeness seem to involve the conscious acknowledgment of unity. So religion proved in the Middle Ages the chief factor in the breaking down of communal barriers—but it was not enough.

To-day the process of the conversion of like into common

interests is further advanced. The civilised world is becoming
more and more rapidly an effective community. Each country
is becoming more and more bound up in the welfare of each.
Every recent advance of science has been a means for the
widening of the area of community, uniting men in ways
impossible before. Railway, telegraph, telephone, Marconi
apparatus, even camera and cinematograph, are they not all
bridging the gulfs of isolation, bringing the peoples nearer to
one another, and enabling them to realise the common factors
of all civilised life ? The will for peace grows with the
means of community. It is solidarity that is making war
unintelligible.

States have carried on schemes of mutual devastation
in cases where no possible gain but only loss could accrue,
in the interests of dynasties or in the name of religion or
of honour. The first two causes, dynastic ambition and
religion, need no longer be reckoned with. The world in
which they operated, in which men fought and laid countries
waste to raise a Habsburg to a throne or " enforce " a dogma,
is also of the unreturning past. Democracy has made the
one and enlightenment the other impossible. And it is to
democracy—of which enlightenment is after all but another
name—that we must look for the gradual removal of that
further cause of war which is itself the legacy of previous
wars, the subordination of people to people. For there is
no assurance that war will deliver the world from what war
has itself created, the subjection of peoples. It is more likely
to substitute new subjections for old. But the growth of
democracy, if it continues, necessarily substitutes (as we
have seen in Book III., Chap. IV.) co-ordination for subordination, autonomy for subjection. The future of peace lies with
the future of democracy.

When we have ruled out these other causes of war, there still
remains the principle of " honour," that strange diagonal
along which the counter-forces of passion and conscience have
driven men—and, if we rule out the idea that commercial
supremacy   follows   military   power—" honour "   alone.
" Honour " stands out as the ostensible exception in international agreements. " Honour " is the last stand of the
argument for war. Nearly all the States of the civilised

world have been in these days binding themselves by treaty
to refer subjects of dispute to the Hague tribunal, but they
have all added the words—" Provided nevertheless that they
do not affect the vital interests, the independence, or the
honour of the high contracting parties." It is thought that
the honour of a nation can be entrusted to no international
tribunal. But the honour which prefers war to arbitration
is the international counterpart of the honour which seeks
justice through the duel, and the reasons which have led
civilised men on the whole to reject the duel, the impossibility
of vindicating honour by the accident of superior swordsman-
ship, the iniquity of a tribunal at which the innocent is as
likely to suffer as the guilty, the wronged man as the wrong-
doer, apply equally to the international duel. They apply
indeed with greater force. For indeed no civilised nation
ever insults another. A statesman may, a newspaper editor
may, an admiral may—but a whole people—never! And
we are as grossly misled in identifying, say, the editor with
" Germany," and the admiral, say, with " Russia," as ever
Louis XIV. was in identifying the State with himself. A
people will readily be persuaded that it has suffered an insult,
but it never regards itself as having first offered an insult.
It never does. " I do not know the method," said Burke,
" of drawing up an indictment against a whole people." But
is not the refusal to refer disputes concerning honour to an
international tribunal the drawing up of an indictment against
all other peoples ?

There is another very significant aspect of the intersocial-
isation of the nations. Community, we said, was a question
of degree. Within it there are groups united by many social
ties, others united by few only. The members of a family are
bound by the most numerous and the closest social ties ;
the members of a city have more than the members of a
State ; the citizens who are also members of a church, of a
social order, of a club, of a council, have more ties than those
who are not. It is the very nature of society to involve
social groups and even strata. This is generally recognised,
but what is less observed is that the lines of social grouping
and stratification tend less and less to conform to political
and national boundaries. There is the society of learning.

Its members are of every nation and tongue. There is " society " in the sense of *le haut monde,* again international. There is the organisation of labour, threatening to bring internationalism into practical politics. Its members have in different countries the same political faith, and a faith not shared in by their fellow-citizens. So the member of the English labour party has even a political community with a German socialist which he has not with his fellow English citizen. And so with a thousand other groupings, artistic, scientific, financial, religious, industrial—unions of men crossing the line of States. The educated Englishman has more in common with the educated Frenchman or German than he has with his uneducated fellow-countrymen. He is more " at home," more in society with him ; he prefers his company. Lastly, do not our royal families, the ostensible heads of our States, intermarry with one another alone ?

In the light of the growth of intercommunity is not war between civilised States becoming unintelligible to-day ?

APPENDIX C.

THE CORRELATION OF LIFE AND ENVIRONMENT IN THE SPHERE OF HEREDITY

In the text (III. 7. 2) we have considered specific cases of the reciprocity of the organic environment and the germ-cells. It may strengthen the position if we here consider the whole question from a more general aspect. To deny the correlation of life and environment in the sphere of heredity is to maintain, if we believe in evolution at all, the constant stability and identity of the germ-plasm throughout all the kinds and stages of organic life. Can this position be in any sense maintained?

The whole conception of an absolutely stable germ-plasm is, as Romanes pointed out in his *Examination of Weismannism*, full of difficulty. If the germ-plasm is stable and continuous, then the germ-plasm of the most variant forms of life must, for all the differences of the expression of life, be somehow the same, not only derived from, but identical with, that of some infinitely remote ancestor. The germ-cells of the inconceivably remote primordial life are seen carrying the " determinants " of all the existent variants in genera and species, as well as of the infinitely more numerous variants which have been and are being lost in the endless " experimentation " of nature. If, again, the germ-plasm is stable and continuous, how can it at the same time be so plastic as to admit these endless variations? Weismann answers that such questions involve a misunderstanding. " I have been asked to explain, for example, how the adaptations of flowers, fruits, and seeds in Phanerogams, could have been derived from a combination of characters acquired by the shapeless primordial ancestors. *The characters were not inherited from the primordial beings, but variability, or the dissimilarity of individuals.*" [1] But we

[1] *The Germ-Plasm*, p. 419. Italics Weismann's.

must still ask, What then is this variability, this power to vary ? *Potentialities too are real characters*, their precise difference from actualities being that they require a particular environment as a condition of development. " *Only* potentiality," " *only* predisposition," this is a favourite expression with those who belong to the school of Weismann, but all life is " only predisposition " until it is made actual in an environment. To say there is a tendency to variation cannot be the last word. We must ask, Has the tendency—or the variation—a cause, or has it not ? Will science here at last, at the heart of life, abjure its faith and speak of " accident " ? Weismann tells us in *The Germ-Plasm* that " *the cause of hereditary variation must be deeper than amphixis* " (the intermingling of germ-plasms involved in sexual reproduction), " *it must be due to the direct effect of external influences on the biophors and determinants.*" [1] But these external influences —the admission of which is in itself most significant—cannot do more, as Weismann reminded us in his Romanes Lecture, than merely provide the environmental stimulus for the development of characters already latent in the germ.

As the life differs, so does its response to any stimulus. Variability cannot be regarded as *mere* plasticity, or variations as mere accidents. Our present knowledge of nature, as the scientist of our day pre-eminent for the fineness of his imaginative insight, Henri Fabre, has striven to show, makes the conception of a world in which *casual* variation (however rigorously controlled by selection) determines species, an intolerable burden on the imagination. If a variation is slight, it can become the differentia of a new variety only if it persists in growth through many generations, and how can it so persist unless it expresses a determinate and directed activity of life ? [2] If it is considerable—and we are beginning to learn how considerable and determinate most variations are in their first appearance—the notion that they are " accidental " in the Darwinian sense, like the grouping of shots round the bull's eye of a target, mere casual divergences from the mean, is contrary to every principle of probability.

Is not the deeper truth implicit in the very expression

[1] *The Germ-Plasm*, p. 415. Italics Weismann's.

[2] Cf. Bergson, *L'Evolution Creatrice*, Alcan, 4th ed., c. 1. p. 95 ff.

" biophors," the bearers or containers of life, life which reveals itself in the creation of new forms ? Since Weismann concedes so much of reciprocity between environment and life, why does he seem to stop short of the admission of its universality ? The answer to this question reveals what seems to the present writer a fundamental difficulty in the doctrine we have been considering—it is a materialistic and mechanical explanation of phenomena which are not merely material and mechanical.

" Heredity is the transmission of the *physical* nature of the parent to the offspring." [1] Is, then, the psychical nature not transmitted ? Does it count for nothing in the process, or is its transmission not " heredity " ? The answer of Weismann may be found in the further statement that " all differences—even the qualitative ones—are ultimately of a *quantitative* nature." [2] Here is the presupposition of this whole doctrine. It is because of this presupposition that Weismann has to maintain at any cost the identity of the germ-plasm through all the countless variations of life. If we limit our explanations to physical or mechanical considerations, we must assume an indefinite number of potentialities in the earliest cells, the potentialities of all the vast organic world. The wonder that a fertilised ovum can contain all the characters of the developing and the mature organism shrinks into nothingness beside this wonder, that a universe of being and an eternity of time should be held within a speck of subtly compounded albumen. Physical nature assumes a majesty so great that life and mind itself can suffer no indignity in being but a form or manifestation of it—but it is always where life is that this physical wonder is also.

" The structure of the idioplasm," Weismann says, " must be far more complex than we can possibly imagine." [3] Doubtless it is so, but the greatest mystery is after all not the complexity of the original cell but its development, not the structure but the power. Now this power reveals itself as life, reveals itself more and more as mind. How then shall we explain heredity, where mind is, if we deliberately rule mind out ?

---

[1] *Germ-Plasm*, p. 410. Italics mine.
[2] *Ibid.*, p. 414. Italics Weismann's.   [3] *Ibid.*, p. 108.

All such methods bring their own nemesis.[1] If we refuse to acknowledge purposive and creative power as determinative where it is actually revealed, we are driven to assume it where it is not revealed. As so often, mechanistic interpretation which denies the immanent creativeness of the life-principle half-unconsciously assumes a transcendental operation of the selfsame power. Many instances could be given, but the following are typical. " I ventured," Weismann says, " some years ago to suggest that sexual reproduction has come into force in order to preserve the variability which had existed since the time of the primordial beings." [2] And again, speaking of the regeneration of the lizard's tail after the loss of the original, he says, " The possibility of such an occurrence is foreseen by Nature." [3] Doubtless the structure of the idioplasm is " far more complex than we can possibly imagine," and certainly in seeking to explain it the work of Weismann is magistral ; but may not his *method* involve something even more difficult than he supposes, the attempt to imagine not merely what is beyond *our* powers of imagination, but—the unimaginable ?

[1] On the other hand it is objected that any assumption of " vitalism " is opposed to the fruitful methods of scientific investigation, substituting an idle hypothesis for active research. It must be admitted that certain forms of vitalistic doctrine have led to that unhappy result in a pre-scientific age, but if the endless correlation of life and environment be recognised, if it be recognised that even in its inmost penetralia and most inaccessible origins life is still as always environed, active in and through the world of mechanical causation, abrogating not one jot or tittle of the law of the physical world, but revealing only the more its infinite continuity and complexity, then, although the outlook of science may be modified by the assumption, the limits of its investigation seem nowise narrowed.

[2] *The Germ-Plasm*, p. 439.

[3] *Ibid.*, p. 111.

INDEX